PRAISE FOR *THE INTENTIONAL LEGACY*

"Far too often the pursuit of money takes priority over relationships, leaving children, coworkers, and employees spiritually, intellectually, and morally bankrupt. This book reveals the legacy treasures that will inspire readers to find ultimate purpose and value in life. McAlvany's insights and solutions to holistic, generational planning make this book a gem! He is transparent and generous in sharing personal experiences as well as professional expertise to deliver a heart warming and practical guide to being intentional about blessing our families far beyond passing along assets."

- Chuck Bentley | CEO, Crown Financial Ministries

"For thirty years I've known the McAlvany family and rarely is a legacy passed, so seamlessly, from one generation to the next."

- Dr. Chuck Missler | Author and Founder of Koinonia House

"McAlvany reminds readers that we both receive and pass on a legacy to others. None of us do it perfectly. We are awkward and broken and therefore need the wise advice and counsel that this book provides. In fact, David, who has learned well, through careful attention and thoughtful reflection, makes reading about wisdom a pleasurable experience. Every page of the book has something memorable, and often quotable. Well written, and profound, all who are serious about living intentionally and leaving in their wake a legacy to benefit those who follow should make this book a must read!"

- Professor Jerry Root, Ph.D. | Wheaton College

"David McAlvany is one of the most impressive individuals I've ever met, so it should come as no surprise that his story of "Intentional Families" is so inspiring. His life story combined with his money management expertise and world view all come together to offer a message that must be told. How to intentionally make the world a better place with a solid legacy featuring faith, family and finance is something that everyone should hear. I'm grateful that Dave was willing to share his "Waffle

House" lesson with the world."

- Mike Gallagher | Salem Radio Host, Fox News Contributor

"Is there anything, anything at all, that matters more in the end than the love and the legacy of our family? As David McAlvany so powerfully demonstrates in both his testimony and in his book, our most strategic lifetime investments are necessarily those that we make at home and across the generations."

- Pastor George Grant | Parish Presbyterian Church

"David has masterfully woven his personal story of rebellion, grace and redemption throughout his book while giving the reader a contagious vision for paving the way for generational unity and intentional families. Legacy is, indeed one's life message . . . it is never too late to begin the journey!"

- Adolph Coors | Coors Brewing Company

"A boy up a tree, a teen slopping pigs, a young man in a diner are together one, a son hungry for the blessing and love of his father. Failure and resentment wafted away with the steam of a cup of coffee as his father offered this—forgiveness. Infused with both gospel realism and gospel hope, *The Intentional Legacy* reminds us of the greatest legacy we have received, and the greatest legacy we are called to pass along. It reminds me that both as a father and a son I am a rich man indeed and calls me to faithfully steward the blessings my heavenly Father has showered upon us. It encouraged me to invest in the one thing under my care that will last forever, the souls of my children."

- Dr. R.C. Sproul| Author Chancellor of Reformation Bible College

"Finally, a thoughtful guide to leaving to the next generation the things that really matter, the things that last—not just property, but the spiritual and intellectual foundations that will ensure we leave this world with no regrets."

- Joseph Farah | Founder and CEO of WND.com

"Question: Why do old men plant trees? Answer: To have a legacy! But might there be a better way to "plant" a legacy? Yes and a remarkable book by David McAlvany *The Intentional Legacy* provides many ways to go about creating and promoting a family legacy. The author identifies how to build a family identity and with it to enrich the personal identity of each family member. Among the chapters are: How to make a financial legacy for your family and its future generations. And many other helpful legacy contributions. So read it and apply it and maybe even plant some trees."

- Paul C. Vitz | Senior Scholar at Institute for the Psychological Sciences and Professor Emeritus, New York University

THE INTENTIONAL
LEGACY

THE INTENTIONAL LEGACY

DAVID McALVANY

BROWN THOMPSON

Brown Thompson Publishing, Durango, Colorado 81301
© 2016 by David S. McAlvany
All rights reserved. Published 2016

Requests for general information, special discounts for bulk purchases should be addressed to: Brown Thompson Publishing, 858 Main Avenue, Suite 203, Durango, Colorado 81301, or call (970) 385-3119.

The Brown Thompson Publishing Speakers Bureau can bring authors to your live event. For more information or to book an event, contact Brown Thompson Publishing Speakers Bureau at (970) 385-3119.

Scripture quotations are from the ESV® Bible (The Holy Bible, English Standard Version®), copyright © 2001 by Crossway, a publishing ministry of Good News Publishers. Used by permission. All rights reserved.

Published in association with The Fedd Agency, Inc., a literary agency.

ISBN: 978-1-943217-43-4
eISBN: 978-1-943217-44-1

Printed in the United States of America
First Edition 15 14 13 10 09 / 10 9 8 7 6 5 4 3 2

To my eternally patient and ever-loving mother.
For my children who I hope will write a better book.

CONTENTS

Introduction

Legacy: An Inescapable Concept

"Our lives are not our own. We are bound to others, past and present, and by each crime and every kindness, we birth our future."
- David Mitchell[1]

This is a book about a future you cannot see or touch, but that is as real as the lives of your children. The subject is legacy—what it means, how to cultivate it, and how to protect it. It is also the story of a real family—mine—and our somewhat circuitous journey toward intentionality.

Here you will read about a modern prodigal son who was reduced to the life of a swineherd, but who found his soul and his future after experiencing a life-transforming act of grace that ultimately paved the way for generational unity.

Here you will meet a woman—actually, several of them—whose indefatigable spirits and refusal to succumb to hopelessness allowed them to provide a legacy of opportunity for their children and to see "years that the locusts have eaten" restored after the pain of abandonment and divorce.

Here you will meet a man whose heroic response as a teenager to the death of two individuals in a plane crash prepared him to maintain presence of mind in the face of an historic catastrophe that claimed the lives of more than 200,000—and, in so doing, modeled for others a principle of survival vital for legacy-minded families.

And before the book is over, I will introduce you to a little boy and his prayers and an island at the end of the world where all of these legacies converged.

But for now, I want to tell you the most important thing I have to say:

Our lives are not our own.

Every choice we make will shape the destiny of children yet to be born. Every act of love or hatred, redemption or savagery, thoughtfulness or selfishness, births a future for ourselves and others. We live lives permeated by legacy—the legacy given to us and the legacy we cultivate every waking moment of the day.

We are the custodians of a generational story. Our lives are but one chapter, positioned somewhere in the index of a book of indiscernible length. The narrative began long before we were born. It continues further into the future than we might imagine. We may not do with our lives whatever we choose. There is a higher call. We are the trustees—the caretakers of our great grandchildren's future.

Our very existence is a gift given by God to be dedicated to His service. That service finds an immediate and practical expression in the context of the life and labor of the family. Our greatest aspirations and highest ideals are reflected in the lives we live with our children. It is not enough that our children succeed; we want them also to build upon our victories and transcend our defeats. It is our children, not our jobs, that are the most important work of our lives.

This book is about the nature of legacy. It is about the duty of families to embrace their legacy with intentionality. Rather than presenting a technical overview of wealth management protocols on the one hand or a spiritual to-do list on the other, I want to present something more fundamental. I want you to understand the very heart of the matter: What is a legacy? What makes it tick? Why is it so often lost? What can you do to cultivate a vibrant legacy that stands the test of time? Why does any of this even matter?

Legacy is an inescapable concept. We may choose to invest in our legacy, or we may choose to neglect it. But either way, you and I will leave one to our children's children. Because human action is inescapable, legacy is inescapable. We may dissipate a legacy, or we may cultivate it. We may prove ourselves grateful recipients or thankless legatees who despise our birthright, preferring a mess of pottage instead. In the end, how we respond to what we have been given—the good, the bad, and the ugly— and what we determine to leave to others will define for future generations the value of our walk on this earth.

The timing of this book's publication is not accidental. It is fair to say we are living in the midst of perhaps the largest legacy crisis in recent history. All fundamentals are in question. What is the meaning of a family? Who determines legacy—parents or the state? What do we do with the dramatic increase in our aging population and the decrease in births? How will we care for the elderly when our financial systems are teetering on bankruptcy? And what about the children who are growing up in a virtual social media world detached from physical flesh-and-blood relationships? What legacy will they embrace? We need to be clear on the meaning of things—in this case, the meaning of legacy.

Legacy is far more than assets on a balance sheet. It is our life message—the total sum of values and vision we leave to others in the form of tangible and intangible assets. Our approach to money, property, business, culture, faith, identity, and virtue are the elements of legacy that we receive, develop, and then bequeath to others. The pains you experienced and the truths you stood for, fought for, worked for, waited for—all of this is the stuff of legacy.

The impoverished father who remembered to pray daily with his children at night leaves a legacy of faith. The single mother who denied herself comforts and pleasure so she could care for the life of a child has given a legacy of self-sacrifice. The business leader who arrived early at work each day to build a company leaves a legacy of hard work ethic.

Here is the heart of the matter: Your children are your life's work. Legacy is not a job, or a credential, or a sum of money, but the totality of an individual's effort on behalf of others. This totality finds its clearest expression in what you leave for your children. Receiving, building, and transferring a legacy to them is a principal objective of your life as you "love God and enjoy him forever." Many may be influenced by the well-lived life of a single individual, but it is the children of that individual who are the immediate and principal life beneficiaries.

Throughout this book I will be returning to several distinct concepts, which converge—legacy, intentionality, and the redemptive ethic that holds them together. Legacy presupposes the desire of one generation of parents to transfer value to their blood and kin in the next generation in the form of tangible and intangible assets. In the context of this book, intentionality means the self-conscious act of purposeful living as it applies to a robust and multi-faceted vision for legacy. The redemptive ethic speaks to an optimistic culture of grace that holds the family together—for better or for worse, in sickness, and in health—in the bonds of love.

As you read, keep in mind three things. First, everything matters because everything was designed to matter. There are no areas of neutrality in your life when it comes to legacy. Second, there are no perfect families, perfect parents, or perfect legacies. There are imperfect, needy families who give up and despair, and there are imperfect, needy families who see beyond challenges and persevere. The single most important common denominator of these latter families is that they have experienced grace in their lives and communicate this grace through an ethic of redemption in the context of non-contingent relationships. Third, there is no crisis so great, nor tragedy too painful, where you are left hopeless and without the potential for redeeming a meaningful legacy. Rather than being an end to the story, broken marriages, absentee fathers, deaths of loved ones, financial ruin, moral failure, and every stripe of personal and familial tragedy are opportunities for grace, mercy, and rebirth.

One common legacy theme centers around people who make terrible mistakes and not only become heirs to a significant legacy, but also become ancestors of those who will inherit an even greater legacy in the future. They are not defined by class, gender, age, profession, intelligence, or financial position, but by faith and perseverance. Often these people are an embodiment of weakness and disappointment. Abraham cowers and sends his wife into a veritable brothel. David lusts, commits adultery, and murder. Solomon, the wisest man in the world, becomes so distracted by his numerous foreign wives that he goes through a season of idolatry. Jacob deceives his family. Noah, Lot, Samson—all are righteous men of faith who sinned. The list goes on. There is pain, there is tragedy, but there is also forgiveness, perseverance, and hope because there is grace. Ultimately, there is victory.

Before you read on, there are a few things you need to understand about me. First, I am not a preacher, and I am certainly not a theologian. I am a husband, a father, a son, and a businessman who takes my faith seriously. I don't know how to divorce my Christian worldview from my perspective, and I would never want to. My faith informs my thinking in economics, finances, aesthetics, wealth management—everything. I recognize that Christians are some of the most inconsistent people on the planet. Ours is a multi-millennia old story of perseverance through generational victory and generational failure. Rather than being a testimony to the weakness of our faith, these strengths and weaknesses remind us of our need for humility and the impossibility of success apart from the grace of God. Our core thesis is redemption based on simple faith in the merits of Christ, who extends that grace to us.

Second, my thinking has certainly benefitted from the writings of many who do not share my own core commitments to Christianity. From Aristotle to Ludwig Von Mises, there is a wealth of economic and practical commentary that speaks to the question on the table. Where appropriate, I draw from the helpful work of these and other giants. But it is the essential message of the Cross that is the heart of the ethic presented in this book.

Third, I have personally been the recipient of much grace, much mercy, and much forgiveness. It is the praise and worship of a merciful Father that serves as the backdrop of both my hope and my ambitions on my own journey of intentionality. I was a prodigal who came home. In Chapter One, I explain how a loving father extended grace to me, opening the door for my own generational legacy. Decades later, I am discovering that the same grace and mercy extended to me as a young man is essential to me as an adult. The process of "coming home" is ongoing. Every new failure, like every new success, is part of an experience that has the potential of drawing us closer to our loved ones and furthering our legacy objectives—if we respond with intentionality.

Finally, I need to be clear that I am not an expert on the subject of intentionality or generational legacy. Frankly, I have never met one. Finding an expert on the subject is like looking for someone to share his personal experience of life after death. You can read about heaven and hell in the Bible. You can listen to people speculate, but until you get there, you're not an expert. The same is true with building a generational legacy. One of the reasons for writing this book is the lack of experts in the field and my own desire to better learn from my own experiences and the experiences of others. My journey as a second-generation businessman and as a wealth management specialist is ongoing. I am, however, a passionate student of the subject and a would-be practitioner. As you read this book, please take what you find to be helpful, dispense with the rest, and dig deeper yourself.

A quick survey of books on wealth management reveals that much that has been written is aimed at the top 3 percent of income earners. There is a reason for that: wealth managers tend to handle larger financial portfolios. This is a book for the remaining 97 percent, as well as those in the 3 percent who wish to transcend the historic problem of shirtsleeves-to-shirtsleeves in three to four generations, a problem that has defined wealth transfers for millennia.

The Intentional Legacy is for college students and grandparents, business owners and blue collar workers. Its principles of legacy and intentionality are not bound by income or social status; they are scalable, transcendent, and practical. They apply to families large and small, to third generational legacies, and families from broken homes—to anyone hoping to see the impact of one family generation extended to the next, and beyond.

- David McAlvany

Chapter 1

The Return of the Swineherd: How Grace Can Save a Family Legacy

"To be a Christian means to forgive the inexcusable because God has forgiven the inexcusable in you."
- C.S. Lewis[2]

In a small suburban community of Colorado, a six-year-old boy climbed on a table to give a speech. The subject was inflation. He was wearing a three-piece suit as he faced an audience of friends and family, unaware that six-year-old boys are not supposed to give speeches on economic theory. There were no notes, only a carefully memorized list of ideas and quotes learned from months of standing next to his father and listening to him give the very same speech.

I was that boy, and I still remember every word.

My first business trip with my father was at the age of three. By the time I was six years old, I had listened to my father give that same speech over and over to hundreds of people and dozens of groups. I knew his points line by line. He was my hero. His words, like his business, were gold to me.

It was a golden season of my life in which I traveled beside my father to mysterious and exotic locations of the world from South Africa to Israel, from England to the Bahamas.

My father was a man of business, strategy, and faith with a growing worldwide business of asset protection and wealth management. He started with a brokerage firm in Houston during the 1960s and later worked for a New York mutual funds manager before starting his own business with my mother in 1972.

What began as the International Collectors Associates sprouted the

McAlvany Financial Group, which included an influential international newsletter and McAlvany Wealth Management. It is fair to say Dad ensured that I cut my teeth in the world of wealth management, learning about financial risk, its appraisal and mitigation, and value recognition. I stood next to him for hours on end as he sat with clients reviewing their goals and priorities, as well as the strengths and weaknesses of different approaches to allocating assets and spending money.

One day, three decades and a lifetime later, I flew across the world to meet my father at a hotel in Shanghai, China. He was living in the Philippines, and my base was Durango, Colorado. Shanghai was a midway point between our two worlds. We told each other that we were getting together to discuss business, but that was just an excuse. The truth was, we wanted time together—time shared between two very busy lives separated by ocean and thousands of miles. Time to talk about hopes, dreams, love, and legacy. Once there, we ditched work and never left our hotel. That conversation, and others like it, have served as one element of the impetus for my theories on legacy.

Today, after running multiple businesses and raising four children, my father and mother serve as missionaries located near Manila. Dad is the director of the Asian Pacific Children's Fund, dedicating his life to serving others. He teaches families how to grow crops and disciple their children. He helps them find redemption in the midst of brokenness and exploitation. It is a good season in the life of a man who does not believe in retirement. Still energetic. Still savvy. Physically stronger than in his younger days due to a rigorous weight-lifting regimen, he is adding a new role to his repertoire—that of elder statesman and sage. He passed the baton of leadership over his company to me just under a decade ago. Like the meeting in Shanghai, that transition is one part of the story behind this book. I am now in the business of helping families secure their legacy, even as I hope to be faithfully building a legacy on my father's foundations.

But it almost never happened.

Six years after I put on that first three-piece suit, I found myself separated and estranged from my father. I was lost, hurting, and angry. By the age of thirteen, I was living apart from friends and family, under miserable daily conditions and up to my waist in pig slop—literally.

My life had become a metaphor for prodigality. It was not just that I was experiencing a crisis of implosion, but the generational legacy of my father was also at stake, including his ability to pass on the benefits of a lifetime of work and sacrifice. Just when things appeared as if they were about to hit rock bottom, I was given a gift—one of the most precious gifts an individual could ever hope to receive. My father forgave me, and I forgave him. It was an encounter with grace. We reconciled, and from that moment on, everything changed. My problems were far from solved, but I had new hope and a fresh start.

That event—to be detailed shortly—launched a lifetime journey through inquiry, success, failure, redemption, further inquiry, self-examination, loss, gain, more redemption, more failure, and even more redemption. It was the beginning of my search for the meaning of legacy—what it means spiritually, philosophically, economically, and practically. It was what opened the door for me to live with some fascinating families in the United States and South America, spend a season of philosophical studies at Oxford, and meet Mary-Catherine—the love of my life. It's what led me to elope with her and start a family, foray into the world of one of the nation's largest investment firms only to return to work beside my father, and ultimately, be given the responsibility of CEO for the companies he had founded more than a quarter of a century before.

My moment of crisis resulted in a conversation on life and legacy between my father and me that has continued for nearly three decades and overlaps our personal and professional lives. It has brought me to the conclusion that great succession plans require great acts of love, great demonstrations of redemption, and great conversations in the context of an intentional vision for family legacy.

Behind Every Legacy There Is an Identity

Here is an experiment. Walk into any diner in America, sit down with any random group of people in their fifties, sixties, or seventies, and ask them about their fathers. It doesn't matter where you live; it's a subject almost guaranteed to elicit a response. They loved their fathers or hated their fathers. Their father taught them about the world, invested in their lives, and loved them. Or their father abandoned them, betrayed them, and disappointed them. I know of men and women in their eighties who remember their fathers with such tenderness they can't even speak of them without shedding a tear, and I know others who still physically recoil at the mention of their dads. Decades can pass. A half-century. It doesn't matter.

No one is neutral when it comes to his or her father.

Why does the subject of fatherhood inspire and motivate? Why does it bewilder or infuriate? The first part of the answer goes to the essence of our humanity—we have been created as relational beings and placed in the context of families where our relationship with our fathers and mothers shape and define our identities as sons and daughters. It is at this precise point—the issue of identity—where the modern world finds itself in such turmoil. Historically, issues of gender, heritage, labor, faith, and culture have shaped our identity. And the core questions never change: Who am I? Where did I come from? Does my past matter? What do I believe about God, government, and society? What does it mean to be a man? A woman? How will I provide for myself? Where do I fit in society? What do I enjoy? What do I dislike? What am I willing to die for?

Historically, these and other fundamental questions of identity were answered less in a didactic manner and more through the daily rituals of family life under the leadership examples of fathers and through the nurturing and grace of mothers. Family and national history gave context to the individual. Family faith rooted the individual as a member of a household, which embraced values that were transcendent.

Even more fundamental to the question of identity than our biological or adoptive parents is the fatherhood of God. God is not only our Creator; He is also our Father. Furthermore, God is a Father who loved His son. God relates to us as a Heavenly Father. We communicate to Him as a Father—"Our Father, who art in Heaven." God has designed earthly fathers, with all of their brokenness and imperfections, to model a defining relationship of strength, courage, compassion, tenderness, and grace. The fact that we carry the very image of God our Father shapes and defines our identity. An Eternal Father who loves us, created us in the Imago Dei, and calls us His children. His fatherhood is not merely a metaphysical reality; it is intensely personal. He asks us to call Him Father and to relate to Him as such. He cares for us, loves us, nurtures us, disciplines us, and communicates to us as a father. And we are designed to have a relationship with Him, which is not only spiritual, but also temporal and practical, finding expression in a life dedicated to "doing the will of the Father." Consequently, fatherhood speaks to a relationship that is fundamental to the order of creation and the humanity of men and women.

The family is an incubator, not just for our own identity, but also for our view of reality. Our understanding of masculinity and femininity, ethics, and the permanency of relationships is all birthed in the family. Children implicitly look to their fathers to model principles of leadership and represent the ideals and heritage of the family. Sons look to their fathers to model masculinity, but so do daughters. Their view of men is often shaped by the respect and dignity (or lack thereof) conferred on them as women by a father. A wise father will reinforce his daughter's sense of self-worth. He will model for her a sacrificial masculinity that shapes her perspective on her innate dignity as a woman. Take either father or mother out of the equation, and the gap must somehow be filled.

It should come as no surprise, therefore, that a disturbance in the relationship between God the Father and His children can be destructive. There even appears to be a causal connection between fatherhood and faith. Paul Vitz makes this point in his helpful psychological study, *Faith of the Fatherless*.[3] He argues that the link between atheism and fatherlessness is not mere coincidence.

> Besides abuse, rejection, or cowardice, one way in which a father can be seriously defective is simply by not being there. Many children, of course, interpret death of their father as a kind of betrayal or an act of desertion. In this respect it is remarkable that the pattern of a dead father is so common in the lives of many prominent atheists. Baron d'Holbach, the French rationalist and probably the first public atheist, is apparently an orphan by the age of thirteen and living with his uncle. Bertrand Russell's father died when young Bertrand was four years old; Nietzsche was the same age as Russell when he lost his father; Sartre's father died before Sartre was born and Camus was a year old when he lost his father . . . the information already available is substantial; it is unlikely to be an accident.

Life with My Father

Of all the joys to be experienced in the life of a son, few can ever top the experience of one-on-one time when a boy is really involved in his father's business—traveling with him, learning from him, and experiencing the ineffable and mysterious wonder of being his confidante and partner in an important quest.

If you have never met my father, Donald McAlvany, then you have missed out on one of the most intense, passionate, opinionated, well-researched, idiosyncratic, humorously paranoid, compassionate, hardworking, and humble men of the last generation. Dad would be the first to deflect praise and tell you he is a man with all the problems of imperfect men living in an imperfect world. All true. Three decades ago, I would have catalogued many of those shortcomings for you, but now I see them and him in a different light. I see them through the grid of humanity and redemption—both his and mine.

My father's own path was not an easy one. Abandoned by his own dad at the age of six, he grew up without a father. What little he knew of a father-and-son relationship was not positive—absence more than presence, philandering, hardship. Hope springs eternal, especially when the object of that hope is the one thing you have so desperately wanted during the most formative season of your life. In the case of my father, the "hope deferred" made "his heart sick." There would be no restored relationship and no meaningful redemption between father and son. Dad would simply have to live with the reality of unresolved anger and sadness. It was a heavy burden for him to carry—one he shouldered well into his sixties.

How do you explain fatherhood to a man who has never experienced it? That is not an easy sell, especially when all he knows is abandonment. But God works in mysterious ways. In the case of my father, he discovered the love of an Eternal Father one day on the Guadalupe River in Texas.

On that day, my father was tubing down the river with some friends when he floated by an attractive woman. The two struck up a conversation—probably not the conversation Dad was expecting. She wanted to know if he understood that God had a plan for his life. Keep in mind that I was not there for this life-changing event, but my guess is that Dad may have been thinking to himself, "Yes, there is a plan, and you're part of it." That is not how the story played out. Within thirty minutes, she explained to him the Gospel, including the story of man's alienation from God because of sin and the hope of redemption because the Son of God took the sins of man on Himself. And she introduced him to an idea completely foreign to him—he, Don McAlvany, was loved by a Father.

The girl from the Guadalupe invited him to a Bible study. He decided to go. It was a new world for my father who began in-depth studies of

Scripture. He saw the world through new glasses. Dad became a Christian. One of the first tests of his faith was through the loss of his mentor. Just a few months after their meeting on the Guadalupe, the young woman died in a tragic head-on collision.

Where does legacy come from? Part of mine traces back to a girl on an inner tube that cared about the soul of my father. From that season on, Dad developed a new perspective on the past and the future. He had an intense confidence in the authority of the Bible and its application to all of life.

All of this played out in my childhood. Early in my life, my father raised questions that repeatedly pointed me to the intersection of economics, philosophy, and faith. He taught me to love our country, but to distrust politicians and bureaucrats. He brought me to conferences on subjects as diverse as Austrian economic theory and biblical eschatology.

I didn't understand it at the time, but he was giving me tools for a lifetime of inquiry about value and virtue, sacrifice and hard work, failure and redemption. That is how my life began. Then something changed.

My Tipping Point

A transition occurred in my own life between the ages of eight and eleven. The little boy who had stood on the table reciting his father's speech was maturing. So was Dad's business. With a growing company and significant international responsibilities, Dad was on the road more and more. Mom ran the household like a single parent, filling the voids created by Dad's travel and business endeavors. My own studies prevented me from the flexibilities of travel we had experienced together when I was a bit younger. By the time I was eight, there was both the expectation and need for a level of relational involvement and intimacy that simply could not happen with Dad away on the road building his business. An unmistakable void emerged. His work schedule changed, and so did our relationship. It came at the time when I needed his influence the most.

It all makes sense intellectually. Dad's response to the pressure of business success was certainly not uncommon. But none of that matters to a boy. At the end of the day, even with his mom's wholehearted effort, he just wants his father. And if his father is not there to the degree the boy feels is right, resentment seeps in.

It is nearly impossible for a ten-year-old to understand the pressure in the life of a father, but it is equally difficult for a father to peer into the heart of a ten-year-old and fully understand his need for affirmation and instruction. Confusion runs deep. I found myself growing resentful. There was just one too many missed hockey games.

Legacies, like confidence, can be lost through inattention. It is possible for parents to spend a lifetime creating wealth for children, only to see the currency of their life's work devalued because they have lost the hearts of their children. This rarely happens from a single moment in the life of a parent and child. Disaffection is usually the result of a continuum of unattended disappointments that lead to broken relationships. It is all too common. One of the great challenges facing modern fathers is that just about the time their business is gathering steam, and work needs special attention, their children reach an age where they too need more.

In the absence of one authority figure, children look for something else to fill the void—peers, entertainment, something. In my case, it was another very special man, my maternal grandfather. While Dad was pre-occupied with business, my mother's father became a special hero in my life. Ellis Augustus Brown was his name—as southern as his style. To me he was Dee Dee. Looking back, I realize that he was the kind of man who set the legacies of others in motion. Dee Dee was a mentor to many. A man's man. He lived in Louisiana where he was a member of the Louisiana Sports Hall of Fame and a highly respected high school principal. He also had carved out a successful career as a twelve-time state champion football coach.

A small return in the life of a child can yield exponential results. Without attempting to quantify value, or even understand it, a child has the capacity to receive and benefit from input at levels uncommon in adults. Compared to adults, the learning curves of children are typically off the charts. The memories, experiences, and impressions of childhood often carry forward into adult life shaping the collective consciousness of the individual. A child spends one day with his grandfather fishing. They barely talk. They just sit and fish. Grandpa cuts the bait. The child casts the rod. They wait. They look at each other. Still, no talking. There is a nibble. The child reels it in. The fish escapes. It does not matter. For the rest of his life, that moment in time is preserved as the experiential definition of happiness. A quarter of a century later, and the boy is now a man who knows that when life is full of lemons, somewhere out there, a lake is calling him back to a moment of innocence and peace. He can never quite replicate the moment with Grandpa, but he is going to try.

Maybe I was with Dee Dee at his home six times. That's it. But they were the right times and the right places. His impact was simply monumental. To me he represented goals, aspirations, and the meaning of being a man.

My own tipping point occurred at age eleven when my hero died. The pain from the loss was excruciating. In the context of my growing disappointments at home, the death of my grandfather was the last emotional and mental straw in a series of disenchanting events. It is nearly impossible for an aching soul to properly interpret the meaning of tragedy when you are under the thumb of grief. My takeaway was this—*God does not hear my prayers. God does not care. My hero is dead.* My father was preoccupied with the grief of my mother. I felt lost in the equation. And I expressed my pain through anger.

Over the course of the next three years, my despair brought me to a point of rebellion and loss of dreams. I interpreted my own reality to myself and to others in the language of hyperbole. And I became an angry teenager. What I did not understand at the time was that I was falling into a generational legacy pit—a downward cycle of destructive experiences and responses to those experiences, perpetuated from one generation to the next. My feelings of loss and disorientation without the knowledge of how to resolve them created a solipsistic world of selfish frustration and anger.

It is a terrible thing for a child to experience the tragedy of abandonment at the hands of a parent. It is even worse when that loss remains unresolved over the course of a lifetime. Dad had suffered greatly at the hands of a father who abandoned him as a six-year-old child, leaving him with unresolved emotional scars he carried with him through much of his life. In their own way, my feelings of disappointment paralleled similar feelings my father had experienced as a young man. Of course, my situation was drastically different. Dad was a God-fearing man who loved me. In spite of the absence of a male role model in his own life as a boy, my father had been a profound influence in my life. But from my vantage point at the time, memories of his influence on my early life were just not enough.

The Great Escape

It is not uncommon to meet children who decide they are sick of their parents' authority and want a break. Their solution? Escape from Mom and Dad to join the military. I took a slightly different route. Just shy of my fourteenth birthday, I ran away from home.

Enough was enough. It was time for some freedom. I had allowed tensions to build, and the precipitating event occurred over something painfully typical and irrelevant; my mom told me not to lock the door to my bedroom. It turned into quite a standoff. "Fine then. If I can't control my own room, I will leave." My father and mother were not about to tell me what to do with my life. I was fourteen, self-sufficient, the master of my future. Hear me roar.

My plan was brilliant—grab a backpack, stuff it with a little clothing, get on my bike, and take off into the sunset. Who needs parents after all?! My journey of independence took me approximately one mile. It started to snow. It seemed to be a good idea to take refuge at a friend's house. Step two of my carefully executed escape plan involved moving in with my friend's family and telling them that I was running away from home to start a new life. News got back to my parents, but they did not stop me. They did not bring me home. A bit surprising, but fine with me. A week or two went by.

Life had changed, but I wasn't going to let that get in the way of things I loved. Hockey, a field of battle where raw aggression and speed converge, was an escape for me. My mom knew that and had compassion on me. She decided to bring my practice gear and meet me at the rink.

Time gives perspective. Today I am a parent—a vantage point that makes it a bit painful looking back on those days. I can picture how Mom selflessly minimized the pain I was causing her to help rebuild a relationship. I can close my eyes and see the look on her face. My wonderful mom, she who was ever conciliatory, ever hopeful. Probably deeply afraid that she was going to lose her son. Her willingness to endure was a means of grace in my life, though I did not understand it at the time.

The day that Mom came to the rink, I took a puck to my knee and was completely immobilized. The puck not only left a dent in my body, but also in my long-term personal exit strategy. It is hard to escape when you can't walk. What was I to do now? Not sure.

Back at my friend's house, I was settling in and nursing an injured knee. Then the world turned upside down.

A car pulled into the driveway. There was my dad. Beside him was a family friend who was an agent for the DEA—The Drug Enforcement

Administration! With them was a police officer. In my absence from home, Dad had been doing some math. He added up the wild friends I was hanging out with, plus my own destructive temper and attitude, and reached the conclusion that I was up to my neck in drugs and rebellion. That was only half right—the rebellion part. During my brief absence, my parents were trying to process the unfolding events in their minds. Dad had reached a conclusion: the only reason anyone would behave like this was if they had a core problem with drug abuse. That was it. David must be a junkie. It wasn't true, but it was the only box my dad knew to check at the time. So he called the police for a bit of assistance, which was probably more of a show of force.

I was absolutely terrified and shocked at my parents' response. In that moment, every expletive of panic and fear rushed through my mind. What was happening? How is this even possible? Police? Really? My heart was pounding through my chest. My mind was exploding with confusion. Eventually, the police officer left. Shortly after his departure, I found myself in a car with Dad and the DEA agent. Destination unknown. Hours later I found myself in a drug rehabilitation center in Houston, Texas. My little exercise in self-emancipation had turned into a living nightmare.

At the drug rehabilitation facility, I sat through classes, meetings, and examinations. It was my first real glimpse into a world of people hurting far more than I was—young men and women with personal stories that should have been the equivalent of neon signs reminding me just how much God had given me for which I should be thankful. That realization would not come for some time.

The team of psychiatrists and doctors quickly figured out that my problem was not drugs. Telling me what I already knew provided little relief, but it was better than nothing. At last I finished the program. About forty days after walking through the front door, I emerged—more defiant, more anxious, and more alienated from my father. Meanwhile, it became clear that my mother was suffering greatly through the entire process. She just did not know what to do.

The next big test was before me. I had made it through drug rehab. Great. Now it was up to me whether or not I would play by the rules and re-enter family society. So while I was still in Houston, Dad presented me with a document, approximately the length of one of his newsletters. Before me was a lengthy list of requirements, my acceptance of which was a precondition for returning home. Was this a test? Was he serious? I refused to sign it.

Apparently Dad was serious because he brought another friend with him to Houston to meet me—one who appeared to me a giant of a man obviously selected as an enforcer. In Dad's hand was an airline ticket with my name on it. The two men escorted me to the airport where I was to board a plane bound for Arkansas.

If Dad was serious, then so was I—about escape. The plan was simple—make it through security, run for my life, and then head for my own "city of refuge," a corner of Houston a friend had told me about during my time at the drug rehab facility. It was a bold plan, except for two things: 1.) The city of refuge was actually one of the most depraved and dangerous locations in all of Houston, and 2.) The idea of escaping by running at breakneck speed through an airport was ill-conceived, to put it mildly.

At the Houston airport I played it cool, waiting for the moment of escape. Then it came. Ready! Set! *Go!* I was off and flying, rocketing through the airport, hurdling over obstacles, and sliding down stairwells with an Olympic resolve. The mad dash to freedom appeared to be working . . .

Then it happened. With escape clearly in sight, my body met a door that simply refused to open. And that was that—flat on my face and essentially down for the count. There would be no escape. Dad's friend scooped me up and escorted me to the plane.

That moment in my life—sort of a Steve McQueen failed motorcycle escape meets Mr. Toad's wild ride—is now a humorous bookmark in a chapter of a larger story I am passing on to my children. Whenever we pass through the Houston airport I point out to my children "the very spot" where I made the crazed run—hallways, hurdles—the whole shebang. It has become a "teaching opportunity" and part of our family lore.

Crisis tests everyone. Sometimes when parents are desperate for answers, they are willing to entertain ideas previously beyond the scope of their normalcy threshold. They are looking for someone or something that will provide a solution—even if the path to get there is extreme.

So I arrived at Glenhaven, a special facility for troubled youth, which felt to me like The Island of Lost Souls. There I would spend the next ten miserable months of my life. The stated purpose of Glenhaven was to "redeem at-risk youth from a broken past." At the time, the operation was under the care of a Christian couple who sought to provide an environment of discipline and order for a vast array of young men and women coming from checkered pasts ranging from drug addiction to violence. My class included several hard-core alcoholics, some drug abusers, and a boy who had been given the choice of Glenhaven or jail after beating his father senseless with a bat.

There are those who believe in a literal purgatory—a middle ground between heaven and hell, disconnected from the living, where time and suffering offer the potential of ultimate redemption. As an estranged fourteen-year-old working off my sins, there seemed little difference. Glenhaven was my personal purgatory—a Twilight Zone universe disconnected from life, family, and the reality I once knew. Located in the wastelands of the Arkansas outback, it was hedged by many miles of unpeopled wilderness. A single, largely untraveled road connected my personal purgatory to civilization. For all practical purposes, there was no escape. Once there, you were stuck. You leave when "they" tell you to leave, and not one minute before.

During my time at Glenhaven, I made few friends. Most of them were angry like myself, but I never quite felt like I fit in with them. I did not feel that I belonged, and more than one person told me I didn't. Heavy on my mind was my status as a McAlvany. While I was like most teenagers in my desire for independence and differentiation, all of a sudden I felt the loss of internal anchoring that comes from family identity.

The circularity of my own position—I have a mother and father—but they are no longer my mother and father—but they are still my mother and father—was confusing. The fundamental laws of life as I knew them had been suspended. I did not know which side was up and which was down, much like an M.C. Escher painting depicting a never-ending maze where the laws of gravity do not apply. In the end, cut off from my family and with no communication from home, I reached the conclusion that my mother and father had abandoned me and permanently disowned me. My vision of independence from the family had come true, just not the way I had planned. It was the closest experience of desperation that I have ever known. And it got my attention.

The Swineherd

The nadir of my internment at Glenhaven was my new calling—caretaker to the pigs. I had become a swineherd. Well, not exactly, but close enough. I was the guy tasked with slopping the pigsty and feeding the hogs. Sounds like a simple enough job description, but the reality was misery. Like Sisyphus condemned to Tartarus and who perpetually rolled his boulder up a hill, my job was never truly completed. How do you maintain order in a hog parlor? As soon as you think the job is done, it is time to start again.

My first job was to clean and replenish the fifty-five-gallon trough barrels. The drums were cut in two and lay end to end. This meant trekking down to the sty, digging the drums out of the mud, lifting the heavy barrels, dragging them down the hill to an ice-cold river stream, rinsing them out, dragging them back up again, and then feeding the pigs. Here is the part of the picture I want you to imagine: To get to these troughs, I had to wade knee deep in swine excrement through an army of aggressive porkers bent on biting me. With every step, I sank deeper. The swine were attacking. My mobility was impaired, and I found myself at the whim of the vicious porcine mob.

I would lose pieces of my clothing often. It wasn't uncommon for my boots to be pulled off my feet by the powerful suction of the wet goop and mud. Splosh. Sploosh. Thwoop. Off came the boots, and down I went, submerged under a sea of mud and pig excrement. My own sinking-sand experience. The more I struggled, the deeper I went. Eyes, ears, armpits, head to toe—nothing was protected. Even now, I can feel it. Slopping the pigs was the gift that kept on giving. Everywhere I went, the scent of pig refuse wafted indiscreetly after me. Nothing helped—not showers, not deodorant . . . not even scrubbing. My body continued to reek. Fetor ruined my personal possessions. Sty stink permeated everything. Do you remember Pig-Pen, pal to Charlie Brown—the comic character known for filthy clothing and a cloud of dust that followed him everywhere? Despite all of his efforts, he couldn't get rid of the mess. That was me, minus the friend part. From beginning to end, it was simply the most miserable experience of my life. The poetry of my purgatorial experience was the stuff of parables. That was my story.

Then one day it came to an end. I got the call. "Do you want to come home? Will you play by the rules?" My heart was not tender, but this time my answer was yes. Anything. Just get me out of here. Now. Please.

It had been nearly a year since I was with my parents. During that time, I had stayed out of trouble, but it was still not clear to me why I was sent away in the first place. Part of the deal for getting released from my own personal purgatory was a document for me to sign—twenty-seven pages long. It was an agreement and a long list of dos and don'ts, which would govern my life henceforth. The content did not really matter to me. I wanted out. I needed to get out. So I signed it and left.

Redemption in a Diner

English novelist Graham Greene observed that "there is always one moment in childhood when the door opens and lets the future in." My door opened at a Waffle House.

Days before my fourteenth birthday, I had run away from home. A year had passed. Now, less than a few months after my fifteenth birthday, I was in trouble again and facing what could prove to be the confrontation of my life with Dad. A lot can happen in a year, but not enough had happened to my will. Ten months at Glenhaven had not entirely humbled me. I was bruised, but unbroken, cautious, but still defiant, when my father invited me to a "conversation" at a local Waffle House. I came spitting mad, dukes up, and raring for a fight.

The issue on the table was a bit of misbehavior that occurred when had I visited a friend from Glenhaven. I had broken some rules, one of which involved smoking marijuana.

The context was a business trip to Indianapolis. Dad had been trying to connect. Taking me with him on the trip was his way of trying to find common ground to rebuild our shared experience. It was his reminder of the "good old days" before darkness set in. Just weeks before, he had reached out to me through an open water scuba diving certification. Both were honest efforts, but not ones I was ready to appreciate. Looking back now, my heart is filled with compassion for my father. He was desperately trying to find a way to connect and rebuild. At the time, though, neither of us understood that something more was needed.

While on the trip with Dad, there was time to look up a friend I'd met at Glenhaven who lived in the same city. Misery loves company, and rebels have a way of finding each other. The combination of the two of us alone, so soon after our release from "prison," was trouble with a capital "T." My friend was an experienced troublemaker. I was the "good" rebel, which only meant that at fifteen I was still sufficiently immature and ignorant of life so the scope of my shenanigans had some limits. Some. When children lose hope, they also lose restraint. Not all at once. It usually happens in stages. Mixing hopelessness with anger is a cocktail for trouble. Despite my father's best efforts, I was still drinking that cocktail, which found its particular expression during that trip in a massive cannabis binge, and then a munchie attack, refrigerator raid, and subsequently getting caught by my friend's father. In sum, it was an exercise in stupidity for a guy who had just been released from Glenhaven.

Angry and hopeless children don't realize when they are breaking their parents' hearts. They are certainly not thinking about legacy. Intentionality is not part of their emotional vocabulary. They get lost in a world of self-absorption. Their responses to conflict tend to be largely reactive. They expect their parents to react in extremes—sometimes capitulation, other times rejection, emotional violence, or punishment. What they don't expect is grace. The kind of grace that does not whitewash wrongdoing, but that provides an offender with the hope of redemption and in the context of tenderness and transparency.

Up to this point in my life, that type of grace was just a concept. I knew the theology of redemption, but not the experience. People who think they know about grace intellectually, but have never understood it experientially, tend to become experts on hypocrisy. They can sniff out inconsistency in others, even as they are blinded to their own. That was me. Which is why I never saw it coming.

It is funny what we remember. I tend to recall great conversations in the context of food. Meals shared with others are a journal entry in my log of life experiences—tastes, textures, and smells that bring me back to moments in time. The menu at the Waffle House that morning was cheesy scrambled eggs and cinnamon toast, accompanied by a concoction of diluted fluid that barely justified the moniker orange juice. But for the rest of my life, Waffle House breakfasts will remind me of grace.

That morning Dad confronted me. He put down his fork, looked at me hard, and asked me what happened in Indianapolis. The jig was up. It would be back to purgatory. The rules had been broken once too many. Time to pay the price. No more family. No more Dad. More pig slop. What do I do? Fight it out? Accuse? I decided to take a risk—to tell the truth. All of it. Not so much because I was sorry for what had happened as much as the fact that I preferred dealing with reality over speculation and falsehood. I embraced it. I swallowed hard and told him everything. Dad choked up. The disappointment was palpable. But he had only one thing to say.

"I forgive you."

That was it. Dad never said another word. He did not rake me over the coals. He did not attempt to shame me. He let me know that he believed me and that everything would be okay. At that moment, the clouds parted in my life. My father believed me! He forgave me! I had a second chance!

Dad did something I never expected. He dealt with me heart-to-heart, like a father to a son. He was vulnerable and compassionate. There was no woodshed—literal or otherwise. He made it clear that his love for me as his son was not contingent on conformity to a set of rules. The rules matter. Breaking them has consequences. But those consequences would not include rejection.

I discovered that my father's love was unconditional.

The conversation was very brief and very quiet. There was no way to verbalize what I was seeing. Imagine being in a dark room with someone turning the lights on suddenly. You are in a tunnel, taking it in, and your eyes are trying to adjust. It was the first time in my entire life that I felt the overwhelming power of miraculous, unmerited grace. Dad invited me to an open discussion about my own hurts and pains. Soon the two of us were making commitments one to another. No matter what would ever happen to us, we would not quit. Dad would not quit on me, and I would not quit on him. That was new. I was flabbergasted. Dumbfounded. There was no strategy formed. It was just a blanket forgiveness, followed by a soul-stirring recognition that, from that moment on, things would be different.

In a very real sense, the next two generations of McAlvany legacy was determined in that diner—work, marriage, children, legacy. Everything. The conversation could have gone a very different direction, one that found me estranged. But my father gave me buy-in instead. He gave me hope. That very hour, my father and I began a journey of reconciliation, which started with our own mutual acknowledgements of wrongs against each other and ended with a lifetime commitment to persevere. Instead of a permanent disruption, in a sense, my father killed the fatted waffle and welcomed me home.

That was the beginning of my journey of intentionality. I told myself that morning, "Everything changes right now. Tomorrow will be different. I want the future to be different from the past. I am changing everything. No more stupid choices. No more attitude." Maturity includes the ability to embrace everything you have been given—the good, the bad, the ugly, and the beautiful—and see it as part of your story. In my life, that process is ongoing. It remains one of my most exciting and challenging personal responsibilities.

On that day at the Waffle House, my understanding was still immature. It would be years before I could begin the process of sorting out the meaning of intentionality—including the ability to take both the good and the bad I inherited from my father, which he inherited from his father, and choose to multiply the best, while breaking with those cycles that perpetuate the worst. But this much I knew—It was time to grow up. I knew what was at stake and what I deserved. For the first time in years, I felt an urgency to be my father's son and my own man—a man of purpose. It was time to "restore the years that the locusts have eaten" (Joel 2:25).

The beginning of intentionality is different for everyone—that moment when you decide to live with purpose. For some it's an epiphany. For others it is a process. For me, it was a specific moment in time when the most important man in my life extended grace to me.

Receiving and Giving Grace

My dad had extended grace. That day I experienced an imperfect human modeling the perfect example of Christ and the commands He has given us regarding forgiveness, peacemaking, and forbearance. My father's act of grace so fundamentally changed my perspective on hope and redemption that to this day—even as I write—it is difficult to think back on that moment without tears. Would I have my family today had my father not extended grace? Would I have peace with God?

We learn about relational grace in the beautiful New Testament passage of Philippians 2:1-16, the center of which is a song of praise for Christ. The passage begins with this exhortation:

> So if there is any encouragement in Christ, any comfort from love, any participation in the Spirit, any affection and sympathy, complete my joy by being of the same mind, having the same love, being in full accord and of one mind. Do nothing from selfish ambition or conceit, but in humility count others more significant than yourselves. Let each of you look not only to his own interests, but also to the interests of others.

In part, the message is about valuation—how our personal value proposition guides our choices. Selfishness directs us to think more highly of ourselves. Christ directs us to "count others more significant than yourselves," which is counterintuitive in the modern world. It fascinates me because I am in the business of value. My staff joins me daily examining markets in an effort to accurately ascribe value to assets. Our ability to properly assess value could mean success or failure with our clients.

The same is true in the life of a family. The message to each family member is simple—value others more highly than yourself, and you will become a person of grace. Forgiveness will be much easier. Healing will come sooner. Family unity can be a reality.

Relational grace does not blind a person to relational problems, nor is it an exercise in pitting mercy against justice. Something more fundamental, more beautiful, is happening. Relational grace is a demonstration of the integrity of the Gospel—a message of forgiveness and reconciliation—in the life of an individual.

We know the meaning of just deserts. Grace is receiving something other than what law and justice mandates. Grace in relationship to other people introduces the idea that we can choose to be magnanimous, forbearing, and selfless in contexts where we might otherwise be justified in seeking judgment proportionate to the action or attitude in question. We learn grace from the life of Jesus. Story after story of disappointing choices met with the response, "Your sins are forgiven, go and sin no more."

Grace should not be confused with a free pass or "mulligan." Grace is never enabling. God's command to "go and sin no more" underscores an intolerance for our waywardness, while at the same time representing enduring love and tolerance for the person with the open arms of a loving father never retracted. While we were yet sinners, Christ died for us (Romans 5:8). Clearly in spite of our choices, God moves toward us in relationship to forgive, redeem, and invite us into a life that transcends our natural inclinations. Grace should be a constant theme in relationship with others to remind us that we are not mere mortals and were, in fact, designed for unimaginable greatness—a reflection of the Imago Dei. Grace transcends ugly and disappointing circumstances to stand as a testimony to the vision of God in and for our lives.

Grace is the gift of God and is cultivated in our lives as we become more aware—spiritually, intellectually, and experientially—of our own desperate need for grace. Those who recognize their own need for grace should be the first to extend it to others. But just in case any of us forget the importance of showing grace to offenders, Christ offered a reminder in the story of a man who was forgiven of his own heavy debts, only to relentlessly pursue another man for a comparatively small offense (Matthew 18:21-35). In the end, the man who was forgiven much, but refused to extend grace to another, suffered great punishment.

In my father, I see a man who is very aware of his failures and does not hide them. He lives bathed in grace with a deep appreciation for it. Extending grace to others is an expression of gratitude for the debts we have been forgiven. That has helped me as a son and brought me to the following conclusion: Without a fundamental redemptive foundation to any generational legacy, our best efforts and practical planning may produce little more than wood, hay, and stubble. Redemption is only possible where grace is extended and received.

Grace wins the day.

The Case for Redemptive Ethics

The message of this book can be reduced to three simple points: 1.) Successful families have a big vision for legacy. 2.) Successful families are intentional. And 3.) Successful families are redemptive. The third point may be the most surprising because it is rarely mentioned in articles and books pertaining to wealth management and legacy, but it is the reason for sharing my journey from the table to the sty to the diner. It is perhaps the single most important point I will make in this book.

There is little hope for your legacy unless you model a family culture of confession and forgiveness, where parents and children experience the peace that comes with having fractured relationships restored. Broken relationships, more than broken bank accounts, are the ruin of family legacy. It is possible to adopt a rigorous approach to intentionality—carefully shaping the legacy you intend to pass on, but without a redemptive ethic driving relationships, it won't matter. With more than fifty collective years in the wealth management business between my father and me, I am convinced that more legacies fail for want of a redemptive ethic than market fluctuations or financial mismanagement. You can work your life and amass a fortune but throw away your successes because you lost the heart of the next generation to bitterness, disappointment, and contempt.

The world is filled with deeply religious people who can speak beautiful moralisms and platitudes about faith, but when it comes time to help real people in the real world, too often the "religious" are graceless. Show me the parent who gives hope, and I will show you a parent who holds the heart. Families who embrace a redemptive ethic realize that children cannot be bullied, shamed, or coaxed into responsibility. They cannot even be educated into responsibility. Education is vital, but it is no guarantee of generational buy-in. Some of the most highly educated individuals are the most irresponsible. The history of wealth management is too often the story of sons and daughters who graduated from elite prep schools and Ivy League colleges only to disvalue their parents' sacrifice and squander their assets.

Throughout this book, I will be exploring three imperative themes as they relate to legacy and redemptive ethics: 1.) Relationships that are non-contingent, 2.) Relationships that are deeply committed, and 3.) Relationships that are humble.

1. **Relationships that are non-contingent:** The hope of redemption that God offers to the soul of man must be replicated in the life of the family. The context for that replication is grace. Children need to know they can be redeemed. No matter what happens, what mistakes they make, they can be redeemed and restored. They are going to make mistakes. They are going to make errors. We all do. But without a redemptive ethic, their lives—and the family itself—break down.

2. **Relationships that are deeply committed:** Intentional families who practice redemptive ethics learn to persevere through difficulties. They simply won't quit on each other. They keep a cool head when things get rough. They learn to improvise, adapt, and overcome. This applies to work, investments, and especially relationships. They keep their eyes on the prize. Too much is at stake. They are constantly evaluating competing priorities to make sure that the most important do not give way to the tyranny of the urgent. Intentional families are concerned about the hearts of their children. They realize the battle is won or lost at the heart level. Children must be won. The next generation must not merely be "told;" they must be nurtured. This requires time and grace.

   We have an expression in our family: "relationship is." Simple as that. Circumstances do not change the "is." Our basic relationships do not change based on the successes or failures of any member of the family. We "are" a family. It is a reflection of our basic commitments.

3. **Relationships that are humble:** Redemptive ethics presuppose humility—the recognition that our children are not programmable robots. We cannot program them and expect them to turn out a certain way and perform the way we designed them. We train, we motivate, we inspire. We sometimes restrain and discipline. We guide and direct, but ultimately they are independent individuals, made in the image of God with unique destinies, each accountable for his or her own decisions and actions. Parents cannot create men and women after their own likeness, and they should never attempt to do so.

   The goal is replication, not duplication. The distinction is vital. Duplication refers to an exact copy. To replicate is to create something similar. We can thank God that our children are not carbon copies of us. They have a life to build on the foundations of our mistakes, by not repeating them. Intentional parents have the humility to embrace their own fallibility.

   There is something even more fundamental—the question of ownership. We do not own our children. They are God's and rest in the palm of His hand. We have been given a window of time with our sons and daughters and are vested with the responsibility of shepherding them.

Wise, legacy-minded parents are those who understand that God holds the destiny of each child. It is His ultimate objectives for them, not yours, that matter. While it is true that ultimately our children are responsible for what they do with the inheritance we give them, our responsibility is clear. We are given a commission of stewardship, discernment, and careful study, which allows us to raise some of the most exciting questions of parenthood: Who are these children? Can I know them? Can I help them grow as individuals of immense worth? Can I help them fully develop the capacities and talents with which they have been endowed?

Asking these questions and more makes parenting a difficult, but beautiful, adventure because it is like managing snowflakes. There is a brief window of time to appreciate them close up. And every snowflake is different. Everyone has an individual glory. The closer you look, the more wonderful and unique.

A Parable for Our Time

A physician named Luke recorded one of the greatest parables of all time, taught by the greatest teacher who ever lived. Here is my summary: Once there was a wealthy father whose son did not appreciate the sacrifice of the prior generation. The son was thinking about himself. So he left his father with disastrous results. The son ended up wasting his father's inheritance, losing everything, and trying to survive by slopping pigs. But then the son came home. He was broken and willing to do anything, if only his father would welcome him home. Rather than rejecting the son or scolding him for his failures, the father welcomed him with open arms and threw a party. In the end, the father was far less concerned about his own disappointments than he was about an ongoing relationship with his beloved son.

The father of the prodigal son understood the heart of the matter. And for the next two thousand years, those with eyes to see and ears to hear have learned from this story. My own story has similarities and differences, but one thing rings true to me—magnanimity from a dad who offered redemption and opened the door for our personal generational victory.

The meeting in the diner was not the last rendezvous with redemption for my dad and me. Over the years, there have been more opportunities for honesty, forgiveness, counsel, healing, rebuilding, moving forward, and vision-casting. The process takes a lifetime because embracing a redemptive ethic is not a one-time event; it is a way of life.

These matters are very tender to my father and me. Dad and I have spent twenty-five years of our lives growing, wrestling, and perfecting our legacy journey. My brothers and sisters will attest to a similar story of thoughtful struggle. It's been three steps forward, one step back. Constant recalibration. Honest conversations, confession, forgiveness, redemption. It has been the process and the ever-present, ongoing reality of redemption that fills us with a deep abiding confidence in the legacy we hope to pass on to the third and fourth generation. It has been grace, glorious grace.

Legacy is a matter of the heart. Vision and virtue—the two foundational elements of a lasting legacy—will only prove successful in the context of a lifetime battle for the hearts of your family. Life, like investments, is fraught with risks. You can make a lot of mistakes financially, and you can make a lot of mistakes in your parenting. But even those mistakes can become assets for you when grace replaces "being right," and redemption is the fundamental ethic of your family. It is a lesson I learned in a Waffle House and have never forgotten.

Chapter 2

Family Foundations: Marriage, Divorce, and Staying on Track

"Here with a Loaf of Bread beneath the Bough, A Flask of Wine, a Book of Verse—and Thou Beside me singing in the Wilderness— And Wilderness is Paradise now."
- Omar Khayyám[4]

Across the street from The Great Hall at Princeton University is one of the most singular plots of land in the nation. It is not unusually beautiful and is frequented daily by only handfuls of people, but it could rightly be described as one of America's most important landmarks for the intentional family. Described as "the Westminster Abbey of the United States," the Princeton Cemetery is the final resting place for many of the literary, political, and theological elite of early American history. Row after row present clues into families who shaped a nation, some of whom successfully passed on a generational legacy to the third and fourth generations.

Of particular interest is "President's Row," a collection of graves, stones, and epitaphs dating to the eighteenth century, which contains the final remains of the early presidents of Princeton and their families. The names tell the nation's story. There is Aaron Burr, Sr., one such president, and his son, Aaron Burr, Jr., the controversial Vice President of the United States who killed Alexander Hamilton in a duel and successfully argued pro se in his own treason trial.

Not far from them is Samuel Davies, also a president of Princeton, and a man to whom both the oratorical style and personal conversion of the great Patrick Henry has been attributed. Several rows away is President Grover Cleveland and his little girl, Ruth, after whom the Baby Ruth candy bar was named.

No two graves in the Princeton Cemetery are as important for our purposes as those of Jonathan and Sarah Edwards, an unlikely couple whose intentional legacy helped shape a nation. Sarah, a woman who is remembered for her spirituality, wisdom, and excellence as a mother of three sons and eight daughters, managed the farm and tended the vines and crops. She was known for being a practical businesswoman and devoted wife. Jonathan is recognized as perhaps the greatest American theologian—a brilliant, but absent-minded, man of letters. Drawing from a rich theological heritage that emphasized work ethic, character, education, and frugality, this simple man and woman created a dynasty far-reaching in its cultural implications.

Theirs was a very special love affair. In her important work, *Marriage to a Difficult Man: The Uncommon Union of Jonathan and Sarah Edwards*, author Elisabeth Dodds explains that what made Jonathan so "difficult" was his singular devotion to his calling as preacher.[5] And what made Sarah so "uncommon" was her singular devotion to her husband, even as she managed the business of a family farm and oversaw much of the education of their children. But their love was palpable. It was known to the children and observable to every visitor who ate at their table. After one such meal, the great American preacher George Whitefield, himself a single man, drafted a journal entry in his diary which read: "Felt wonderful satisfaction in being at the house of Mr. Edwards. He is a son himself and hath also a Daughter of Abraham for his wife. A sweeter couple I have not yet seen."[6]

Now imagine if the love of your home was of such a quality that visitors were inspired to seek a spouse because of your example. Speaking of Sarah, Whitefield wrote:

"She is a woman adorned with a meek and quiet spirit, talked feelingly and solidly of the things of God, and seemed to be such a helpmeet for her husband, that she caused me to renew those prayers, which, for some months, I have put up to God, that he would be pleased to send me a Daughter of Abraham to be my wife."

What came of this couple? Scholar A.E. Winship asked that very question, and what he found was remarkable.[7] Tracing the progeny of Jonathan and Sarah Edwards for 150 years after Jonathan's death, Winship made the following astonishing discovery. The legacy of Jonathan and Sarah Edwards includes:

- one Vice President of the United States of America
- three United States senators
- three state governors
- three mayors
- thirteen college presidents
- thirty judges
- sixty-five professors
- eighty public-office holders
- 100 lawyers
- 100 missionaries

Leaders in law, politics, theology, academics—this was the fruit of Jonathan and Sarah Edwards. Notably, these children and grandchildren produced more than 135 books. The family's influence extended to commerce as well. Winship claims "There is scarcely a Great American industry that has not had one of this family among its chief promoters."[8]

In contrast, Winship also studied a contemporary of Edwards' named Max Jukes whose descendants had become well known within the New York prison system. The descendants of Jukes appeared to be a more pitiful group: seven murderers, sixty thieves, fifty prostitutes, 130 other convicts, 310 paupers who lived a combined 2,300 years in poorhouses, and 400 offspring whose lives were destroyed by excess.

The message? Legacy matters. The kind of legacy you leave will impact untold numbers of lives. What you plant today may not sprout for years, but the choices you make now may yield thorns, thistles, and weeds, or they may prove to become the choicest grapes of the most fruitful vineyards.

For our purposes, the vineyard and its fruit stand as model and metaphor to the legacy-minded family, especially those who desire that the story of their children's children will be of a people of blessing, whose "barns will be filled with plenty and your vats will be bursting with wine" (Proverbs 3:9-10).

Your Own Vintage

There are people who spend the better part of their lives looking for the perfect bottle of wine. Instead of perfection, my interest is in personality. Every bottle has one. Its personality is found not just in the finished product, but in the story of the journey from vine and grape to bottle and cork. It is all about the journey.

A bottle of wine is like a family—it comes with a history that shapes its character and gives it a distinctive flavor profile. That history reflects a series of strategic decisions and the consequences of those decisions. Where to plant? What type of environmental exposure is desirable? How much pruning should take place? Chance has little to do with wine or families; both are the product of a process. The more thought and care that goes into the process, the more likely the product will reflect excellence.

Every blend is unique, and the product of the decisions—intentional and de facto shaped the journey and resulted in a finished product. Perfection is the wrong objective for vintners and family legacy planners. Like great bottles of wine, seasoned families have imperfections that make them interesting. Discerning individuals can recognize and appreciate both the subtlety and nuance that makes them special.

Sampling a bottle of wine is like experiencing the company of family—both come with a history, character, and nuance, which makes them unique and gives them a personality. Both have levels of complexity. Some are approachable. Others less so. Both are the product of years of careful decision-making and response to natural happenstance. Vines and legacies share many common denominators, but the most prominent one is that both tend to yield great fruit as a result of intentionality. Winemaking, like legacy building, is a slow, lifetime exercise in careful thought and hard work. Both involve understanding the foundational and enduring elements that will promote growth. Both require a mastery of how to handle stress and change.

The first question in winemaking is, *What do you have to work with this year?* And the second question is, *What are you going to do with it to best coordinate the existing elements and characteristics into something that will develop to an acceptable and hopefully ideal outcome?* Every good vintner knows that winemaking is a painstaking and deliberate process, developed over many years, that combines both science and art. The most enduring element in winemaking is the soil. The soil creates for the vine its own unique character. The vine is nourished according to the soil content and quality. Some soils allow for fast growth and mass quantities of fruit. Others less so. Speed means a quicker yield. Quantity has obvious benefits. But speed and quantity can compromise quality.

Some soils introduce stress and strain to the vine. Rocky soil is one example. Like the challenges we encounter in life, which shape our character, in rocky soil or mountainside planting, more energy is typically spent maintaining the health of the vine than the quantity of the fruit. The uniqueness of the grapes tends to stand out, though. With these conditions, you get nearer to the essence of the soil's contribution to the wine. Oenophiles call this terroir. The choice of land determines the terroir. You can only control this element by deciding where you will plant your vineyard.

Environmental elements are not static. Many are uncontrollable. Like external circumstances, which bring ebb and flow to family life, the environmental life of the vineyard is one that changes annually. Grapes, like children, respond differently to each unique season in their lives. There can be huge fluctuations in temperature and wide variance in rainfall from one year to the next. In the end, the fruit of the vine will reflect the enduring elements as well as the transitory ones. As a result, some years a wine may be exceptional, and others may be less-so based on factors that are only marginally controllable.

On the other hand, winemaking, like legacy-building, also involves controllable factors that also affect the end result. Vintners must choose: organic farming or non-organic? Positioning of the vines to capture more, or less, sun exposure? How much trimming of the vines and leaves is needed to maximize energy put into the fruit? We make choices to focus our efforts and limit distractions in family life, not unlike cutting back fruit (and throwing it away!) so as to concentrate energy into the grapes that remain.

Of course there is a long list of things that happen to the grapes once they leave the field. Winemaking is organized according to a philosophy and with specific goals in mind. The process is managed down to the last detail, which can create either a masterpiece or a disaster—just like cultivating and growing a family legacy.

The God of Your Vineyard

When it comes to analogy of vineyards and legacy, the single most important metaphor was given by Jesus Christ who reminds us that "I am the true vine, and My Father is the keeper of the vineyard" (John 15:1).

Now is the time to recognize that great results require scientifically informed artistry. However, because you are attempting to shape a future contingent outcome with limited insights and limited control, you had better start praying, looking to the true keeper of the vineyard. There is simply no substitute for research, work, and prayer. The age-old dilemma of just how man's responsibility interacts with God's sovereign influence will not be resolved in this book. But here is what you can take to the bank: God blesses faithfulness.

Families have a duty to be intentional. They must prepare and plan. They can make reasonable predictions. They can develop expertise in the science of legacy-building. They can learn, for example, that certain approaches tend toward failure and others toward success. They can bring an artistry to their parenting and legacy-building that reflects wisdom, experience, and their unique gifts. When all is said and done, however, they should never confuse success with mastery of a mechanistic process or with their own artistic brilliance. Lift your prayers up to God and never underestimate His response to your prayers. "Trust in the LORD with all your heart, and do not lean on your own understanding. In all your ways acknowledge Him, and He will make straight your paths" (Proverbs 3:5-6).

With a healthy respect for the mysterious antinomy of God's sovereignty and man's responsibility, it is time to explore some of the fundamental elements in your own family's intentional journey from vine to bottle.

The Three Decisions

In our lives we will play two distinct legacy roles—heir and visionary. Think of these roles in the context of our wine analogy. The first role is as the heir to a cellar of bottles containing the legacy bequeathed to you. That cellar may contain fine wines, mediocre wines, or even rancid wines. But in whatever shape or form they come, they are fabulously valuable because they were given to you. They constitute the archives and past collective brain trust for your future legacy. Without them, you cannot properly take on the second role. The second is your role of vintner to a new, as of yet, unbottled legacy. This is a long-term responsibility with constantly changing factors, and yet there is one clear objective: excellence.

The first role comes with the responsibility of gratitude and stewardship for everything you have received—each element of which serves as your life curriculum, allowing you to study and master what must be done to improve so that you can bring forth your own special vintages. The second requires vision and oversight and builds on the knowledge of past crops. Both roles converge to form the person that you are.

There are three vital, foundational decisions that every heir and legacy visionary must make. How you address them will shape your path. These are: the decision to embrace your parents' legacy, the decision to marry wisely, and the decision to intentionally build your own legacy. Sounds simple, but the fact is, the majority of heirs to great fortunes squander the legacy they receive, develop lifestyles that lead to divorce and broken families, and seek to avoid altogether the type of advancements of maturity that prepare them to build their own legacy.

Shirtsleeves to Shirtsleeves

There is an old Scottish proverb: The father buys, the son builds, the grandchild sells, and his son begs. This is known as the problem of shirtsleeves-to-shirtsleeves in three-to-four generations. Wealth was created by parents, which was then dissipated by children. One generation labored to provide a reward for the next generation, and that next generation subsequently squandered the legacy, leaving future generations to start from scratch.

The problem of generational legacy failure is as old as the earth. It is recognized in the literature and aphorisms of diverse cultures. A proverb from Lancashire England states, "There's nobbut three generations a tween a clog and a clog." The Italians say, "Dalle stalle alle stellle alle stalle." From stalls to stars to stalls. The Japanese say, "Rice patties to rice patties in three generations." The Chinese say, "Wealth never survives three generations."

The core problem with a dying legacy is selfishness. One generation sees the bequest of their parents as a cul-de-sac. The gift goes to them and no further. It is a problem of the heart and mind, more than the balance sheet. The recipient makes the mistake of thinking that a gift is about themselves, rather than about their own duty to others. This is why one of the first principles of legacy is generational responsibility—the understanding that our resources are given to us by God and held in trust for the benefits of a greater purpose. We are merely stewards.

Insofar as any parental generation fails to teach this stewardship principle of transcendent purpose and selfless duty to their progeny, they should not presume that their lifetime of labor and sacrifice will reap a meaningful dividend in the lives of their children. James Hughes, author of several books, including *Family Wealth: Keeping It in the Family*, explains that despite the fact that nearly all wealthy families have a finance preservation strategy, less than one-third are successful in passing it on to their grandchildren.[9] What was once a shirtsleeves-to-shirtsleeves problem in four generations has been reduced to three. And the legacy gaps are getting bigger. Some would argue that the breakdown is presently verging on two generations. The breakdown between boomers and their parents can be attributed to a fundamental disconnect in communication, values, and family culture.

This shirtsleeves-to-shirtsleeves phenomenon looks something like this:

- **The Shirtsleeve Generation:** The first (or founder) generation starts from scratch. They roll up their shirtsleeves and get to work. Husband and wife share an ethic for life and hard work. Their efforts pay off. The result is wealth. They usually achieve this wealth without any fundamental changes to their values and lifestyle. Often these same parents want "something better for their children." They want their children to benefit from these successes and enjoy the fruits of prosperity. They don't want to see their progeny endure the hardships they had to endure to create the wealth.
- **The Spendthrift Generation:** The second generation is able to leverage the benefits of their parents. They move to their version of the Hamptons, drive nice cars, eat at the best restaurants, and rise in society. Because they have learned to spend money, rather than make money, the family fortune begins to decline. Consumed with the good life, they lack the values of their parents including hard work, savings, simplicity, and delayed gratification for long-term benefit.
- **The Cynical Generation:** With few core values and even less vision inherited from their parents, the third generation dissipates the remaining wealth. They identify the hypocrisies of the past generation, grow cynical, and perpetuate the problem. The devaluation of family values and vision, which their parents allowed in moderation, they take to an extreme.
- **The Shirtsleeve Generation:** The fourth generation is back to the beginning—with nothing. This generation must find its way by once again rolling up shirtsleeves and starting from scratch. There is a net loss, however, in that the values of the founder generation must be rediscovered or replaced by a more lasting vision.

In their book *The Fourth Turning: An American Prophesy*, authors William Strauss and Neil Howe examine how social change occurs from one generation to another.[10] Experiences are lost, and stories of the past fade with time. New generations think and act differently, drawing upon a new and distinct interpretation of the world. It has been argued that four generations, just like four seasons, mark a full revolution of time, or social thought. For Strauss and Howe, this implies a cyclicality in history. We see a similar pattern in families. Time erodes the clarity of message from one generation to the next. We learn from either formal study, or we learn from direct experience. Failure to duplicate these instructional journeys means that each family will see a generational disconnect, each drawing on a different knowledge base. Santayana famously said that if we don't learn from the past, we will repeat it. This is the inherent and inevitable danger of collective amnesia, which is only prevented with deliberate effort and a recast vision in each generation.

Lack of a financial succession plan is only one reason why families lose their wealth. Of the 70 percent who succumb to the shirtsleeves-to-shirtsleeves epidemic, nearly all of them have a financial succession plan. What then is the problem? In each family the issues involved are unique and complex. It seems, however, from one generation to another, if parents do not cast an adequate vision, foster strong relationships, and replicate in the next generation those essential qualities that were required in their own generation to make progress, then the path to starting all over again (back to shirtsleeves) has been initiated. Choosing to take a financial inheritance, without understanding or appreciating what it took to create it, leaves the heart of a legacy behind. So to avoid the shirtsleeves-to-shirtsleeves cycle, one must with gratitude value what has been received and put to use the practical tools needed to steward that legacy for the benefit of the generations that are to come.

You cannot just give a legacy to a child and expect positive results. They have to receive it. That is a key point of this book. You must prepare children to receive their legacy through a lifetime of intentional choices as a family. Intentionality presupposes that for children to properly receive a legacy, they must understand it. More importantly, they must want it. Their growing realization of their familial identity and their valuing of their spiritual, intellectual, cultural, and financial inheritance is a process that may take years.

The Decision to Embrace My Father's Legacy

After the Waffle House, my new world began. Thus commenced the first step in a journey of maturity, which for me was often two steps forward and one step back. But it was always exciting. The formal concept of legacy was still fuzzy to me. What I knew was this—I was rediscovering what it meant to be a McAlvany.

My tendency towards self-absorption and seriousness morphed into a newfound, and often annoying, earnestness. In this case, it was what my father *did not do* which opened the door for me to receive his legacy. He did not stop me from exploring, thinking, testing ideas, or going through the often-painful process of owning a worldview. My own journey began with books. I entered a world of men whose faith was more than words, and grace moved from a theoretical idea to a living reality between my father and me. As I began to explore the lifelong impact of grace, my thinking was deeply influenced by the books of Francis Schaeffer, GK Chesterton, and C.S. Lewis. Reading *Pilgrim's Progress* was instructive for discerning the life choices that would help or hurt my effort to grow and mature.

At the age of seventeen, I read *The Cost of Discipleship* by Dietrich Bonhoeffer. Part of the intellectual defense of Christianity and opposition movement to Adolf Hitler during the high point of the Third Reich, Bonhoeffer would ultimately die a martyr at the hands of the Nazis, just days before the liberation of Germany by allied forces. Bonhoeffer underscored the high cost of grace and reminded me that my previous treatment of it had been to devalue and diminish it. More than any other volume, it became an aide-mémoire, marking the transition from an adolescent myopia to a robust vision of love, sacrifice, and maturity.

Dad started treating me as a man-in-the-making. He gave me the freedom to grow and to learn. He sent me out into the world where I enjoyed robust experiences. He encouraged me to draw from his personal reputational life capital with business associates who welcomed me into their offices and homes. This generosity not only allowed me to master new skills and be exposed to new ideas, but it also allowed me to see my father through the eyes of other men—as a patriot, a businessman, a Christian, and a leader. That alternative vision was good for my own soul. It tempered me when I was inclined to reflect on his shortcomings and reminded me that my life was a part of something much larger than I was.

Throughout this season I took mental notes. What was I supposed to learn? To believe? What were the values I was supposed to embrace both as an individual and as a member of a respected family? I did not always have answers, but some things became increasingly clear. One was that being a McAlvany not only came with opportunities, but also responsibilities. I was emerging into my own man. My father wanted that. I needed that. But being a distinct person with a unique identity did not expunge my family identity.

Life as a Single Man

My journey through higher education began to build on that breakfast at Waffle House. It was my personal time to begin the process of recasting vision. Here I would find inspiration in new worlds of ideas. These ideas would stretch me, challenging me to test and expand the values and beliefs of the first twenty years of my life. Thus began my season of self-reliance.

My academic training consisted of two defining experiences: my three years as an undergraduate at Biola University and my year at Oxford University. At Biola University I studied under great apologists and philosophers, men and women of character and insight who opened my mind to three thousand years of Western intellectual tradition in the context of Christian thought. I found the core worldview given to me by my father reinforced, even as my mind broke new ground exploring the worlds of classical philosophy and supplementing the "what" of our family catechism with the "why" of philosophical insight. Where Biola reinforced my worldview, Oxford tested it. In both cases, the net effect was the spark of maturity.

Experience informs intellectual curiosity. In my case the personal pains and disappointments of the past piqued my interest in issues of redemption, integrity, and hope. It was here where I first began to study the visional ethics of Stanley Hauerwas—a Christian philosopher and theologian writing of hope and redemption based on the premise that we should see others as God sees them—completed, grown up, mature individuals living into their fullest capacities—whether they presently are or not.

As a single man, my life was something like a musical gathering at an Irish watering hole—spontaneous instrumental explosion meets endless regaling of adventure stories, philosophical debate, and futurist speculation. That was David McAlvany the emerging man. I was a grape-laden vine, ripening in the sun, but untested. My roots were still searching for depth.

Sometimes reality was a step removed, and there was never a plan for tomorrow. The present moment and future extemporaneous feat was too easily disrupted and bound by the obligations of a charted course.

That was the B.R. period: "Before Responsibility." Of course it was an era where a lot less was actually accomplished. Goals were life goals. They were for the future, and the future was a long way off. I had a lifetime to accomplish them.

The Decision to Marry Wisely

I met the love of my life in the usual, completely unexpected way these things happen. The location was Texas, and the circumstance was a lecture on the influence of postmodernism on contemporary dance. She was the teacher.

In the span of fifty-five minutes, this sprite of an intellectual powerhouse spit out volumes of information so quickly that I wrote in the margins of my notes, "who could ever keep up with this gal?" My intrigue grew at the conclusion of her message when I discovered that this Mary-Catherine was not only an accomplished lecturer, but also a dancer and a connoisseur of all things artistic and intellectual. But it was the line of sculptures that finally got to me. There in the hallway outside the lecture room were these amazing creations made by the woman whose encyclopedic knowledge of dance theory had just wowed me. I was sold.

I was nervous. I was excited. So I made my move and began the first of ten thousand conversations. To my astonishment she, too, not only had attended Oxford but also had been part of Keble College like I had. We had just missed each other, but we took the same courses, studied under the same professors, read the same books, and had studied on the same parallel track, asking the same kind of questions.

How could all of this be an accident?

A romance began, but a cautious one, which matured largely in telephone calls and letters from a distance. For two-and-a-half years, we wrote and called each other. The phone bills were astronomical, but we did not care. The synchronicity of our interests continued to manifest.

During this season, I had an experience that changed the way I looked at my world. One day, at the age of twenty-five, I found myself making a five-course Easter feast—just for myself—when I realized the singular state I was in. What kind of life is it to create experiences and memories for yourself, which will never be shared with another human being? Meals, like life, are meant to be shared, particularly five-course Easter feasts! Was this my future? What was I thinking? It was the pinnacle of loneliness, so I grabbed my journal and went to the park and wrote this: "How rotten to live life alone."

The only person I could envision creating life-long memories with was Mary-Catherine. She was always on my mind, but something more was needed to cinch the deal. That something was the Shakespeare Festival in Boise, Idaho. For three glorious days we watched epic performances of plays written by the Bard, went rock climbing and river rafting, and talked over picnic lunches and luxurious meals. I was insanely, head-over-heels in love, and down for the count.

With that long weekend, the second great life-legacy question— Whom will you marry?—was answered for me.

Returning for just a moment to the analogy of the vineyard, marriage can be likened to the press whereby the choicest grapes from two differ- ent vines can be selected and combined, thus generating a blend with the highest concentrate of excellence. This is how I see my marriage: a Cham- pagne blend of chardonnay and pinot noir with appealing notes that is still maturing.

The advent of marriage also served as a wormhole through space, somehow shrinking time and allowing me to cover greater distances. Mar- riage is a multiplier, and not just of children. Where unity exists between man and wife, marriage can increase effectiveness exponentially.

I feel it. The multiplying effect is real. Together, Mary-Catherine and I create a space where dreams and reality meet in an unmatchable dyna- mism. We share responsibility. We daily divide to conquer. We operate in social gatherings and with our kids like tag team wrestlers, with one allow- ing the other to recoup while the team still presses onward with energy and spirit. In business she has the practical experience and depth of insight that comes from being raised around a family enterprise. In the home she is a practical visionary guiding our children through the minds of the great thinkers and the heart of great literature, encouraging creativity and play, both precursors to the innovation and vision-casting in their future. In her I have a trusted counselor, long on wisdom, deep on intuition and instinct.

As it is true that "love covers a multitude of sins," so too the charity of a good woman covers the blemishes and peccadilloes of her husband. That is my experience. Where I am cautious in my interactions with others, she is appropriately daring with dignity. For all the gaps in my interior life, she seems to fill them with grace and strength.

When a marriage is born, there is a sacrifice of self-interest. Because a marriage is made up of two imperfect individuals, even the best marriages will involve challenges, which usually can be traced back to one or the other spouse forgetting the prime directive and placing self before other. It is a battle that will remain throughout life and marriage, but the sooner you realize the stakes that are on the line, the more likely you are to make efforts to fix the problem. Without an effort to elevate "us" and sacrifice self, you cannot presume success with your legacy as an intentional family. A legacy of love and self-sacrifice is inherently other-oriented.

As grapes must be crushed to produce wine, so married life does not mature without pressure and time. Understandably, marriage has many challenges. Good relationships take hard work. The dividends of this God-blessed labor cannot be calculated. Then too there is the deeply satisfying sense that hard work invested now, in our family and in our business, is giving life to what is next—a future we don't control but can imagine even in a blurred form.

Marriage and Maturity

Marriage matures men. It takes desire and energy and gives both a focal point and an outlet for expression. It directs their sexual impulses towards fruitfulness and responsibility. It teaches men that love comes with a price—self-control and self-sacrifice. The advent of children should speak to the soul of a man, reminding him that his life is not his own. In all of these ways, marriage has the potential to give a meaningful context to masculinity.

Marriage harnesses a man's energy. The very nature of healthy family life encourages a process allowing men to exchange the emotional, psychological, and relational acne of their youth for a social and spiritual countenance of maturity. Men are at their best in marriage—at least that should be the case for most men.

Within our modern culture, there are a thousand distractions luring men from the path of maturity and beckoning them to adjust their appetites towards a fantasy world of pubescent proclivities and irresponsible behavior. Perhaps more than any generation for the last two centuries, ours is the epoch of the perpetual child. And it's not child-like wonder that we are perpetuating, but childishness.

When men remain children, families disintegrate. The next generation rebels. Marriages crumble. These distractions are legacy killers. Unchecked they would enslave men to an unending frat house mentality. The ever-present lure of pornography, the Madison Avenue emphasis on perpetual youth, the social expectations for immediate gratification—all this and more are signs of the times.

Marriage and Risk

I have always been a risk taker. But as a first-born male with an ingrained sense of duty and responsibility, I have historically taken calculated risks. (Okay, when I was a teenager, they were less calculated.)

As a wealth manager, I am very interested in the relationship of risk to legacy. Wealth management is a constant process of risk-taking, risk-mitigation, and the cost-benefit analyses that help decipher both. One of the consequences of marital maturity is that on a very personal level marriage impacts risk analysis. Responsible, married men become more thoughtful before betting the farm. Marriage does not remove risk, but because the heart of marriage is responsibility, that relationship does change the cost-benefit analysis. It is not that risk takers like myself suddenly become risk averse. It's simply that we approach the cost-benefit analysis of each circumstance with greater thoughtfulness, which is why the last time I attempted a winter ascent on a large glacial peak and was confronted with unstable snow pack and a higher-than-average probability of avalanche, the decision was easy.

There is a reason why the United States military handed P-51 Mustangs and Thunderbolts to thousands of eighteen-year-old boys during World War II and had them engage the enemy with daredevil maneuvers. Eighteen-year-old young men are the demographic with the least realistic sense of mortality. They will do what the twenty-four-year-old men will not—engage in ultra-high-risk maneuvers without flinching. Maturity and responsibility changes a man's risk quotient. The principle extends beyond combat training. It is one thing to risk your life as a single man. It is another to take disproportionate risks with a wife and children depending on you to return home.

Facing a decision as to whether to take a slope where the possibility of an avalanche has increased from a mere 5% to 10%, I realize that something more has changed than the probability of an icy catastrophe. My own mental calculus has changed, and dramatically so, since I was eighteen, more so since I married at twenty-five, and even more still since I started to have children! Marriage breeds responsibility. Responsibility births intentionality. Intentionality precedes legacy.

Now there is a different vision of the future, which has been refined and clarified as the family has grown. I'd like to stick around. There is an enormous impact in the way a married man and or a family man lives his life, and the future, as well as present, family needs are huge factors. No, if you are wondering, I didn't proceed to the peak. We turned around. And yes, the snowfield we found suspicious did slide a few days later, taking seven climbers off the mountain in the process.

The Disappearance of Marriage

One of the issues that has added complexity to the dialogue on wealth succession plans in the context of family legacy is the disappearance of marriage. We have reached the point in history where marriage is no longer the presumption as a foundation for a grounded society. It is not even the presumption in many Christian churches. As a wealth management specialist, this creates some practical challenges. As an author, it means I can no longer assume that a general audience of readers will share the common ground of the family as the primary vehicle for legacy. Nor can I assume that the presumption that marriage is one man and one woman for life will be embraced by the next generation. Since beginning my work on this book and the publication of its content, the United States has already undergone a radical transformation with the Supreme Court's ruling legitimizing same-sex marriages.

So I am going to say it, clearly—I am an advocate for traditional marriage. One man and one woman for life in an institution designed and blessed by God for our benefit. I think we give up on our covenants too easily. Ours is a culture that is training its children to think lightly of marriage. This, more than inadequate succession plans, threatens the highest ideals of family legacy.

The family is the bedrock of society. It was the first institution and remains such. The family, not the state, is the basic locus for generational care, education, and commerce. Those of you who are considering a life well-lived and a legacy well-crafted and given should do so in terms of a family unit.

There are exceptions to the rule. Even in the Bible, there appear to be unique individuals given a special gift of celibacy, as well as others who, through unique circumstance, simply find themselves in prolonged single-ness. There are even seasons of cultural upheaval and imminent death where the Apostle Paul reasons that it may be best to wait on marriage "for the present distress." But such are the exceptions.

The presumption for an efficient, happy, fulfilled life of significant love and labor is marriage. I have found marriage to be an incubator for personal growth and formation as I've learned, first from being married and then from raising a family, the extent of my ingrained self-centeredness and comprehensive need for transformation.

Legacy after Divorce

A very practical issue today concerns the redefinition of a family following divorce. Divorce is a form of death—a person has ceased to exist. Before, there was you the individual, and there was the unique person created when you became one as man and wife. But that person is now gone. The world necessarily looks different. Legacy must be reevaluated and re-crafted. Divorce brings added complexity to the question of maintaining a context for the transmission of values. Notably, it introduces a regressive math into the equation as well: Take resources and divide by two!

Divorce is an epidemic crisis of modern society. Probably fifty percent of you reading this book will have suffered the pain of divorce, either as one who has personally suffered a marital break-up or as being a child of divorce. The norm today is not an enduring relationship of love and grace, but the death of love and commitment as a consequence of hardening hearts.

If ever there was a season in our history that called for compassion for broken families, this is it. Few people are untouched by it. My own father is a child of divorce. My wife is a child of divorce. Their lives were profoundly influenced by coming from a broken home. Rather than being the end of their stories, it was the beginning.

Divorce is another form of legacy, encompassing the disappointed hopes and expectations of a life together. Children carry it forward as an inseparable part of their identity. Adults grieve a real death. But divorce is not the end. No circumstance is beyond redemption. I recall those closest to me, both family and friends, who have demonstrated dogged determination to adapt, heal, grow, and reestablish a vision tragically broken by divorce, but never cast off.

Legacy Beauty for Ashes

There are examples of people who model grace—grace under fire, grace to overcome seemingly insurmountable obstacles, grace as a reflection of the love of God in their lives. These men and women remind us of God's mercy and the power to overcome.

My friend Kim is one example. When Mary-Catherine and I think of a hero, we think of Kim. She is a brilliant and beautiful woman who suffers no fools. Tragedy struck her life when she discovered one day that her husband's constant absences from their home were because he was a sex addict engaging in numerous (potentially hundreds) of affairs and the hiring of prostitutes. His adultery introduced sickness into the family. The situation was simply nightmarish, but she had three children with her husband. What to do?

Kim made the toughest call of her life: divorce. Using her degree in education, she became the primary financial provider. And determined to be emotionally available for her children, she chose not to date until her last child was off to college.

The years went by. She kept all of her promises. She did not date a single person until the youngest left for college. She never spoke an ill word against her former husband. She never uncovered his wrongs to their children. She was respectful. She was circumspect. One day a child asked, "Mom, did Dad cheat on you?" Her only reply was, "Yes. You are going to have to come to terms with this and reflect on how anyone's selfishness can impact those around them." Consistently she proved herself to be a woman of honor, more concerned with raising her children in an environment of integrity than with exercising her own rights. She created a substantial legacy by prioritizing her children and investing in the development of their gifts and talents.

God is bigger than any seemingly insurmountable problem. He is the one who designed marriage and legacy. He is the one who can restore "the years that the locusts have eaten." We have seen this over and over again.

My own family involves the story of mercy and redemption after divorce. Dad was raised by a single mom who did her very best. She understood what psychologists like Paul Vitz have reminded us—it is one thing to lose a father, but it is another to lose a father and never have a father surrogate. Children must have a masculine, fatherly influence. It is essential. My grandmother understood this. After she divorced, she knew that in Texas there was a loving family with a friend who seemed to be uncle material. So my grandmother decided to pick up everything she had and move to Texas so that my dad and aunt would grow up with male role models and solid companionship. She never married again, but she gave my father hope. She did something else well too. She made a decision that shaped my father's life forever. She refused to allow negativity to govern her home. Home would be a happy place and a world of laughter. My dad would tell you they had the happiest childhood because they laughed all the time. His mom was always able to bring joy into the family. She made smart decisions surrounding him with positive influences. She worked with what she had. As a mom, she was willing to say, "Don, it's not ideal, but let's do the best we can with what we have got."

As I found redemption when grace was extended to me in a Waffle House, broken families can give and receive grace all the time. The Apostle James writes, "God resists the proud, but gives grace to the humble." Even when our very best is a failure, God's grace is sufficient. It allows us to be men and women of vision, ever looking forward.

I know God has done something with our imperfect family. Perhaps He has done the same for yours. Imperfection makes us more dependent on Him. It reminds us that we are needy. We need to have God "forgive us our debts even as we forgive our debtors." It is one of the reasons why legacy presupposes an ethic of forgiveness and grace. It is a reminder that God grants legacy to the widow, the fatherless, and to divorced men and women hoping to rebuild the rest of their lives.

The "C" Word

Sometimes it takes the emotional equivalent of a bat to the face to wake a man from the drunken slumber of immaturity. I was a thirty-year-old husband still wrestling with relational infancy. In 2004 I received one of those shattering blows, and my infancy ended.

Mary-Catherine was diagnosed with cancer.

I thought she would always be there, but then I heard the word "cancer." You hear this word all the time. It is no big deal because it is always someone else's problem, not yours. It can't happen to someone you love. But then it does. In one moment, all of your hopes and dreams stand at the precipice of a cliff from which there is no return. It was the birth of clarity. It was the birth of a much deeper love.

In the nanosecond that it took me to process the potential imminent loss of my wife, everything else became meaningless. Every idiotic fantasy, every wasted moment not poured into the life of the one true object of all my earthly affections and dreams, became less than worthless.

What do I do?

Yes, there were doctors and diets and treatments, but in the end, all I knew was desperate prayer. "God, save my wife." Every day and every night the same prayer. "Please, just save my wife." And He did. She was spared. God strengthened her to beat cancer.

One of the greatest mistakes we make in life is to minimize mercy. There is a moment of despair. We cry out to God, and He shows mercy. For a brief moment we experience gratitude, but then we are back to the business of life. We forget the magnitude of the gift of mercy. We forget the nightmare from which we have been spared. I learned to be grateful in the midst of chaos and fear, and I find that remembrance of that mercy continually draws our hearts together. Painful disturbances in life can be a blessing.

The Decision to Build My Legacy

The greatest impediment to any endeavor is lack of resolve. The greater the focus, the higher likelihood for success. Find any great Olympic athlete, and you are likely to discover a person with extraordinary commitment to a personal mission objective. They recognize that the tiniest distractions can derail a vision. Big distractions can deep-six it.

Great legacy presupposes great intentionality. No great legacy vision can survive a non-redemptive atmosphere closed off to grace. These problems may be the reason why some of you reading this book cannot sustain a commitment to become the intentional family you desire. As an idea, legacy is desirable. Becoming an intentional family sounds great. The end results are attractive. But the commitment to maintain resolve over many years is daunting. It requires something unusual, something modeled by couples like Jonathan and Sarah Edwards whose simple commitments led to progeny who would shape a nation. On the most basic level, they would not be dissuaded from the simple commitment of an intentional life.

I entered my thirties with two great transformations. The first was the recognition that life as I knew it had almost ended, but God showed mercy on us by sparing my wife. The second was the revitalization of a vision for family legacy with a renewed clarity of vision, empowered by the removal of distractions. I was all in.

The results were almost immediate. Our life objectives began to mature. Our time spent together matured in quality. Our transparency as a couple matured. Most importantly, our dreams expanded to encompass a far-reaching vision for our children— beginning in the heart, cultivated in the home, and ultimately extending to others through business, art, and culture.

Chapter 3

The Blessing of Disturbance

"After a great blow, or crisis, after the first shock and then after the nerves have stopped screaming and twitching, you settle down to the new condition of things and feel that all possibility of change has been used up. You adjust yourself, and are sure that the new equilibrium is for eternity . . . "
— Robert Penn Warren, *All the King's Men*[11]

Life is beautiful, but it is not pretty. If you plan for a life free of chaos, you will be sorely disappointed. Every lasting legacy is built around preparation for the inevitability of disturbance—those moments that introduce havoc and threaten your best hopes and dreams.

Disturbance can take the form of a financial, environmental, criminal, personal, ethical, or spiritual crisis. Disturbance can be a crash in the financial markets, a debilitating sickness, the unexpected death of a loved one, a public scandal, a government audit, an act of betrayal, or a catastrophic environmental event—anything that undermines the status quo. In those moments, it is your response to upheaval, not the interference itself, which can make or break your legacy objectives.

With most life disturbances, three messages speak to the nature of crisis itself:

- **Crisis often emerges because problems have been ignored.** Most disturbance is predictable, usually emerging in the context of unresolved problems. With better analysis and preparation, the deleterious effects of crisis can be mitigated.
- **Crisis is preparation for the next crisis.** Disturbance must be a presumption of life, not an unexpected singularity. We spend our lives moving from one disturbance to the next. The smaller

disturbances prepare us for the larger ones.

- **Crisis is opportunity in disguise.** With every disturbance we encounter, we can choose to be a helpless and disoriented victim or an innovator who not only survives, but thrives. It is largely a matter of perspective.

Crisis Often Emerges Because Problems Are Ignored

Disturbance does not emerge in a vacuum. There are signs and predictors. Causes go ignored. You and I are not always directly responsible for disturbance. We may have little to nothing to do with some of them, but that does not mean we cannot anticipate their arrival. More is involved than reading tea leaves. We must understand the times, like the sons of Issachar (1 Chronicles 12:13), and do the analysis.

The Bible presents the sons of the tribe of Issachar as a family of wise men of action who lived during the Old Testament era of Israel. Three observations are noteworthy: First, they were part of a family culture that emphasized analysis. Somewhere in the generational line, the family patriarchs had determined that their survival as a family required the gathering and processing of social, cultural, and economic realities. Second, their unique virtue was the ability to "understand the times"—to evaluate trends that could adversely affect them or result in calamity. Third, they not only predicted the potential of disturbance, but they understood how to respond to it. They were problem solvers capable of making intelligent decisions about how to prepare for crisis.

Intentional families need to be like the "sons of Issachar" families who are purposeful to understand the times so they can make informed predictions that lead to action. Tragedy predominates where leaders deny the imminence of disturbance in the face of incontrovertible evidence. Whether the subject is families, companies, or nations, an unwillingness to assume disturbance leads to failure. One of the clearest examples of this occurs with the absence of a succession plan in a family, business, or nation. People age. They die. The need to replace leaders is inescapable. Lack of a plan will create a disturbance that inevitably breeds insecurity, jealousies, divisions, and often even violent responses.

Alexander the Great was one of the most important men in world history. Prophesied in the Bible, and having successfully conquered more of the world than any other man, his death at the age of thirty-three in 327 B.C. sent shock waves. Although there is a certain degree of historical controversy about the nature of Alexander the Great's wishes at the time of his death, most scholars agree that the absence of a clear succession plan plunged the empire into civil war as survivors scrambled for power and resources.

Families and businesses routinely are guided by larger-than-life leaders with a clear vision and confidence that makes decision-making seem effortless. This is a benefit until that clear direction is lost. Developing a succession plan is more than a will or last testament; it is the living, breathing mentorship necessary for a leader to be replaced and able to step aside as a lynchpin. A confident leader, building something that will last in his or her absence, can address succession failure through a vision of the organization cast selflessly.

While it is difficult to predict a specific day of crisis, it is easy to anticipate when crisis will occur based on context. The stock market crash of 1929 was a predictable event. Exceptionally loose monetary policies made it easy for people to speculate in the stock market. It created a feeding frenzy driving prices continually upward. It was an unsustainable environment. Implosion was inescapable. But only handfuls of investors prepared for the inevitable implosion. When the crisis hit, it hit hard.

Winston Churchill was visiting New York on Black Tuesday, October 24, 1929, when the stock market crashed. Financial turmoil resulted in widespread panic. People abandoned hope and made rash decisions. Churchill was awakened the next day by a noisy crowd outside the Savoy-Plaza Hotel and would later write, "Under my very window a gentleman cast himself down fifteen stories and was dashed to pieces, causing a wild commotion and the arrival of the fire brigade."[12]

While there are tragic tales of lost savings and upset dreams when a market does the unexpected, it's worth noting that a market moving down is not, in fact, unexpected. Since 1877 the U.S. stock market has spent 40 percent of the time moving down and not up. With this kind of cyclical predictability, it is possible to inform a family perspective on markets that sees the creation of value in episodes of collapse. Only the fully invested feels the destruction of value and the loss of hope in such a spasmodic period. Is it any different than forecasting the weather (admittedly challenging) and carrying a raincoat or umbrella on a day it may rain?

Denial is another form of crisis preparation avoidance. There are hundreds of millions of people who choose to live near volcanoes, including several highly populated cities. Usually this is not a problem because eruptions are rare and predictable. The benefits of living near a volcanic region include geothermal energy, fertile soils, availability of valuable minerals, and tourism. Notwithstanding the predictability of many volcanoes, it is not uncommon for some local residents living near a volcanic mountain to choose to remain in harm's way, rather than heed warning signs of imminent disaster. Influenced by personal experience and misplaced loyalty to a location, rather than clear factual data, some ignore the warning of scientists.

Fifty-seven people died when Mount St. Helens erupted in Washington state on May 18, 1980. Autopsies showed that most of the people killed in the eruption likely died from asphyxiation after inhaling hot ash. One of those to die was eighty-three-year-old widower, Harry Randall Truman, who lived alone with sixteen cats. Officials repeatedly urged Truman to leave the mountain. Truman owned a lodge on Spirit Lake for more than fifty years. When asked about the volcanic threat, Truman responded with colorful interviews to the press: "I'm going to stay right here because, I'll tell you why, my home and my life's here . . . My wife and I, we both vowed years and years ago that we'd never leave Spirit Lake. We loved it. It's part of me, and I'm part of that mountain."[13] On May 18, his home was hit by a mud-and-snow avalanche, and his remains were never found. He is still a part of that mountain.

Perhaps that is poetic—being old and OK with becoming a part of the mountain. Embedded in this disposition of denial seems to be a presumption of historical uniqueness. Either it can't happen to me, or this environment is different for the following reasons and therefore will not pose a threat. Denial has grounds. It's important to analyze the assumptions and presumptions that undergird it.

You may not live on a volcano—you may live with one. Allowing conflict to go unresolved for months or years within family relationships can allow for pressure to build under the surface until one day the emotional eruption occurs.

Crisis as Preparation for the Next Crisis

In the winter of 1999, a private plane carrying a mother and father plummeted into the mountains outside of Durango, Colorado. The precise whereabouts of the plane was unknown, and the prospects for survival was grim. If any of the passengers were alive, they would be facing the prospect of freezing to death at a high and largely inaccessible altitude. Time was of the essence.

At the base of the mountain, traffic gathered, and police assembled to survey the situation. The authorities on the scene either did not know what to do or were unwilling to do it. There was a general state of confusion. Banter was exchanged over who was responsible for the search-and-rescue, or whether they should wait for back-up. And the clock continued to tick.

Into this stalemate of jurisdictional chest-puffing and general disorientation, a sixteen-year-old local mountain climber named Scott arrived on the scene. Standing five-foot-nine, he was tough-as-nails and scrappy, but he had never before faced a crisis of life and death. Scott had grown up in a household where the language of preparedness in the context of personal, political, and economic instability was part of the routine family vocabulary. But he had never been tested. Within seconds of his arrival at the base of the mountain, Scott noted the disorganization and inactivity of the people at the scene. Their behavior was inefficient and self-serving. As he interacted with police, his mind was processing the stalemate between officials. Then something clicked. Scott made the decision to take command of the situation. "I am going to find them."

In the absence of a better plan and unwilling to put themselves in harm's way for such a low probability of success, the authorities on the ground stood down and let him go.

Taking a close friend and grabbing some gear, Scott attempted an arduous ascent of the mountain in search of the plane and any survivors. Hours of intense climbing in the inhospitable winter climate ultimately yielded success, but the discovery was tragic. The plane had crashed into the side of the mountain, shattering into pieces. No one survived, but there were bodies—or rather, body parts, strewn over the snowy mountain crags and rocks.

Once again Scott had to make a decision—what to do? Return to the ground and report to authorities? Wait for someone to find them? It was the first time he had looked death in the face, but he kept a clear head and resolved to take action. If this had been his family, he reasoned, he would hope someone would do the same for them. So he carefully collected the body parts and prepared them to be transported off the mountain. Scott and his friend had done what no one else was willing to do.

Full disclosure—Scott is my younger brother, and for the last three decades, our family has had a front row seat watching the transformation of a tough-as-nails, wave-riding, hell-raising wild man into a tough-as-nails man of God with a passion for his wife and children and an authentic love for his fellow man.

Here is the problem: At some point, it is the destiny of elder male siblings to succumb to the temporary illusion of power they wield over the younger. That usually happens during a season of temporary insanity known as puberty. What they are oblivious to at the time is that it is the destiny of younger brothers to take the thrashing, bide their time, and then develop the muscle and skill set to beat the living tar out of their older brothers. It can all be in good clean fun, of course, but really it's not. On a recent trip to Durango, Scott gave me a long-awaited schooling on the Jiu Jitsu mat. I walked away with broken ribs, but it was worth it.

The real education I have received from Scott has been watching his personal journey. Ridiculously strong, he was the kind of guy whose idea of recreation was taking on a half a dozen guys twice his size in bar room brawls. He practiced marksmanship with his buddies by shooting beer bottles out of each other's hands. Scott once walked into a hut in Indonesia to experience the equivalent of a local rite-of-passage by picking a live cobra out of a box, chopping off its head with a machete, draining its venom and blood into a glass of moonshine, and drinking it as a cocktail. Some businessmen talk about "swimming with the sharks," but Scott does it literally. During an expedition to Australia, even the best of the surfers on location fled the water during a season of record swells because of a significant shark infestation. Not Scott—after all, why worry about sharks when you can surf fifteen footers by yourself?

He should have been dead ten times over, but God had other plans for Scott McAlvany. While I don't presume to understand the mysterious work of God's grace in the life of my brother, one thing seems clear—a proper response to epic crises has shaped the life of the man. In moments of epic disorientation, those who keep a clear head, adjusting their mental map to present realities, become the survivors.

Today Scott is an entrepreneur and aspiring Jiu Jitsu master instructor living in Bali. The locals call him "Turbo" because of his unstoppable energy on the mat. Fluent in the local language and respected by his fellow Balinese, he personifies Teddy Roosevelt's maxim "speak softly and carry a big stick." This quiet and commanding manner, backed by decisive action, has allowed Scott to repeatedly resolve intense conflicts.

Scott has learned that those who learn to point their boards into the wave and ride over the swell develop the skill to survive. But those who successfully ride a tidal wave of crisis to shore and who return to take the next wave are the ones who own the beach.

The plane crash crisis of 1999 had mentally prepared Scott to handle an even bigger crisis. In December 2004, five years after he had pulled bodies from the side of a Colorado mountain, Scott found himself surrounded by tens of thousands of dead and dying at the heart of one of the largest natural disasters in recorded history. The confusion and panic he had observed on a small scale in the mountains of Colorado were multiplied exponentially.

In this new crisis he would find himself negotiating through an environment of chaos that required him to make hundreds of split-second decisions that would determine whether people lived or died. Time had passed, but the message was the same—in moments of fundamental disturbance, something more is needed than fear and a visceral panic reaction.

It was the challenge of a lifetime, but one that became a laboratory for understanding right and wrong responses to events that precede and follow life-threatening disturbances.

Wake-Up Calls

Disturbance has consequences. The destruction of business property by fire can make or break a situation. A plane crash into the mountains of Colorado may not only take the lives of the people on board, but forever change those family members left behind. The significance of any grand disturbance cannot be diminished. Great loss, especially where human life is in question, can be devastating and deeply personal.

Closer to our daily experience are the wake-up calls, or signals, which tell us that more is occurring than is obvious at first. Verbal intonations we hear or use suggest a relational problem or tension may be under the surface. There are subtle signs of unhealth our bodies send in the form of changed skin tone, general fatigue, or localized pain. My father was approached once by a doctor who in plain language told him that the ashen gray color of his skin suggested high levels of toxicity in his body and an over-dependence on coffee. He listened. He changed his habits, and his health improved. In more extreme wake-up calls, a heart attack can send a clear message that adequate exercise and proper diet need prioritization.

But there is another type of disturbance—the type that has the potential to reshape life for an entire generation of people, an epic crisis. They include war, genocide, international economic collapse, and natural disasters. The bigger the disturbance, the clearer the message to future generations. Every once in a while, the people of the world get one of these wake-up calls, reminders that disturbance is real, and more is coming. What they choose to do with that warning is another matter.

At times there seems to be an inverse ratio of danger to response—the more significant the danger, the less likely people are to take precautionary measures. You have seen this with individuals who refuse to discuss their own mortality. They simply will not make plans for their death. That death is coming is one of the certainties of life, and yet no amount of certainty about future disturbance can arouse their attention in the present to address practical matters that will define their own legacy, let alone spiritual matters which will define eternity. They prefer to live in a state of denial as if not thinking about the disturbance will make it go away.

The same problem affects nations and bankers and politicians. There are reasons why truth is often ignored and even suppressed. Sometimes the reasons are political—leaders may view disturbance preparation as contra to their own power objectives. They believe that an appearance of instability or weakness will undermine their power base. Other times the reasons for ignoring warning signs are related to deliberate short-term thinking—why focus on the worries of another generation when the worries of our present are sufficient? A third reason for ignoring warnings of future disturbance is cost. The expense of managing the tyranny of the urgent is overwhelming. There appears to be no additional emotional and financial resources left to worry about the problems of tomorrow.

Krakatoa's Message in a Bottle

One of these wake-up calls occurred on August 27, 1883, when the volcanic island of Krakatoa exploded, sending rocks and ash around the world and rendering the loudest recorded blast in history.[14] The impact was staggering. People heard the sound thousands of miles away in mid Australia. The volcano released twenty-one cubic kilometers of ash and pumice into the atmosphere and was so dense that sunlight was blocked for days. Global temperatures dropped for five years. The fine dust was carried all over the world and created eerie vivid red sunsets in North America and Europe. There were even reports of fire engines being dispatched in Poughkeepsie, New York, after local residents reported fire in the distance, which was actually a red sunset generated by Krakatoa. In an article for *Sky and Telescope* Magazine, "When the Sky Ran Red: The Story Behind *The Scream*," physics and astronomy professor Donald W. Olson makes a convincing case that Edvard Munch's famous 1893 Expressionist paintings depicting a psychedelic sky was inspired by a sunset the artist watched in Norway after Krakatoa's explosion.[15]

The volcano and tsunami of 1883 was one of the most documented blast events of that century and launched the modern science of volcanology. After it, people searched for answers. Will it happen again? The answer to that question was largely resolved: Yes. Not only could new explosions erupt on Krakatoa (and the rising island of Anak Krakatoa—"Son of Krakatoa"), but the entire region also remained ripe for more cataclysmic events resulting in tsunamis. This portion of the world sits on tectonic plates with highly volatile subduction zones that produce significant seismic events. In fact, over the course of a century, this region of the world has witnessed one-eighth of all the worlds seismic moments released by earthquakes. In other words, the Krakatoa event, followed by many other volcanic and seismic events, pointed to core issues that remain harbingers to the modern world. Future disturbance events might be coming.

But these harbingers are frequently ignored.

Lack of Seriousness about Catastrophic Threats

At the beginning of the twenty-first century, all the signs were there. There was a history of earthquakes and tsunamis in the region. There were scientific warnings about an imminent event. Scientists had been appealing for disaster preparation. But by the time the waves hit the beaches of Indonesia, India, Sri Lanka, and Thailand on December 26, 2004, causing an ultimate loss of life of more than 230,000 men, women and children, it was simply too late. The failure to assess and mitigate risks led to a historic death toll. Those who survived the initial wave found themselves acting as confused victims, often making choices that ensured that they would not survive the second wave.

The Sumatra-Andemann earthquake and 2004 Indian Ocean Tsunami occurred during Christmas week in the vicinity where Krakatoa had exploded just over a century prior. The earthquake registered a magnitude of up to 9.3 and was one of the deadliest natural disasters in recorded history. A massive undersea disturbance, it triggered a chain of tsunamis that hit coastlines in fourteen countries bordering the Indian Ocean. Coastal communities were hit with waves up to 100 feet high.[16]

Where others flee, Scott McAlvany runs toward danger. So into this maelstrom of destruction he flew on a mission to rescue the injured. Scott was in Indonesia at the time of the earthquake, but his location had been protected from the brunt of the tsunami. Within minutes of realizing the magnitude of the disaster, he decided to put an outfit of gear together and talk his way onto a plane bound for the epicenter of the crisis.

Preparing Your Resources

Crisis had prepared Scott for more crisis, so he mustered his street smarts and began his journey in Jakarta where he talked his way as a medical relief worker onto a transport. His currency at the time was not merely his ability to operate in crisis situations where others were losing their heads, but also the fact that he followed the first rule of disturbance mitigation—gather your resources in advance. Be prepared.

There were many impediments to Scott's getting on the transport plane—not the least of which was the fact that the government was at war with the Tiger GAMM Rebels, and Scott had no government identification or affiliation. What he did have was a sharp mind and four duffel bags full of medical supplies he had pre-prepared for the daily disasters kids experience at the orphanage where he volunteered, and just in case of a larger crisis.

My brother and I have learned to develop a MacGyver-esque resolve to solve most field problems using simple tools like duct tape and wire. Somewhere down the road of life, Dad had given Scott and me the book, *Where There is No Doctor: A Village Health Care Handbook.*[17] It became our Bible of field medicine resources. From the ever-valuable duct tape to bandages and syringes, Scott knew what to bring. And it paid off. Those who have the resources help define the resolution to the crisis.

Here is how he described the events to me:

We were trying to get into a mess that everyone else was trying to get out of, knowing that there was going to be a lot of red tape. We had to avoid the formal rules of entering a closed area. We knew that the main airport was knocked out. We did our recon and discovered that the military base was out of the impact zone. We knew flights would be touching down there, so we made that our point of contact.

Once there, we sold ourselves as the solution they needed. We simply walked past all security and guards, asking them to step aside and not get in the way, explaining we were the solution and warning them that we would be contacting their supervisors if they slowed us down.

Indonesia is a shame culture. No one wants to rock the boat, so we pulled that card and walked through any obstacles by being above the rules. It was acting; it was bluffing; it was knowing what we knew of the culture and navigating through to get to our goal.

Scott made the plane. The BBC offered numerous reports from survivors including this eyewitness account: "People had very confused emotions, and nobody knew what to do next. We saw the wave strike just 100 meters away from us. We were lucky to escape, but before long, mothers came crying . . . they had lost their small children in front of their very eyes and seen them floating to the sea. They were unable to hold them since they hadn't been able to grab them under the water."

And this one: "Everyone was running frantically and urged us to beat it as the sea was coming further inwards. My brother-in-law and his parents had gotten engulfed by the "killer" wave, the second one. They had hardly entered the hotel nearby when they were submerged by this huge wave, which came dashing over them and into the hotel. Furniture was floating in the water, and my aunt was hanging on to a floating table for dear life, glad when it struck a pillar and remained stationery."

By the time Scott arrived at ground-zero, the body count was in the tens of thousands, and chaos reigned. Doctors were in short supply, and those available were having nervous breakdowns. Frenzied people in a state of shock were rushing back to the beaches. The entire area was flooded, and bodies and debris created a cocktail of death.

One of the first principles of surviving an unanticipated crisis is adaptation. Get a grip on your emotions, survey the relevant information, adjust your mental map to present realities, and solve problems. Scott was ready. Years of past experiences dealing with disturbance had him thinking outside the box and free from the emotions of panic and despair.

On the other hand, people on the ground he watched were dying hour by hour because they could not adapt to changing circumstances. Here is how he described the situation that he found on the ground at his arrival:

> There had been no education to these people in the impact zone regarding the nature of tsunamis. Simple education might have saved thousands of lives. Survivors recalled the surreal event as the tide was rapidly dropping and the water moving out. Families and kids were running towards the ocean, picking up fish, looking at a newly exposed beach, and losing every precious minute they could have been running to higher ground in the city. Survivors of the earthquake were in shock for days. They were trying to make sense of what they had just experienced. In those precious minutes, instead of running, they were walking around in disbelief, completely unaware that the worst was yet to arrive.
>
> From my perspective they had no plan, no prethought response. You fight the way you train; you react the way you plan to react. Higher ground was not in the plan because there was no plan. In the chaos of the event, there was no anchor of objectivity. This was all uncharted territory, but it did not need to be.

Hope in the Midst of Chaos

Once on the ground, Scott found the makeshift medical center and went into action. There were almost no doctors and few supplies. He worked furiously in twenty-four hour stretches to save the dying. He demonstrated one of the virtues vital to deep survival in a crisis situation—the presence of mind to communicate encouragement and hope to those who are fearful.

When we were treating patients, most times I had no clue what to do, but I never wanted to bring any doubt or more gloom to an already-dark time. I figured that hope could do some good, perhaps, to turn the tide. And as it turned out, hope was the difference between the upturn or downturn.

For many patients, I saw first hand the difference between life and death. It often hinged on hope. I remember two patients—both septic and on the way to death. One was handled by an Indonesian health worker who told the patient, "You are going to die; no treatment can help you; say your last prayers." I countered those words with the opposite, but the wrong seeds had already been planted. I threw that worker out of the room for saying that, and he avoided me from then on.

Compare the patient lying next to the one who got the negative report. This one I told he was gonna make it fine. I'd fix him up with a few shots, some good food. He wanted to tell me all about his family, names, faces, ages, memories. I lied through my teeth, smiled big, and said he was in great shape, but there would be a lot of pain. I told him that I needed him to fight the pain, so he could find his family soon. Would you believe it? He was the one who was able to hold on three days until we could amputate his legs and nuke his body with the proper antibiotics. The other man rolled over and died that very night even though his wounds and injuries were far less serious.

Those drowning from fluid and mud in their lungs only lasted as long as they had hope to hang onto. It was the one life line amidst the current of death. I kept remembering the words from the Bible, "The tongue has the power to bring life or death" (Proverbs 18:21), and "people perish for lack of vision" (Proverbs 29:18), and "I know the plans I have for you says the Lord, plans to prosper you and not harm you, plans to give you a hope and a future," (Jeremiah 29:11). Without hope, people die. With hope, they can overcome more than any doctor could ever imagine.

Scott's observations from the beaches of Banda Aceh, Indonesia, are revealing. The events surrounding the 2004 Tsunami, before, during, and after evidenced each of the classic wrong responses to disturbance.

Loss of Historical Information and Legacy Gaps

There was an historical record of a disturbance even within miles of Indonesia: Krakatoa. But it would appear there was little knowledge of and complete disregard for the dangers that had previously devastated the people groups in the Krakatoa area. Except for a brief historical record, there were next to no living survivors who could pass on any first-hand knowledge of the Krakatoa explosion, thus creating a void of knowledge concerning the potential of disturbance for the present generation. No one had been through a massive event to that extent. In a certain sense, Krakatoa became more of a child's tale to the people of the region than an historical warning of something that could repeat itself.

Denial and Ignoring Warning Signs

To the extent that some people were aware of the potential crisis, there was still a complete lack of receptiveness and forward thinking on the part of both the government and the population. No one was willing to take seriously the real and present danger that earthquakes can create. It was something no one had experienced and therefore could not be real. One example which highlighted the problem involved a renowned scientist from the U.S. who was watching the fault lines and activity. He had his own seismic monitors in place to track what he was describing as "the event of the century."

One month prior to the fault line slip and earthquake, this scientist met with Indonesian government officials to inform them of the eminent danger. On his own initiative, he printed flyers and posters to warn the masses of a huge event that could claim many lives.

He was laughed at. Officials tore down his posters and threw his fly-ers away. They completely discounted his data and would not endorse his theory. Nor could they be bothered with putting money towards risk mitigation. After the event, survivors recalled how they had laughed at the posters and the notion of a catastrophe.

If you counted the days it took Noah to build the ark, he spent most of his life being wrong. Noah's project was discounted, and he personally was beyond the fringe for looking ahead and planning ahead.

Failure to Initiate Minimal Risk Mitigation

When the undersea earthquake event first occurred, a seismic station in Java picked up the reading. The seismic disturbance was big, and they knew it, but they did not have the telephone technology available to warn others. Even the most basic forms of communication were unavailable. The phone line had been disconnected, so no one could make a warning call to the government offices. This meant that tens of thousands of people on the beaches and in the local areas were sitting ducks. But even had the phone call come in, there was no pre-prepared mobilization effort capable of handling the situation. The outcome would have been largely the same. Protocols to follow are essential to pilots, the military, and emergency med-ical responders who know what to do under pressure, not by instinct but by forethought, training, and education. Simple protocols could have saved tens of thousands of lives.

It is not surprising that many of our greatest leaders have emerged in times of crisis. Leaders emerge as those individuals who keep a cool head, viewing crisis as an opportunity for problem solving. It is a mentality, a dis-position, and an ability to maintain perspective. Such individuals are able to communicate hope and peace to others, often saving the day.

Intentional families recognize that one disturbance can change life, plunging a family into a survival mode from which they may not recover. Intentional families are about the business of reverse engineering their response to disturbance preparation.

They know disturbance is coming in one form or another. They know that there are classic inadequate responses to disturbance. So they look to history to anticipate disturbance trends and the key repeatable themes concerning unwise responses to disturbance. The history of the world is replete with such examples where the wrong responses result in tragedy.

Predicting Disturbance

My business is market analysis, which is to say that predicting economic disturbances is my livelihood. My father and I have spent the better part of our lives anticipating disturbance—market fluctuations and implosions that might unsettle a family's wealth portfolio. Our objective has been to do more than help our clients survive a crisis—we want them to prosper and get ahead of the game. This requires using all available information to properly assess the landscape, anticipate problems before they arise, mitigate risk, and find creative solutions to problems on the horizon. In a way, I am sort of a financial seismologist, watching the fault lines and recognizing that the tectonic shifts in the economic basin have a volatility that can't be ignored. That being said, tremors can be predicted and measures taken to minimize the devastation caused by catastrophic events.

My version of a seismometer is Monday research—a day dedicated to charts, graphs, books, and analysis for my weekly radio broadcast on Tuesday. The interdisciplinary world I inherited from my father's globetrotting, conference-rich, newsletter-focused routines introduced me early in life to a community of philosophers, economists, and men of faith. Each week I interview one of these men or women for my broadcast. Their insights are a rich source of experience and reflection that enhances my ability to see and anticipate cycles of volatility in the financial world. This anticipation allows for the avoidance of some market disturbances and opens the door for unique and otherwise unforeseen opportunities.

Not surprisingly, one of the more common questions I get from my clients concerns economic disturbance: What happens if and when the system crashes? What if years of bad policy and debt accumulation result in a financial apocalypse? What if the government issues another "Executive Order 6102," like they did in 1933, and decide to confiscate gold from private citizens? What if the state seizes assets and shuts down accounts as they did in Cyprus? Is there a Plan B for legacy-minded families in the wake of economic or political implosion?

The answer to that question is its own book. But the short of it is this: wise families take time to develop Plan B. The issue of Plan B has been part of my life for as long as I can remember. When your family is in the business of market projections, safety nets, back-ups, exit strategies, and practical means for surviving disturbance are fundamental life ingredients. My dad always put it in terms of the "Boy Scout" way: always have a backup plan. The first step in crisis management is risk mitigation.

Disturbance, Risk, and Gold

We have learned a lesson from our international clients who have lived through devastating wars, physical displacement as refugees, and even the break-up of their nations. In times of crisis, there is only one completely dependable asset that is portable, valuable, universally recognized, and capable of purchasing the fundamentals of survivability and sustainability: gold. The rest of the world remembers what Americans have forgotten: paper burns, molds, and certainly devalues. But gold is largely indestructible and maintains value everywhere in the world. Gold is the defining monetary instrument in times of transition and crisis.

This principle was memorably illustrated for us in 1977 by a family from Vietnam fleeing Southeast Asia. They were less than three weeks off the boat, walked into our office, and proceeded to cut open their shoes to remove wads of devalued Vietnamese paper currency called dong. It wasn't the currency which interested us; it was what was inside the paper. Hidden in each wad of cash were taels, or bars made of gold. This family left everything they had behind them except the shirt on their backs and the shoes on their feet and the gold they smuggled into America in the heels of their shoes. They did not speak a word of English, but they spoke the language of the one enduring money: gold. The value of gold translates in any part of the world. Gold is a financial Rosetta stone. If you are liquidating gold in a Spanish-speaking nation, all that is needed is one word—how much? The same is true in any country and continent.

As the family removed the currency wrapping from the gold, they threw the Vietnamese dongs into the trash. The paper currency was as worthless to them as old newspaper, but the gold was the basis for a new life. We gave them cash for the gold, and they took the cash and bought a grocery store in Arizona. Months later they returned to us with a brown bag full of U.S. paper dollars. Gold, turned into cash, plus hard work, equaled financial success. Now they wanted to turn the cash back into gold. They bought the gold back knowing full well that gold had been their only means of economic salvation. They immigrated with the shirts on their back and the gold in their shoes. They knew gold. They trusted gold. They were right. When the Vietnamese family came back with their paper bag of money, they were simply reloading because they felt naked and vulnerable without the ounces of gold that were a part of their enduring wealth legacy.

Gold ownership is simply one form of "disturbance insurance." Our company has provided this kind of insurance for nearly fifty years, but I will tell you, intentional families must go beyond economic risk mitigation. The only way for an intentional family to achieve an across-the-board strategy for risk mitigation is to develop an approach that benefits from the mental, historical, and practical preparation needed to have the mindset of a survivor.

Intentional Families as Survivors

This is a book about intentional families, which is another way of saying this is a book about hope-givers, dream-casters, and survival experts. It is about people who will not quit, people who can see beyond disturbance because they *must* see beyond disturbance and reshape legacy vision in the face of it. It is about people who are, as of yet, untested, but who will someday be called upon to handle a crisis that will make or break their legacy. When that day comes, I want you to remember Scott. Remember the Scriptures he referenced: "Death and life are in the power of the tongue, and those who love it will eat its fruits," (Proverbs 18:21) and "Where there is no prophetic vision the people cast off restraint," (Proverbs 29:18) and "For I know the plans I have for you, declares the Lord, plans for welfare[a] and not for evil, to give you a future and a hope," (Jeremiah 29:11)."

For today, assume that your best efforts to build a family legacy will someday, sooner or later, be subject to a crisis that will threaten the future of your legacy. As a redemptive ethic is to the cornerstone of a house where a vibrant family legacy resides, so survival is to the estate security of the intentional family.

Most family legacies will suffer one or more significant threats to their existence or ideal trajectory. It may come in the form of an internal crisis or an external attack, but it will come. Plan on it. Prepare for it. Choose now that you will adopt the mentality and practices of a survivor, not a victim.

The Day Disturbance Saved My Life

I was thirteen when my father received a phone call from the manager of a hotel in Cape Town, South Africa. The message was simple: "We are unable to honor our commitment to you and your eighty-five guests."

The context was one of my father's world-class international geostrategic tours of sub-Saharan Africa. Dad and his good friend, political commentator Howard Phillips, had worked together for years taking teams around the world to economic and political hotspots from Angola to China. Their particular passion at the time was sub-Saharan Africa. It was a season of international upheaval in South Africa and its environs, as the Soviets, Cubans, competing political parties, and local terrorist organizations scrambled for hegemony.

Back in America, conservatives battled liberals and the U.S. State Department over policy objectives for the region. The controversy over Apartheid and the call for financial disinvestment in the nation was in the news daily.

On the ground, the politics of the region were far more complex than reported in the States—tribal group versus tribal group, terrorism in the streets, daily bloodshed, economic pendulum swings, fortunes made and lost, the old world versus the new, conspiracies, and collaborators. In other words, the climate was precisely the type of chaotic and incendiary vortex of intrigue in which my father thrived. Into this maelstrom my dad proposed to bring eighty-five high-paying guests—businessmen, commentators, investors—men and women who were subscribers to his monthly newsletter, some of whom just wanted a vacation. And the issue of gold was no small concern to the guests. Most were gold investors who realized that seventy percent of the world's gold supply came from South Africa. The trip was planned, the flights booked, the guests registered, the fees paid, and the hotel secured. Then came the call telling us our accommodations had been cancelled.

The Afrikaner relaying the message to dad was speaking in English, but I am sure my father's first response was to translate the message into dollars, cents, and relationships. But there was good news—a possible mitigation to the catastrophe: If Dad could persuade his eighty-five guests to change all of their travel plans and come earlier, the hotel was willing to rebook their flights with the airline and provide the necessary rooms for them. If you have never been around the trip organization business, then perhaps the monumental nature of the request is not immediately apparent. People plan trips months, sometimes years in advance. They build the micro details of their calendar around the up-and-coming "trip of a lifetime." Many of these travelers are elderly, which tend to be the most schedule-sensitive demographic on the planet. The odds of getting buy-in from paid guests to reconstruct a trip on short notice is scant. The response is normally disfavor and cancellation.

My dad did not blink. Taking a deep breath, he made the calls. The response appeared to be a miracle—nearly 100% buy-in. The guests were willing to switch the dates.

The next trick was for the hotel to work with the airlines to change plane tickets. It was a disturbance and a genuine inconvenience to everyone—our would-be team of adventurers, the hotel, and certainly the airline. But somehow they did it. The airline agreed to switch out their tickets, including the return flight from South Africa to London to America. The trip concluded successfully, and we were home. But that was not the end of the story. Sitting in our home one day, we received the news report that Pan Am flight 103, London to New York, exploded over Lockerbie, Scotland, killing 233 passengers. A Libya-backed terrorist had successfully mounted the largest aerial terrorist strike of the decade.

Pan Am flight 103 was our original plane—the plane that we were booked on for a return flight. The flight we missed by a hair's breadth became the object of the greatest terrorist bombing of the 1980s. We missed the plane—eighty-five of us—because of an unexpected disturbance.

If you were to ask my dad to interpret the events of December 1988, he might describe the disturbance that forced the crisis leading to the change of plane reservations as a supernatural intervention of God. Twenty-five years later, it is still difficult for me to process. Why me? Why Dad? Why did we live and others die? I cannot answer those questions. What I can tell you is this: I have experienced the reality that crisis can save your life, if you chose to overcome it rather than become a victim to it. We are much more relaxed today about things that occur, which we have no control over. Missing a plane connection because of mechanical issues and delays, or being stranded in an airport overnight because of inclement weather, we count as blessings and maybe even gifts.

How to Think Like a Survivor Family

The lessons of history ring true. Disturbance often emerges because problems are ignored. A correct response to disturbance will better prepare you to handle the next disturbance in your life. Properly handled, disturbance is opportunity in disguise. Grasping these three concepts allows the intentional family to think like survivors, not victims. But there is another important point: Despite our best efforts, we cannot plan for every eventuality.

In my family, the humbling nature of each disturbance experienced is a reminder that despite our best efforts, we cannot plan for every specific disturbance, but we can live and learn in a manner that will allow us to meet each new crisis with fresh perspective and clear heads.

From our life experiences, my father and brother have shepherded our family and helped us think like a survivor family, the heart of which boils down to these four principles for handling a major disturbance:

- **Focus:** Turning fear into focus is the first act of a survivor. Calmly assess the situation. Separate emotion from reason.
- **Adapt:** Recognize that something has changed—and you cannot change it. You must adapt to it. You must adjust your mental map to changing scenarios and modify plans.
- **Reject Victimization:** Don't wait for someone else to save you. Cry out to God for wisdom and guidance, and then act.
- **Do the Next Thing:** Remember Dory's words in the film *Finding Nemo*: "Keep on swimming." Don't stop. Don't curl up into the fetal position. Keep swimming. Do the next thing.

In this chapter, I advocate analysis and preparation, but that is only one part of the equation. The other part is the reality that we can never predict everything. We lack knowledge, time, and resources. This practical reality was on the mind of Nobel-prize winning author John Steinbeck when he fashioned the title of his 1937 novella, *Of Mice and Men*, after a stanza from Robert Burns poem "To a Mouse."[18] The Burns stanza has become part of the lexicon of disturbance—a recognition that even with the best planning, things go awry: "The best laid schemes o' mice an' men/Gang aft agley." —which is to say, even the plans of mice "go awry."

With this in mind, please consider that when disturbance comes—and it will— there is an upside. One of my literary mentors, Dietrich Bonhoeffer, likened "crises and war to stop motion photography in its capacity to make changes plain that are ordinarily too gradual to be seen." Herein we begin to see the great blessing of disturbance: it is a window to those issues that must be addressed to make us men and woman of greater confidence and ability. Those who survive disturbance become the visionaries and entrepreneurs and legacy-builders of the next generation.

Chapter 4

Legacy Baggage: An Inquiry into the Proper Disposal of Generational Junk

"I don't believe in a lot of baggage. It's such a nuisance.
Life's too short to fuss with it. And it isn't really necessary."
- Hugh Lofting[19]

This is the story of a bag. Not an especially beautiful bag, and not a well-used bag, but a bag that is very important to my personal family legacy. It's the kind that a gentleman might have once carried traveling on a steamliner across the Atlantic, or perhaps boarding a train to leave his family on an important business trip.

Somewhere, sometime, probably three quarters of a century ago, an animal was slaughtered, its hide taken, and the Hartmann Luggage Company fashioned it into this very bag that is presently sitting on the floor of my living room. What makes the Hartmann bag particularly important for our story is that it has not been opened in half of a century.

Long ago the keys were misplaced—or deliberately lost, and its mysterious content relegated to conjecture. That the bag contains artifacts from the past is beyond dispute—shake it, and the elements unsettle. What those elements are has been the source of much speculation.

Inside the bag may be the answer to a family mystery that has shrouded the past in controversy and unresolved conflict. There are those who believe that hidden inside the antique Hartmann are documents or love letters that prove the legitimacy of a scandal once suppressed, the source of which added to unresolved family dysfunctionality that seeped down through the generations.

I am inviting you to join me on an experiment in real-time. Before this chapter concludes, a gathering of McAlvanys will congregate in our family's living room where we will pick the lock and open the trunk. Once opened, we will view the documents and determine whether the mystery has been solved and what lessons might be learned from the revelation. We will remember the past, toast the future, and conclude both a chapter in our own family story and this chapter in your hand.

But to get to this destination point—you, like me—must deliberate through an inquiry into baggage that has less to do with a specific piece of luggage and more to do with the cumbersome and debilitating burdens we lug from one generation to the next.

Like the albatross around the neck of Coleridge's ancient mariner, "legacy baggage" is a heavy burden that can drain the life out of parents and children alike and hamper the best efforts of an intentional family.

The broader context of our investigation is the question, Why do even the best legacies fail? The simple answer is that legacies dissolve for lack of vision and planning. They fail because there is little buy-in from the next generation. They cannot be sustained in a graceless environment that lacks a redemptive ethic. Often these failures reveal deeper, longstanding problems—negative patterns unresolved, sometimes unidentified, and passed from one generation to the next.

Because there are no perfect families, there are no perfect legacies. Everyone has legacy baggage—elements of your inheritance that can be defined as negative. For example, you may inherit the financial debts of a prior generation. Or maybe financial debts are the least of your concerns. Legacy baggage can be unhealthy physiological and psychological proclivities for chemical or emotional dependencies. They can include a history of promiscuity, misplaced priorities, broken relationships, or absentee parenting.

Anything negative, unredeemed, unhealed, or burdensome passed from one generation to the next can be defined as legacy baggage.

Who was J.R. Thompson?

The Hartmann bag in my living room had an owner. His name was J.R. Thompson, and he was a successful businessman born in the year 1906. Legend has it that one day, many decades ago, J.R. placed something very important to him in a safe that was sealed until after his death in 1989. J.R.

was nearly eighty-three years old. After his death the items were secretly removed by a loyal staff member. The contents were never revealed to J.R.'s widow but are thought to have been relocated and locked into the Hartmann bag. Eventually the key was misplaced—lost or thrown away. The bag was set aside and largely forgotten until it was recovered and preserved unopened by one Mary-Catherine Schmidt of Houston, Texas, the woman who would one day become my wife.

I never met J.R., never read a book by him, was not included in his will, and never attended Texas A&M where Thompson Hall was named after him. Even so, J.R. became one of the most influential men in my life. Back in the day when energy companies were on the rise, he was a man dedicated to a life of hard work and focus in the pursuit of commerce. In time, his labors were rewarded. He emerged as a noteworthy philanthropist and the first-generation family wealth creator of an energy empire valued in the tens of millions.

J.R. was born in Georgia in 1906 during the presidency of Theodore Roosevelt. It was the same year as the birth of actor Lou Costello, Supreme Court Justice William Brennan, and cosmetic magnate Estee Lauder—the beginning of new century, the age of the industrialist, and a season of tremendous optimism. America's military and economic position in the world was on the rise, and the Great War was more than a decade away.

J.R. came into the world as a legacy beneficiary—heir to a heritage of irascible, gun-toting Scotch-Irishmen with a determination to carve a future for themselves and their families, by force of will if necessary, out of a new experiment in freedom called America. They arrived in the colonies during the decades preceding the War for American Independence as one of the five waves of Scotch-Irish immigrations to the continent. In his book, *Born Fighting*, author James Webb suggests that, as a group, these Scotch-Irish immigrants were defined by three key traits: loyalty to kin, extreme distrust of government authority, and a determination to bear arms and use them whenever necessary.[20]

One of these immigrant men was J.R's ancestor who fought for General George Washington as a member of the Continental Army—a fact that would be remembered with pride from one generation to the next. Perhaps it was that ancestor who became the inspiration for J.R.'s pearl-handled revolver, which rested on the desk of his corporate office underneath a sign that read, "I shoot every third salesman that wants to meet with me. The second just left. How can I help you?"

One hundred and fifty years had passed since the Thompson family arrived on the continent, but the immigrant ethic persisted. Loyalty to kin was a dominant theme. Duty to parents and siblings was inculcated. Families fought for each other. They did what was necessary to stay alive. Before he was a corporate magnate, J.R. was a teenage boy with a big mission. Like a scene from an early "talkie" from that era, in 1926, he was placed on a train headed for Houston, Texas, and given a simple objective: "Go to the big city. Make money. Send it back to the family. We are counting on you."

J.R. was a big, strapping, home-fed boy. The years of working for his mom and dad as pig and peanut sharecroppers reduced to this simple declaration from J.R: "I am tired of looking at the rear end of a mule." He was ready. Off he went. Duty, adventure, and hard work—the quintessential pull-yourself-up-from-your-bootstraps-and-don't-forget-your-family American story.

By 1933, the world looked a bit different than it did in 1906. J.R. was the eldest of seven surviving children scraping by during the height of the Depression. The economic downturn affecting the entire country had reached a crisis level within the Thompson family. Little food and less work meant something had to be done, so the family turned to the first-born son, already out of the house, for a solution.

J.R. was glad he had put everything he owned into a burlap sack, boarded that train, and headed for Houston, Texas. At the time, Texas was the capital of America's burgeoning energy business, and with its access to oilfields and a port, Houston was the hub.

As the train pulled into the station, J.R. looked out the window, and the first thing he saw was an electrical company. He disembarked the train, crossed the street, walked in the door, and offered his services. He would do anything and work for little. Sweep floors. Pack boxes. Anything that would pay. Moments later, his burlap bag was in the corner, and a broom was in his hands. It was the beginning of a lifetime working in the energy and electrical distribution business.

J.R. sent paycheck after paycheck back to his mother, father, and seven brothers and sisters. Now a young man in his early twenties, he had become the primary breadwinner for a family of ten. Then, at the age of thirty-one, the indomitable spirit of J.R was tested when he contracted gangrene after his appendix ruptured. Doctors decided to remove a large part of his stomach lining and told him to prepare his estate because he was not long for the world. The entire family traveled across country to pay their final respects.

For twelve months J.R. walked hunched over from pain, but against the prediction of the medical experts, he pulled through. In Houston he met a beautiful girl named Mary Claude Williamson on the steps of Woodland Baptist Church. They married. After being told that they could have no children, one was born. The baby would prove to be their only child, Cheryl Lynn Thompson—a little girl who grew up to love her father very much and whose life may have become quite complicated because of the issues giving rise to the contents hidden in the Hartmann bag.

In Houston J.R proved himself trustworthy and hardworking. He moved up in the ranks from one booming company to another until he met Mr. and Mrs. Warren, a childless, elderly couple who were the owners of a competitor company who maintained friendly relations with others in the industry. Galveston, Texas, was the American Riviera of the 1930s. The Warrens vacationed there and would often stop by the business J.R. was then managing. They were impressed by J.R.'s work ethic, his knowledge of the business, and his character, so they hired him.

J.R. showed devotion, industry, and compassion to the aging couple. He filled in gaps, took initiative, and demonstrated unswerving loyalty to their interests. Whatever they wanted he did—and then some. Great attitude. Hard work. Lots of gratitude. Realizing the gem they had in J.R., the Warrens offered to start a new electric company with him where they would share ownership in a business to be called the Thompson Electric Company. But sometimes epic events intervene in the lives of ordinary men and women changing their best-laid plans.

On December 7, 1941, the Warrens and J.R. were standing with a realtor on the site of the building that was to become their corporate headquarters when a man ran across the street shouting to them, "Pearl Harbor's been bombed! Pearl Harbor! We are at war!"

That was the end of "The Thompson Electric Company." The reality of America at war meant greater state and federal regulation, as well as a general sense of impropriety about a man in his thirties starting a new company while others would go to fight.

Finally, the distribution of critical commodities was controlled and limited to the existing businesses at the outset of the conflict. The answer was to make the Houston location the new corporate headquarters for an expanding Warren Electric Company and to put J.R. at the helm. In his will, Mr. Warren left fifty percent of his company to the man who had become like an only son. It was a big break, and one that became bigger after the death of Mrs. Warren, who ultimately gave to J.R. the remaining interest in the Warren Electric Company.

And that was the beginning of a multi-million-dollar fortune. J.R. took a local business and grew it internationally. By the next generation, Warren Electric Company expanded through the United States and to the Caribbean and the Middle East.

The Generosity of J.R. Thompson

J.R. had notable virtues—He was often generous to a fault and exceedingly compassionate to those who were suffering. In the course of his life he gave away millions of dollars, paid for medical operations, helped build hospitals, and acted with magnanimity to any who came to him for help. Even at the height of his fortune, J.R. Thompson lived modestly. He was comfortable, but neither his home nor his cars told the story of the vast resources he had accumulated through industry and business acumen.

On matters of personal finances, he was circumspect. He never spoke to his own family of the scope of his wealth but contributed generously to every member. Notably, he provided for his wife—a sturdy woman whose childhood had been a life of poverty and who had eked her way through the Depression serving as a clerk for the Great Southern Life Insurance Company. Every month J.R. liberally endowed her bank account, giving her the freedom to buy what she wanted, when she wanted—furs, food, anything. He did the same for his daughter, Cheryl. J.R. wanted them to enjoy life and not suffer from the privations that he had endured as a child. Throughout his life he continued to provide for his extended family—brothers, sisters, cousins, aunts—a vast network of extended relatives became the beneficiaries of J.R.'s kindness and sense of familial duty.

Man as Breadwinner

In his groundbreaking 2001 book, *Bias*, media insider Bernard Goldberg argues that one of the biggest sociological and demographic news stories of the 20th century was simply not reported—the historic reconstruction of the family model away from a single breadwinning strategy and the monumental transformation of childhood due to the mass exodus of mothers from the home.[21] The merits and weaknesses of that model is a subject beyond the scope of this story, except as it applies to our bag and its owner—Mr. J.R. Thompson, a man well qualified to become the poster-child for breadwinning males.

Like many who rightly recognize their duty to provide for family, the error comes not from a commitment to provide, but from making "breadwinning" the principal focus. The tendency, especially on the part of men, to define their success in terms of providing for their family bank accounts, college tuitions, vacations, and trust funds—IS the problem.

The Bible has much to say about money and relationships, and one point especially bears mention: "For what does it profit a man to gain the whole world and forfeit his soul?" (Mark 8:36) And perhaps this application is appropriate. What shall it profit a man to give his family all the good things the world has to offer, but to lose his heart? More than fancy vacations and toys, children need flesh-and-blood interaction from loving parents who recognize that they must provide relationship to their children—real, interactive, soul-stirring parent-to-child relationships.

Where J.R. excelled as an entrepreneur, he was less successful at family discipleship. Money is helpful. It is a tool. But it is no substitute for a rich relationship. And money is never a solution to the aching hearts of a family who needs the direct involvement of a father. Like many first generation wealth creators, J.R. lived an unbalanced life. He failed to demonstrate the full array of values needed to preserve wealth and a robust family culture to future generations. He was unwilling or unable to guide his family through difficult moral and emotional issues.

In the end, J.R. fell into the trap that has defined fatherhood in the twentieth century—great intentions, but no follow through. Absent any financial succession plan rooted in family values, culture, and heritage, his wealth by the third generation was largely expended. Despite the tens of millions of dollars J.R. had amassed through corporate successes, the business was gone, and the wealth dissipated within three generations.

And yet despite the loss of a fortune, J.R. did leave much behind in terms of legacy—a heritage of lessons, which includes both legacy treasures and legacy baggage.

Buried Treasure

A tangible inheritance is easily identifiable, but the greatest legacy wealth comes in other forms that are less obvious and can sometimes be elusive. The closets of our past often yield more than lost baggage. Sometimes they contain passageways to vaults where legacy treasure is buried. It is our duty to push beyond the baggage and find the secret doors that reveal the wealth.

From J.R. Thompson I have received two defining legacies. The first is my bride —formerly Mary-Catherine Schmidt, granddaughter to J.R., and a woman whose own life has been sculpted and shaped through a healthy, redemption-drenched response to both the assets and liabilities of her grandfather's bequest. The second was a lesson in generational continuity and discontinuity from the life of J.R., which I received vicariously through Mary-Catherine. This inheritance is the result of many hours Mary-Catherine and I have shared reflecting on lessons from her grandfather's life.

There may actually be a third item of inheritance—depending on what we find in the bag. The locked Hartmann luggage piece to be opened at the conclusion of this chapter is believed to hold secret correspondences between J.R. and a family friend that could provide some answers to the questions "What?" and "Why?" What held J.R. Thompson back from a level of transparency and personal leadership so desperately needed by his family? Was it the general character of that time period, or had J.R.'s personal choices created barriers to his heart? Why did such a promising family legacy fail so quickly?

It may have been that J.R. Thompson had high aspirations for his family that far exceeded wealth acquisition. He wanted to be there for his wife and children. He wanted them to thrive, "but there were meetings to hold and planes to catch." He may have experienced the "cat's in the cradle"—where a father has the best of intentions, but simply does not follow through.

Harry Chapin's Conundrum

On December 21, 1974, America woke up to a new song topping the Billboard charts. Ten days before, on December 11, 1974, my father woke up to news of a new son— me.

Dad was out of town when my mom's water broke in the back seat of a friend's new 1975 Volkswagon Beetle on the way to the hospital. Typical of my mother, she was more concerned about making a mess than with her own health. But she made it to the hospital.

I can't prove this, but I feel confident that somewhere, sometime, in the days following my birth, Dad joined millions of other Americans in listening to Harry Chapin's "Cat's in the Cradle," a song that would become the defining folk-rock anthem for a generation struggling with dysfunctional fatherhood and legacy implosion. Told from the perspective of a father, Harry Chapin presents an homage to the angst of millions:

A man's wife has a baby boy, but there were "planes to catch and bills to pay," so he missed the birth of his son. In the next verse, it is the boy's birthday. His dad buys him a baseball. The boy just wants to throw the ball with his father, but his dad is just too busy. The son says "that's okay." As he grows, his desire is to be with his father, and to someday be *like* his father.

> *My child arrived just the other day*
> *He came to the world in the usual way*
> *But there were planes to catch, and bills to pay*
> *He learned to walk while I was away*
> *And he was talking 'fore I knew it, and as he grew*
> *He'd say, 'I'm gonna be like you, dad*
> *You know I'm gonna be like you.'*

Harry Chapin had one number one song—only one—but it left such a dent in the American psyche that out of the hundreds of thousands of songs recorded in the twentieth century, it was named 186th of the 365 most important. The chorus is an homage to the symbols of childhood: a string game called Cat's in the Cradle, a christening present of silver spoons, and familiar childhood characters like Little Boy Blue and The Man in the Moon.

> *And the cat's in the cradle and the silver spoon*
> *Little boy blue and the man in the moon*
> *'When you coming home, dad?' 'I don't know when*
> *But we'll get together then*
> *You know we'll have a good time then.'*

Cat's in the Cradle was once a cultural universal. The CEO, the Vietnam biker vet, and the guy down the street working construction each had the same basic response. By the third stanza, the manliest of them was reduced to a teary-eyed, snuffling, weepy mess. Everybody "got" it, but perhaps none so much as the song's author. "Frankly," Chapin remarked to a live audience, "This song scares me to death."

Chapin was not merely a performance artist; he was also a human-itarian, a documentary filmmaker, and the son of a musician who had played with Tommy Dorsey and Henry James during the Big Band era of the Second World War. He was father to five children, each with a name beginning with the letter "J." *Cats in the Cradle* was written for his first-born Josh. The folk-rock anthem became somewhat of a self-fulfilling prophecy, when the very busy and hard-traveling Chapin died in a car accident at the age of thirty-eight.

The final two verses reverse the roles. In the third verse, the son returns home from college, and his father wants to spend some time with him. Instead, the son just wants to go out and asks the father for his car keys. The fourth verse advances the story quite some time, as the father is long retired, and his son has started his own family and no longer lives nearby. The father makes a phone call to his son and invites him for a visit, but the son has his own issues with his job and his children who are sick with the flu. The final two lines of the song reflect the father's observation of what has happened:

I've long since retired and my son's moved away
I called him up just the other day
I said, 'I'd like to see you if you don't mind'
He said, 'I'd love to, dad, if I could find the time
You see, my new job's a hassle, and the kid's got the flu
But it's sure nice talking to you, dad
It's been sure nice talking to you'
And as I hung up the phone, it occurred to me
He'd grown up just like me
My boy was just like me.

Continuity and discontinuity is the stuff of life. Look a little deeper, however, and you may discover a generational symmetry that can be more than a little surprising. There are often parallels to the past that inform our own life journey. My father and I were thirty-two and thirty-four, respectively, when our wives gave birth to our first and second child. Not only were we the same age, but we were also at the same season of our lives with similar pressures and professional responsibilities. *Cat's in the Cradle* hits home to both of us. In the case of my father because he was the son who was abandoned by a dad who then died young. In my case, I almost became another "Cat's in the Cradle" statistic.

My father and I are painfully different and often alarmingly alike. There are aspects to both of our lives that neither would want to see future generations perpetuate. But as to the defining redemptive message of my dad's life, I hope he will one day be able to say—and without regret— "he'd grown up just like me. My boy was just like me."

It has been the ongoing and sometime painstaking process of identifying generational strengths and weaknesses that gives us hope. We are determined to understand and appreciate the sometimes-buried treasures of legacy, even as we recognize the need to own, and then toss, the legacy baggage that weighs us down.

Receiving your Legacy

Here is a helpful rule of thumb: Before you can disown your baggage, you must first own it. Consequently, you must stop running from it. Stop fearing it. Stop hating it. Own it.

This means an honest appraisal of what you have inherited—the profitable and the painful. You have inherited much—more than you may realize. Understanding your true legacy "balance sheet" is vital to your own success. It could help to define the nature of the legacy you hope to give to your own children. As Churchill observed, "the farther backwards you look, the farther forward you are likely to see." The more you understand the past, the greater you can plan for the future.

Some people inherit hard assets. These are quantifiable in terms of specific dollar amounts and include real property, like lands and estates, as well as personal properties like boats, cars, and furniture. They can also include financial instruments, trusts, monies, and, of course, gold and silver.

Hard assets are appraisable, meaning that it is possible to identify their specific market value. Keep in mind that market value is not the same as subjective value. The home you inherit may have a fair market value of $250 thousand, but in your present financial position, you would be unwilling to sell it for $2 million because it was the home you lived in as a child. It was at this home where you enjoyed Christmas dinners, first threw a baseball with your father, and owned your first dog. You associate the home with happy memories that reinforce your own family identity. Perhaps your subjective valuation is based on more than just sentiment. You believe that the continued ownership of the property will help you build a stronger family legacy as you plan to use it to connect the present generation to the past. Maybe you intend to invite extended kin back to the home of their ancestors for family celebrations or provide a retreat for family vacations.

More important than the tangible assets is the intangible inheritance you receive. While some receive lands and monies, many more people inherit a treasure trove of intangibles that have greater impact on life and future than the physical assets. Intangibles are the assets often overlooked by wealth managers and families alike. They include a legacy of culture, family history, and values. These intangibles may encompass your family reputation in the world of commerce and the community. Intangibles also include experiences with far-reaching spiritual, emotional and psychological implications. Most intangibles are not quantifiable in terms of dollars and cents on an excel spreadsheet. They speak to your values, reputation, appetites, proclivities, attitudes, experiences, and beliefs.

With respect to these treasures, we often take our parents and grandparents' greatest assets for granted. We benefit from them without really examining the underlying sacrifices expended to develop them. Success is rarely an accident. What were the insights and qualities required to achieve a particular outcome? How were these variables cultivated, and can they be replicated?

Overemphasizing Personal Hurts

Most of us tend to look at our parents' legacy in terms of what we liked and disliked. We tend to focus on what we perceive an ancestor did correctly, or what they did wrong, and how that benefitted or hurt us personally. In the case of legacy baggage, we tend to expend much energy on resentments and insecurities created by past negative behavior. It is not uncommon for disappointed children to live lives of frustration, bitterness, and resentment over unresolved issues they inherited from a mother or father. Little effort is expended to understand the personal and historic context of their shortcomings, or even to recognize the existence of intangible inheritance treasures, which exist side by side with legacy baggage.

In our own relentlessly selfish and self-centered vision of reality, we can be guilty of doing the very thing we pray our own children will never do to us—reducing the meaningful lives of our ancestors to one-liners and emotionally-driven oversimplifications. What is needed is a grateful, prayerful, and compassionate reflection on those who came before us—one that acknowledges their humanity and causes trembling as we consider our own frailties.

The same duty that compels intentional families to understand the past also requires that they approach even the most derelict of fathers or mothers with a spirit of generosity. There is a difference between bitterly judging our parents and graciously identifying those shortcomings we may not wish to repeat. The delicate tightrope must be walked. In the end, it is a matter of the heart that speaks to one of the fundamentals of generational legacy— honor. "Honor your father and your mother, as the Lord your God commanded you, that your days may be long, and that it may go well with you in the land that the Lord your God is giving you," (Deuteronomy 5:16).

Both errors—resentment over wrongs and indifference over successes—are not only a waste of energy and resources, but also a missed opportunity. What a waste of emotional energy and time, a waste that breeds a poisonous spirit of victimization and blame-shifting. Far better is the admonition from St. Paul: "Let all bitterness and wrath and anger and clamor and slander be put away from you, along with all malice. Be kind to one another, tenderhearted, forgiving one another, as God in Christ forgave you," (Ephesians 4:31-32).

Breaking Negative Generational Cycles

You have been given a rich story. For most people it includes moments of heartbreaking disappointments and undeserved acts of goodness. It includes legacy treasures and legacy baggage. It is your response to the past, not the past itself, that will define your future. You have the same duty to your ancestors that you hope will be embraced and exercised by your children's children—recognize, evaluate, forgive, learn, grow, move forward! You received something, maybe not a physical inheritance. Perhaps your parents are spiritually bankrupt. You get to reset the trajectory from this point forward. You get to be a founding generation.

Be aware of your own propensity to replicate the error. Embrace it wholeheartedly. Be free from anger, resentment, and disappointment. Learn. Forgive. Move on. Only by wholeheartedly embracing what has been given to you can you hope to achieve your potential as an intentional family.

We are heirs to the specific legacy God has given us. Each legacy is unique to the individual who receives it. We have it for a reason. What we do with our legacy will shape our lives and the lives of others. Learning from past failures is precisely what is necessary for our own legacy success.

Receiving a legacy requires an honest appraisal of the past. It means recognizing the strengths and weaknesses of our parents or grandparents and specifically identifying those attributes we wish to dispense with and those we should perpetuate. Intentional families embrace their place in the generational story. Rather than mourning the imperfections of an earlier generation, we see even their failure as legacy education. The failure of our parents can become assets in our legacy arsenals when we understand that trial and error, success and failure, sin and redemption, are building blocks for growth.

Here is how this concept plays out in the Bible. Psalm seventy-eight gives a generational admonition that includes some of the following: First, make sure to tell future generations about the work of God in the life of the family. Second, make sure not to follow the bad example of past fathers. Third, make sure to follow the good example of past fathers. Fourth, make sure to set the right example for future generations by teaching them to do the same.

Intentional families want, in a spirit of confession, humility, and grace, to acknowledge past mistakes through honest and open conversation so that the mistakes will not be repeated and, where possible, relationships will be restored. They want to be freed from the emotional, psychological, and spiritual bondage that comes with unaddressed wrongs.

If you are a man struggling with drunkenness, sloth, pride, or pornography, don't be surprised if your father struggled with it. You may have inherited aptitudes or predispositions that have remained unaddressed and unidentified because they were covered by fear or shame. The same principle applies to all vices and character problems. Most education is caught, not taught, and that includes the subtle and not-so-subtle attitudes parents often unwittingly model for their children.

As it concerns vice, the caught portion can in fact be the void or the silence experienced on a particular issue. Voids are filled. Nature abhors a vacuum, and when a parent does not address a significant personal foible the consequence is a loss of authoritative voice to address that same issue with the subsequent generation. Authority in this case describes a sage, or a specialist, who can speak to a subject without pretense or hypocrisy. This authority is powerful and protective. Unspoken, the lack of authority often serves as an invitation for the repetition and recycling of problematic behavior or pain.

Left unaddressed, generational error will often be repeated. When kept in the dark, pain and neurosis tend to recycle like scratches on a record. Generational error can grip and enslave a family, substantially limiting its effectiveness, killing its joys, and disrupting its unity. Many families will simply never experience their true potential because they harbor resentment over long-standing, unaddressed issues. So address them. Bring them into the light. Talk about them. Graciously work through the difficult and uncomfortable realities of imperfection.

Children who perpetuate the errors of their fathers will suffer the consequences for doing so. Children who learn from these errors and forsake them will experience love and kindness. Everyone is responsible for himself or herself. Love God. Don't worship yourself, or false gods, or anything. Be faithful. That is the message.

The prophet Ezekiel put it this way: "The son shall not suffer for the iniquity of the father, nor the father suffer for the iniquity of the son. The righteousness of the righteous shall be upon himself, and the wickedness of the wicked shall be upon himself," (Ezekiel 18:20). This message stands in sharp contrast to any idea of fatalism. No one is "doomed" because of the choices or proclivities of an earlier generation. No one is guaranteed to repeat the errors of the past. Many of us, however, are susceptible to the same weaknesses that afflicted our parents. When these weaknesses are left unaddressed, they tend to be handed down in the form of weighty legacy baggage. Generational sin simply cannot be merely "managed." It is the very nature of sin that it perpetuates unless it is stopped.

The key is to embrace the good of past generations, but identify and turn from their weaknesses—even as we maintain a deep abiding respect for them—and show compassion for their own humanity. Their weakness will either become our victory, or just another step in a generational cycle of decline. That means we need to do an honest and informed appraisal of the past. We need a level of generational transparency.

For the redemptive-minded family, it should become natural to see areas of weakness and failure as the areas out of which healing, insight, and strength can be built. Ultimately too they can become a resource for ministering to others. Like a bone that has been broken, the greatest area of strength is that part, which has fully healed. The choice to live transparently with our own past or that of other family members can convert empty space into pillars that support a legacy. Paradoxically, bad news can be good news for the family who seeks healing, wholeness and redeemed relationships.

The Girl Who Made Breakfast

Returning to J.R. Thompson, he was a very busy man. His only child, Cheryl, understood that. Dad was a workaholic, gone six days a week, fourteen hours a day. He left before 6:00 a.m. and returned home long after Cheryl was asleep. No family dinners. Her only window to be with him was in the early morning over a meal. From the age of ten, Cheryl woke every morning at 4:30 to make her father breakfast. It was the only time she consistently saw him. And she loved him so much that she was willing to fight for that daily brief window of time. It was just Cheryl and her dad. Mom never made it to breakfast.

But there was one thing Cheryl was never able to do—she could not be the boy her father had always wanted. Even making breakfast could not fix that problem. Dad related to her as her provider, but not as the father of a daughter with specific needs for fatherly affirmation. Of course he gave her any material possession she could desire, but the one thing she craved—the attention that comes from a mutually reinforcing relationship of tenderness between a father and daughter—J.R. did not know how to give.

It does not take rocket science to figure out that voids will be filled. When a father fails to speak to the heart of his daughter, someone or something else will. Cheryl went looking for love in all the wrong places, and at the age of eighteen she conceived a child. The circumstances and scenario were almost a stereotype—all too predictable and unfortunate. But the tragedy was not the conception of a child. The tragedy was those things that didn't happen before and much that did happen afterwards— events that may have brought unresolved conflict in the secret life of J.R.

Thompson colliding with his own daughter's misfortunes.

Scarlet Letters

There was a time when a woman was shamed for having a child out of wedlock. It was not necessary to wear Hawthorne's infamous scarlet letter to experience the same practical consequences—social and emotional shunning and rejection. Today the pendulum has swung. We have largely lost our moral compass. Rather than acknowledging the incompatibility of a culture of shame with human redemption, our society increasingly dispenses with the notion that virtue and truth even exist. The principal reason why shaming a woman for an extra-marital pregnancy is gone is that marriage is no longer viewed as relevant. If marriage is passé, is there an ethical or practical difference between having babies in or out of a marital covenant?

There are better reasons why scarlet letters of every shape and size have no place in civilized communities. First, they tend toward the de-humanization of the individual. They seek to reduce a human made in the image of God to mere status. If you can minimize the humanity of another human being, you can justify every form of social and ethical atrocity against them; after all, they are something less than human. Scorn, contempt, rejection, gossip, caricature, and objectification of an individual can all manifest as variations on a theme—the dehumanization of a human being of great worth.

Second, badges of shame (scarlet letters) are the enemy of a truly redemptive ethic, one which is able to navigate away from the dangerous waters of moral equivalency on the one hand, while wholeheartedly extending a message of safe harbor to any who will receive it, on the other. The family must be a city of refuge to its members.

Third, scarlet letters stand in implicit opposition to a visional ethic bathed in compassion, which "bears all things, believes all things, hopes all things, endures all things," (1 Corinthian 13:7).

Shame

Just under a half a century ago—sometime not far from the time that the Hartman luggage bag was closed and locked—Mary-Catherine's mother,

Cheryl, became one of those woman required to wear a scarlet letter.

It was an era in the South where social status did not mix with social shame. Bad behavior was tolerated, even encouraged, just as long as it remained private and covered up. It was one thing to make mistakes; it was another for mistakes to become public gossip. Scandal could ruin business and position in society.

When his only daughter became pregnant out of wedlock, J.R.'s first response was rage. It manifested in a one-time event of heartbreaking physical violence against Cheryl. Up to that point in her life, her father had never even spanked her, but he had also never been faced with the prospect of seeing his life's work come crashing down through public scandal.

Next he insisted that she get an abortion. But the girl who had always wanted to please her father just could not comply. Even in her own state of emotional confusion, aborting her own child was a line she could not cross. When he was unsuccessful at convincing his daughter to kill the baby, J.R. turned to another man for reinforcement. The year was 1968. Roe vs. Wade was several years from hitting the Supreme Court, and abortion was still something that polite people only whispered about. The pastor of their local Baptist church, wanting the issue to be kept quiet because J.R. served as treasurer, stood with J.R., urging Cheryl to abort her own child and get on with her life.

Thanks to the determination of Cheryl and the intervention of a Roman Catholic family doctor, the push for an abortion came to an end. The baby would be born.

And yet even the problem of social intolerance did not completely account for J.R's response. Something else was going on behind the scenes, something that may relate to the locked Hartmann bag.

J.R.'s prior relationship with Cheryl may have been emotionally insubstantial, but his plans for her life were not. She was to go to college, acquire land and houses, and obtain all the externals of social advancement. They were fatherly expressions of provision and perhaps even love as understood through the mental grid of a superior breadwinner.

Now with the pregnancy, there would be no higher education and no "big plans." Everything came to a screeching halt—including, and perhaps especially, breakfasts with Dad.

Cheryl's "scarlet letter" came next in the form of rejection from her mother—J.R. Thompson's wife—who was so concerned about the social stigma associated with teen pregnancy that she escaped to Alaska for a season, leaving her daughter behind to carry the baby to term. Throughout the "crisis," J.R. was distant and embarrassed, but not absent or without compassion for his daughter. For some reason, he simply lacked the clarity and moral authority to help her navigate the turbulent waters. There were enormous resources available to J.R., but those resources did not include either fatherly wisdom or the intensely personal emotional assets that Cheryl needed.

The unplanned pregnancy also lacked a plan for the future of the young couple, so a shotgun marriage was arranged. To help his daughter along, J.R. invested a small fortune and gifted a business to his new son-in-law who proceeded to abandon it several weeks later. In less than a year, he moved in and out of twenty-five different jobs. The marriage simply failed to launch. A little over twelve months after the child was born, and with the encouragement of J.R., they divorced.

It was the first of three divorces and four marriages for Cheryl. Regardless of the circumstances surrounding conception, the birth of a child is never a mistake. It is often the children of misfortune who bring the greatest blessing to the world around them. In this case the baby was not Mary-Catherine, but her older brother, John.

Family Secrets

Probably around the same time that Cheryl conceived a child with her best friend, her father J.R. may have been having an affair with one of their family's best friends. Does this account for J.R.'s silence and emotional distance? Perhaps. But if that was true about J.R, it remained a secret. Something dark and unacknowledged. What we do know is that maintaining silence is often because of guilt and shame that mutes the voice of the one who would otherwise speak with authority on the issue. If we are hardwired to appreciate truth and beauty, it makes sense that we experience an awkward silence when our actions and words are inconsistent or hypocritical. So we keep secrets instead.

In *The Book of Tomorrow*, Cecelia Ahern offers this insight: "All families have their secrets, most people would never know them, but they know there are spaces, gaps where the answers should be, where someone should have sat, where someone used to be. A name that is never uttered, or uttered just once and never again. We all have our secrets."[22]

Rather than being a source of protection to children, keeping secrets from one generation to the next builds distrust. Cassandra Clare wrote, "Lies and secrets . . . are like a cancer in the soul. They eat away what is good and leave only destruction behind."[23]

The Death of J.R.

J.R. Thompson died on October 11, 1989. The funeral was an event that drew friends from across the nation. Grateful individuals J.R. had helped came to pay tribute. The building was filled to capacity, overflowing into the hallways.

J.R. was a man with great strengths whose weaknesses were cultivated during an epoch of American social history that struggled to find balance between the Christian ethics of another era with the changing values of modernity. The result was a culture that included social elites who tolerated hypocrisy, sometimes even encouraging moral failure as long as it remained hidden from public scrutiny. In this world a man could write a check to make a problem go away. If personal failure were brought into the light, the only appropriate response was disgrace, shame, and disapprobation. Empires and reputations might be on the line. That was the world in which J.R. Thompson had lived.

There were many grieving people left behind with J.R.'s death, but perhaps none so broken as his daughter. The closure she had dreamed of would never happen. He was gone. The window of opportunity for personal healing between father and daughter had ended. In the years that followed, Cheryl spoke openly to Mary-Catherine of the hole she carries in her heart to this day—having never had the relationship that every daughter dreams of and every daughter needs.

Finding Treasure Amidst the Wreckage

Looking at the legacy baggage that my mother-in law inherited, and trying to understand all that she endured over the course of her life, my heart is filled with gratitude. She made three decisions that have become my own legacy treasures: The first was her willingness to endure heartbreak, pressure, and personal rejection in order to carry a baby to term. She fought for life. In so doing, she modeled for the generations who would follow the most basic truth—greater love has no [person] than they lay down their life for another (John 15:13).

The second was her decision to honor her father's legacy by fighting for his company. She had no formal training and no college degree, but she had something better—a sense of duty, determination, and work ethic. She poured every penny and every ounce of energy into managing a company that reached close to 1000 employees and more than tripled in size on her watch. She did it magnificently. At its peak, and under her watch, it produced $350 million in revenues a year.

The third was to speak to her daughter—my wife—with crystal clear transparency about the legacy baggage in her own life. Cheryl did not flinch when talking to Mary-Catherine, both as a girl and as an adult: "Here is what I did wrong." "Here is where I should have refused to quit." "Here is how I felt and how that affected me."

There is something innately humbling about parent-to-child honesty. It is an approach to family life that spurns both idealization and self-vindicating revisionism—an honesty that allows the next generation to move beyond shame and actually benefit from the mistakes of the past. Transparency opens the door for the next generation to come to terms with their own identity in light of an honest appraisal of both legacy treasures and legacy baggage.

How can I properly thank her for the gift of transparency? I cannot. Through her transparency, she has nurtured the character of my wife— a woman who is hopeful for her future because she is at peace with her past.

Time to Decide

Here then are the questions: What vestiges of folly and bad choices will you reject? What honorable legacies will you perpetuate? How can you learn from both? How can you be thankful for both?

Gratefully receiving legacy treasures and coming to peace with legacy baggage is necessary for your own journey of intentionality. Your children are watching your example.

Gratitude for the excellence and virtues of your ancestors, even while maintaining a spirit of compassion and forgiveness for their errors, is vital if you hope to receive the same response someday from your own children who must also identify error and excellence and make choices of their own.

In this, as in so many parts of our marriage, Mary-Catherine has become my mentor. Her deep abiding faith in the power of redemption and her generosity of spirit, have allowed her to translate a complicated family legacy filled with three generations of treasure and baggage into a message of abiding hope for our children. And it gives hope to me.

When crisis emerges with one of our children, how will we respond? Try to decide that now, before the stress-filled moment of pressure and disturbance. The exercise is particularly helpful in clarifying whether our response to a child's failure stems from how it reflects on us, bringing in our own issues of pride and shame, or relates specifically to the child.

The exercise also benefits us by reiterating the need for grace in relationships. Do our children know they can speak freely with us? If they have a concern or question, will they be met with grace, or do they know the sword of Damocles is ever hanging over their heads? Don't shy away from thinking about a worst-case scenario, and decide now how you will respond. Don't wait.

Mary-Catherine and I have already made our decision. We pray for God's grace and mercy on each of our children. We hope to cultivate a welcoming environment where our children will embrace truth and virtue, where their physical and emotional purity will be honored and preserved before marriage. But if "the worst-case scenario" occurred, our relationship with our children would not be changed. Our relationship with them "is."

Even if I were prone to forget this commitment, God has allowed weekly reminders to keep it at the forefront of my mind: Most weeks I have a conversation with a three-foot-tall, five-year-old, ethereal woodland elf with the last name of McAlvany. Sometimes she comes dressed like a ballerina and other times like a princess, but what she lacks in height and maturity, she makes up in moxie. And often she comes with the same question:

"Daddy, do you love me?"

"Oh yes sweetie, I love you so."

"But Daddy, you don't love my fussiness, do you?"

"No, I do not love your fussiness."

"But you love me, even though you don't love my fussiness?"

"I will love you always and forever, and your fussiness cannot change that. When you choose to be fussy, have a bad attitude, or disobey, I don't like what you choose, but I love you all the same. I love you with all my heart, and I always will."

That is my message to her, and God's message to me—non-contingent, unconditional love.

Being a father or mother requires having your receiver on 24/7. We simply cannot afford to lose the connection, even as we realize that the battle for a wandering heart is not fought in the middle of a crisis, but long before, when the decision is made to love unconditionally and whole-heartedly.

Opening the Bag

But what of the bag—the non-fictional, non-metaphorical bag that once belonged to Mary-Catherine's grandfather, J.R. Thompson?

The moment has arrived to open the time capsule.

Into the living room I went as the children gathered around. Down from the shelf came the Hartmann. I had an idea. What if I can open it by testing various combinations on each of the two three-digit combination locks? Each set of three had a potential 1,000 variables. Doing about twenty-five a minute meant that I should be able to discover the first set of combinations in no more than forty minutes.

Twenty minutes into the first set I cracked the combination. The second set was even easier. No locksmith. No property destruction. Just good old-fashioned deliberation and patience.

Then came the moment of truth. The Hartmann opened for the first time in decades.

Inside the case were artifacts from various vacation destinations around the world. Ticket stubs, match boxes, brochures, and leftovers from the traveling life of J.R. Thompson. Missing were specific clues for the reasons for the trips or the person with whom he was traveling.

But why were these documents so important that he chose to lock them into the Hartmann? We may never know for sure. What we do know is that around the same time J.R. was struggling with a correct response to developments in the life of his daughter, he was in a long, ongoing affair with the wife of a close friend, a subject on which he chose to remain silent to his dying day. Perhaps these mementos are evidence of that affair. We can only speculate. The love letters, known to exist, were not in the Hartman case as suspected. What was done with them?

It has taken three generations for us to begin the process of getting a handle on a problem that has affected our family. Now, with Christ's message of love and forgiveness as our interpretive grid, we cannot only understand the past, we can also forgive those who came before us, even as we prepare to abandon their legacy baggage. Rather than bringing new grief, the unfolding mystery of the life of J.R. Thompson helps us to better understand how we can break with generational sin cycles and chart a fresh course. Now it's your turn. Where will you begin?

You have one crack at being a parent. Don't blow it! If you have blown it, join the crowd of 100% of all parents who have ever lived. Now repair the problem. Stop whatever you are doing and fight for the most important relationships in your life. It does not matter where you are on the continuum from failure to success. As long as you have breath, the story is not over. Do not underestimate the power of resolve and redemption.

Chris Hodges correctly observed that "the problem with baggage is that it affects other people's trips."[24] This is precisely the point: It is one thing to sink your personal vessel, but what of your children's? One of the greatest gifts you can give to future generations is to jettison all unnecessary baggage off the side of your ship: Family secrets—gone! Redemption-less shame tactics—goodbye! Unconfessed wrongs to one another—treat them like toxic waste in a container. It all must go. Every single bag.

There is a delicate balance to legacy navigation. Too much weight will sink your vessel. Identify the legacy baggage. Take note of contents, and then throw them overboard. Don't replace them with fresh bags. Don't mourn their loss. Just chuck them forever.

Chapter 5

The Times of Your Life:
Creating a Family Identity

"When I discover who I am, then I will be free."
- Ralph Ellison[25]

My home is Durango, Colorado. It is a walking town—a quiet and friendly "peace be with you" kind of a town. With a population just under twenty thousand, we are small enough to recognize one another on the streets but large enough to keep to ourselves when we want. Our identity as a community is inextricably linked to our history—one of gold and gunslingers, trains, and movies.

We are an artsy, culinary, cowboy town that gives new meaning to the word *eclectic*. In Durango conservative Christians, western ranchers, creative entrepreneurs, vagabond musicians, and New Age aficionados have somehow learned to live side-by-side in relative harmony. One person described it as "a city of black sheep from different flocks that have decided to graze together—most of the time."

Beyond the center of town, the warp and woof of life is in the streams and valleys, the bluffs and downhills. Durango is a haven for skiers, triathletes, mountain bikers, ice climbers, and anyone who wants to defy the vertical. Where others prefer cocooning, our life is spent outdoors—it's our culture. Just a shout and a holler down the interstate highway are the Great Sand Dunes and the Anasazi Cliff Dwelling Palaces of Mesa Verde National Park. We are within a two-hour drive of some of the greatest environmental treasures of America.

As a community we owe our existence to the railroad boom of the

1880s. Durango was birthed when the Denver and Rio Grande Railroad first laid their tracks where we now call home. Down the street from my in-town office is the depot of the old Durango to Silverton Narrow Gauge Railway. Where most tracks were four feet, eight-and-a-half inches in width, ours only a "narrow" three feet. This allowed the trains to be lighter, using smaller cars, bridges, and tunnels, and to take tighter turns—a benefit for a world that beckoned men around and through the local mountains in the search for gold.

Durango is known to much of the world as a Butch Cassidy and Sundance Kid kind of town where the four-time Oscar winning movie was filmed. People still trek to the spot where Redford and Newman once made their famous jump into the Animas River. The appeal of Durango to Hollywood has remained strong for more than a half a century. They call us "The Hollywood of the Rockies." It is a moniker reflective of the flavor of our gunslinger-meets-avant-garde attitude as a community. Dozens of other famous films were shot here, including Around the World in Eighty Days (1956), Viva Zapata (1952); The Sons of Katie Elder (1965), City Slickers (1991), and The Lone Ranger (2012). The streets, railroad lines, and mountain switchbacks speak of an America that has all but disappeared. It's a setting which makes Durango evergreen as a cinematically desirable location.

We are just far enough from Denver to keep our sanity and close enough to the mountains to revive our spirits. For Mary-Catherine and me, our decision to live here is intentional. I am not sure that it actually started out that way, but it has become exactly that. We love our community. If we were starting fresh, it would still be our first choice as a place to settle and start a family. We have one of those unique types of national and internationally oriented businesses that could be operated from almost any reasonable location. Durango provides a quiet environment where we can accomplish our mission and maintain a relatively low profile.

When it comes to reverse engineering a legacy, the question of identity is perhaps the most fundamental to be resolved. Who am I? Where did I come from? What makes me me? Are there others like me? Do I fit in? How does my relationship with my father or mother shape the person I am today? What is the significance of my personal journey? My experiences? Will my response to the past define the person I will become in the future? What is my mission? Does my life matter? These are questions of identity. They are fundamentals, and they have been asked in one form or another as long as man has been on the earth.

These questions form the basis of philosophy and religion because they are matters of ultimacy. From Moses to Aristotle, Augustine to Nietzsche, men have searched for answers that give insight to identity. Even something as basic as Descartes' proposition—Cogito ergo sum ("I think, therefore I am") relates to the identity of the individual. But despite the need in the heart of man for answers that establish identity in terms of the transcendent, the practical reality is that our answers to these questions tend to emerge more in the context of personal relationships than they do in philosophy class or even Sunday school.

Every Family Has an Identity

Every family has an identity. Some are clear and articulable. Others appear ambiguous and undefined, but are no less real. Some are inconsistent. Others appear schizophrenic. Some are attractive and promote buy-in from family members. Others appear toxic to the children who end up rejecting their family identity. Identity can be shaped and molded or transformed, but in the end there will be an identity. Like legacy, it is an inescapable reality.

This is a chapter about identity, especially as it relates to the cultural legacy of your family. To be examined are the environs, the rituals of life, and the character that shapes the identity of the family. Everything matters. Even eccentricities and idiosyncrasies that make your family unique are part of the culture that binds you together as a family in a common experience. Your identity finds expression in your citizenship within a nation as well as the various professional, social, and religious organizations of which you are a part. But more than anything, your identity is an expression of the three relationships that define your life—your spiritual relationship with the Creator, your relationship with your family, and your personal relationship with yourself—who you are as an individual.

Identity is shaped by many factors and is always tested in adversity. Families that confront significant disturbance and survive tend to experience a strengthening of their identity. Struggle either bonds people together or drives them apart. Struggle is a necessary component in the unfolding story of your identity as a member of a family.

With all of this discussion about family culture, it is important to note the importance of individuality. Wise parents will cultivate a distinctive family identity that promotes buy-in from future generations, even as they encourage individuality for each of their heirs. Unity and distinction can exist side by side when family culture is redemptive, inclusive, vibrant, and hopeful. Having an identity as a Smith or a Martinez is not exclusive of the need for each person to flourish as an individual. Freedom to individuate within the context of a culture where the members share core values and experiences will go a long way toward ensuring that the next generation embraces the most important aspects of the family culture. Family identity creates a context for understanding a personal identity that is refined over one's lifetime.

Our names remind us of the principle. Think about it this way: in Western cultures each of us has at least a Christian name and a surname. The surname, or last name, identifies us as members of a specific family. It is our tribal name. It is a mark of identity that remains with us throughout our lives. But even though we formally identify ourselves through the use of our surname, we are known to friends by our first name—an example of family identity and individuality existing side by side.

One way to think about identity is in terms of the way you choose to respond to the story of your life. It's a long story—one that predates your birth and will continue long after you depart this earth. Your identity begins with the collective generational influences of your ancestors: the past history, language, present legal system, social structures, cultural ethos, and economies, which make up your national citizenship, and your personal perception of them. Intentional families further recognize that identity is not merely a function of faith and philosophy, but of community and environment. You are an American, or Fijian, or Moroccan, or Mexican, or Balinese, or Texan.

Very little of our identity is truly original. We are the combined effort of people who have come before us, of events and circumstances that predate our birth as well as the contributing influence (for good or evil) of the people who surround us. Notwithstanding, there is a sense in which our ultimate identity transcends all of these factors. We are who we are because we were made in the image of God and are loved by Him. This means that, regardless of circumstances or identity confusion that may exist, there is value to each individual. If nations fall, and families disappear, if all the externals of life were to evaporate before your eyes, your ultimate identity would not change because it is based on a transcendent relationship with the Creator. That relationship is the single most important mark of identity. The decision to recognize or reject your identity as a child of the Heavenly Father is the defining identity crisis of your life. Choose wisely.

Identity Shapers

Every family has a story. The delights, disciplines, and deeds of the family emerge in the context of choices that make up the backdrop for that life story. What your family views as "normal" will shape your identity. Structures and strategies are important, but normal is what people think about when they think of family life. The decisions you make that define "normal" for your family often have greater impact on how your children perceive themselves and whether or not they self-consciously buy in to the family identity. Who you marry has direct bearing on the delights, disciplines, and deeds your family will prioritize.

For the rest of this chapter we are going to explore the circumstantial factors that shape your family's identity. Where and with whom you live, the rituals and routine events that bind you together as a family, and even the idiosyncrasies, attitudes, and general atmosphere of your daily life shape your family identity.

Somewhere down your own journey of intentionality, environment and community become defining issues. Environment is the physical backdrop of your lifestyle. Communities are those social groups that intersect with your life. Small or large, country or city, free spirit or traditional, your choice defines your family lifestyle. The truth is, choosing your environment and community may be the least flexible decisions you ever have to make, but they are probably in the top five most important decisions for the intentional family. Of course, there are different communities for different types of people and different stages in life. Being in the military, starting a family, or approaching retirement are just a few of the factors that might influence your choices and available options. Environment and community may influence more elements of your family identity than you realize. Your musical preferences, entertainment choices, view of relaxation, and diet are all influenced by where you choose to live.

Time is another issue. Life is short. Your time is one of your most valuable assets. A decision to spend fifteen hours each week in bumper-to-bumper traffic has direct implications on family life and must be weighed against other available options in terms of the consequences it creates.

Delights, Disciplines, and Deeds

Legacy-minded families recognize that the journey of intentionality involves a reevaluation of our lives from top to bottom. Basic choices relating to the culture of your family will shape its identity. These choices can roughly be broken down into three distinct categories:

1. **The Delights of the Family:** Here is an exercise. Don't think too hard about it. Just stop and try to write down five areas of delight mutually shared by members of your family: music, food, work, spiritual life, entertainment—the categories are numerous. The question you are answering is this: What does your family enjoy doing together? What brings you delight? How is that delight cultivated? For example, are you a baseball game family? Would you say your family characterized by loving the company of children? Do you delight in the mountains or the beach? Both?

2. **The Disciplines of the Family:** Disciplines are the rituals and protocols that govern daily life in the family. What are the daily rituals that shape your identity? Can you list five that are known to every member of your family and create a common thread in the course of life? For example, when do you rise in the morning? What does hygiene look like in your household? Do you pray as individuals or as a family? What disciplines do you follow with respect to finances? Do you prioritize healthy foods? Do you read on a routine basis? Do you work together around the house?

3. **The Deeds of the Family:** The deeds are the way your family invests in the lives of others. Deeds are a means of expressing your family identity beyond the household. Some families are involved in philanthropy. Others participate in coaching. Some have a robust hospitality calendar and a dinner table populated by guests. Some families are involved in politics or the life of the church. Your family "deeds" are the externalization of the identity of your family in the real world.

A few years ago, I met a fascinating couple whose life was dedicated to the world of words and ideas. The husband was a writer for *Harpers, The Atlantic,* and *The New Yorker,* and the wife a distinguished television critic with *The New York Times.* I met them for dinner and spent a very happy evening swapping life stories and observing how the delights, disciplines, and deeds of their childhoods shaped their identity and direction in life.

The husband came from a family of Rabbis and bookworms. The wife was from a family of academics. The two shared a common denominator. They came from families who embraced similar delights and disciplines. Both came from religious homes. Both grew up in an environment where reading and talking together as a family was the norm. "Our family read all the time," he told me. "Saturday was sports day for other families. For us it was a day devoted to reading."

These disciplines reflected their delights and resulted in a life of deeds; both went on to devote their own careers and marriage to sharing the world of ideas and thought with others. While many view them as a New York power couple, my experience of them was of two deeply inquisitive and expressive souls.

Your lifestyle shapes your identity. Whether it be watching television, playing golf, reading and discussing ideas, or getting outside to run, you are cultivating a social norm, and with it, an identity. Whether these identity influences are deliberately chosen or not, they define the nature of a legacy.

There are, of course, elements of your family identity which are hard to categorize. Do they emerge from idiosyncrasies? Are they philosophically driven? Are they the result of a unique cocktail of mixed influences that makes your family your family? In your family, these hard-to-categorize elements of your identity may find expression in the fact that every member of your family, for as long as you can remember, brushes their teeth five times a day. Or perhaps, yours is the family that always feeds stray animals. But when your family culture combines a keen professional interest in political and economic trends with expertise in survival skills and passion for outdoor activities, the results are "bug-out" bags and boulders.

I grew up in a world of bug-out bags. There has been one in my room since I was fifteen. A bug-out bag is what happens when a portable escape pod meets a treasure chest. Bug-out bags are designed to do what their name implies—bug out. They are light, portable, and contain "the most important things." Dad taught us that if things ever got really bad, if the fire was coming over the hill, and the house was about to burn, or if the enemy was at the gate, and you had just minutes—maybe seconds—to get out, there would be time for just this—to grab your bug-out bag and your family, and get out of Dodge. The principle behind bug-out bags was this: Everything can be replaced except for your flesh-and-blood family, and yet, there are just a few things that are not easily replaced: your "lovey" that you cuddled as a child, the 1921 peace dollar your grandpa gave you before his passing, a letter from your father. Those very few items that have become sacred artifacts in your life, or even tools for rebuilding your life— only those (and they'd better be light) go in your bug-out bag. He taught us—Choose it now. There won't be time later.

In our home, we grew up reciting Kipling: "If you can keep your head when all about are losing theirs and blaming it on you . . . then you will be a man, my son." This philosophy was defining. Bug-out bags were one way Dad taught us to keep a cool head in times of crisis. We also learned it dealing with the environment of the physical world of Durango. Because we are Durangans, we live in an outdoor culture where physical interaction with ice, snow, rocks, and mountains is an assumed part of our life. One result of that is that when it comes to accidents, weather issues, and natural disasters, we are problem solvers. For our family, problem solving and figuring out solutions is routinely practiced in the outdoors while climbing on the boulders.

People come to Durango to go hiking, tour the mountain passes in jeeps, or downhill ski. It is a remarkable once-in-a-lifetime getaway. But what for some people is an extraordinary experience is more common for us. It is not that we take these experiences for granted. The fact is that our environment has such an impact on our identity that we cannot think about life apart from the terrain. What the neighborhoods in the Bronx are to New Yorkers, or the North Shore waves are to the surfing culture of Oahu, the streams and boulders and slopes of Durango are to us.

Part of our family identity is that we are rock climbers. Our children start bouldering and rock climbing from the age of three. It is a way of thinking and a lifestyle. It comes from being close to a very distinctive and inviting environment. Walking down the street to summit a small mountain or climb a boulder might be a revolutionary experience to others, but for Durangans, it is part and parcel to our lives. It is not uncommon to see the banker with whom you just transacted business or the waitress who served you the other night both hiking the trails or summiting a boulder on any given day of the week. Life in the outdoors is very egalitarian.

Our family culture approaches rock climbing in much the same way we approach investment strategies. We are willing to take risks, but not to bet the farm. When it comes to climbing, we want to push ourselves, not shorten our lives. But it is really a matter of perspective: one person's perilous climb is another person's walk in the park. We approach bouldering as a family—identifying the boulders we hope to climb, assessing their difficulty level, identifying the best routes to execute our ascents and descents. We rarely use ropes, opting for a spotter and placing bouldering pads (similar to gymnastic mats) on the ground. It means we all have to stay alert. We have to work as a team.

Boulders can be rated for difficulty based on technical grades. The American system is called the "Huaco Scale," and rates boulder routes from V1 to V16. As with investments, we approach boulders by first evaluating the level of risk against the potential benefit. It is a mentality we have adopted as a family. We have a risk threshold, which is a reflection of our present priorities and past experience. In the case of investments, my father and I have a fixed money number we are willing to risk, lose, and not miss a minute's sleep. This is known as a position limit and is vital to risk management. We apply the same mentality to bouldering. Summiting a boulder requires a combination of analysis, presence of mind, and physical skill. Because this is a form of free climbing, there is a special emphasis on teamwork and cool-headedness. There is no place for panic. Directions must be calmly communicated. Experience makes the analysis more intuitive. Presence of mind comes by learning to manage difficulties—to find finger holds and routes that previously seemed impossible to tackle. Practice leads to increased tendon strength and flexibility. Small failures allow for greater successes when you get back up after the failure.

With seven years of training and experience on the rocks, my ten-year-old is capable of climbing a V6 boulder. There is a risk-mitigating safety drill we always follow, involving a crash mat, route surveillance, and spotting. He can do it. He knows it, and I know it. More importantly, he is now able to lead and guide others.

Family Identity Marks

There is an even bigger question than the decision of where and with whom you will live. Environment and community are important identity issues, but not the most important. More defining than the world outside your home is the one inside. The dinner table trumps the ski slopes. To put it another way, family culture is first and foremost a function of real life lived out in the context of home life.

Everything matters. Every detail of the life of your family is crafting a unique cultural identity. All of it matters: praying beside the beds of your children at night, dancing in the living room, gardening in the backyard, caring for a pet gecko, changing baby diapers, the prints you put on your walls, the candles you light for ambiance, the music that wafts from room to room, learning the best time to speak softly and the right time to be loud, bringing friends and guests into your home, reading, talking, thinking, singing. The great nineteenth century commentator on family life, J.R. Miller, observed: "There is nothing in the daily routine of the family life that is unimportant. Indeed, it is oft times the things we think of as without influence that will be found to have made the deepest impression on the tender lives of the household."[26]

Family idiosyncrasies: you see them every day in the routine course of life. They are marks of identity. Because they are so familiar to us, they often fly below the radar screen of our analysis. But these idiosyncrasies are key elements that shape the identity of your family culture—a culture which, in turn, shapes you. I am referring to those idiosyncrasies which are distinct to your family and make you a Smith or a Martinez. They include mannerisms, tastes, preferences, stylistic traits, and that which are representative of your family. They take a thousand shapes and forms. These are the types of behavior that are usually not formally taught, but *caught* over the course of your childhood. These idiosyncrasies may be the product of nature, nurture, or both. Many will remain with you till your death. Sometimes consciously, but often on a subliminal level, they inform your approach to human interactions.

A family idiosyncrasy could be that all the men wear suspenders, or that the women apply make-up that is just a bit over the top. Perhaps in your family there is a universal disdain for putting mustard on hot-dogs. Maybe you are one of those enlightened families who embraces an across-the-board pro-canine position towards man's best friend and acknowledge cats to be self-absorbed creatures of general indifference to humanity. Maybe your idiosyncrasies are clearly genetic—you have a distinctive nose, receding hair-line, or stature that marks you as a member of your family. Or maybe the idiosyncrasy is stylistic—you are a hat-wearing family, a family of gigglers, or singers, or cut-ups, where every member is known for a quick wit and a sharp tongue.

Sometimes you see these marks of identity on the facial expressions of family members. They can be so subtle as to be barely perceptible, like the way every member of your family drops his or her jaw ever so slightly when they feel uncomfortable in a conversation. It could be that family members share the same basic scowl when disappointed or deliver a signature whinny laugh when they hear something very funny. You might be a family of huggers, or hand holders, or not. Perhaps there is a similar cadence to the speech, or a particular gate, to the way the men walk.

McAlvanys have at least a thousand eccentricities that identify us as members of the same tribe. One is that we are a family of whistlers. We whistle all the time. My children grew up hearing their dad whistle. I belong in the 1920s as a cheesy tunesmith. Now they are cheesy tunesmith whistlers. It does not matter if you find us when we are happy or sad—you are likely to hear us whistling. We are even a bit like Snow White's seven dwarves because we whistle while we work, whether that is at the office or the home school. Pretty much anything is an occasion for a good whistle.

Family idiosyncrasies are usually benign, but not always. Some really bother you, so you react against them and vow that you "will never be that way" when your turn comes to run the show. Often they are so much a part of who you are that you don't realize when you are replicating these same marks of identity in your own life. Your friends see you doing it. Some find it endearing, others annoying. But the more they get to know you in the context of your relations, the more they recognize that these idiosyncratic marks of identity are directly linked to a society of individuals you call family.

The message is this—More often than not, idiosyncrasy is a good thing. Embrace it. Find the humor in the marks of your family identity. Wherever possible, learn to enjoy the peccadilloes and eccentricities that make your own family unique.

Tribal Signs and Cultural Barometers

Now is a good time to survey the ethos of your family culture. You have an opportunity to shape it and see it transformed in the direction most desirable. Here are seven categories of questions that may help you to identify the spirit of your household, which will shape how your immediate heirs perceive their own identity:

1. **Humor:** Do you smile a lot or only on occasion? Is home a place of humor and joy? Is the only kind of laughter you know the kind that comes from mockery or sarcasm? Are you a somber family? Hypercritical? Laughter is an antidote to anger. The two do not coexist at the same time. Laughter allows people under great stress to make it through the most difficult of circumstances. Homes without laughter are like hives without honey—a shell filled with stingers. Are you a laughing family?

2. **Delight:** Is there delight in your home—the kind where children are allowed to enjoy the experiences of childhood, and young adults and parents retain a sense of wonder and mystery about the joys of life? Does your family stop to see the beauty of life? Do you take time to smell the proverbial roses? Is your home a place of inquiry, discovery, and adventure? Isaac Asimov said, "The true delight is in the finding out, rather than in the knowing." Most importantly, is your home a place where family members enjoy worshipping God? "Delight yourself in the Lord, and he will give you the desires of your heart, (Psalm 37:4). In what does your family delight?

3. **Hospitality:** Is your home open and inviting to others? The Bible has much to say on the subject. Hospitality is to be extended to strangers (Hebrews 13:2), and offered without complaint (1 Peter 4:9). Are friends comfortable in your home? Do your children's friends want to spend time at your house? Is your family life marked by hospitality?

4. **Sound:** What are the sounds that fill the walls of your home? Babies? Teenagers? Are they happy sounds? Violent sounds? On the loud versus quiet spectrum, where does your family fit? Is it a cheerful loud or an angry loud? Is it a peaceful quiet or a lonely quiet? If you were to walk into your home on any given day, what would you most likely hear? Is your home filled with music? Do children and parents enjoy the same types of music, or is your home a cacophony of cultural segregation? Is there an appreciation for syncopated, melodious, or harmonized notes? What is the message to future generations that comes from the sounds that fill

your family culture?

5. **Order:** Is your home orderly? Is it so orderly that it feels like a museum? Is it so disorderly that it seems like a pig sty? Is it a comfortable place that feels safe and inviting to every member of your family? Is it child-friendly? Some homes have organized clutter; others feel like sterile environments. What is the feel of your household? Do people tend to congregate together, or do they perpetually avoid one another, disappearing into their own private rooms? What is the message you want the design and order of your home to communicate to your family?

6. **Service:** Some families perpetuate a culture of generosity. Dad is always giving. Mom is always giving. The children follow suit. Generous parents are less likely to generate selfish cultures. Do your children see you helping others? When you think of your family culture, does generosity come to mind? Or is your family prone to the "gimmes," always taking and wanting more? Can you think of memorable examples of service and generosity?

7. **Smell:** Yes, homes have distinctive smells. Smells are important because we tend to associate them with emotions and events in our lives. Do you remember how your grandma's home smelled different from your own? Visit a home from a foreign culture, and one of the first things that stands out is the smell—it is just different. Different foods, different standards of hygiene, even different philosophies of the use of design and space can result in a different olfactory experience. Are there incense or scented candles burning in your home, or does the scent of kitty litter pervade? What distinctive scents fill your home?

These categories are all part of the cultural experience that will inform your children's collective consciousness about the experience of home life, providing the subtle details that create nostalgia.

Toxic Identity

Sometimes the development of toxicity is subtle, spreading slowly and gradually alienating various family members. Other times it is devastating and sudden. Physical and sexual abuse, hatred, anger, cruelty, destructive addictions that poison the ethos of the family, and anything that results in relational disconnect between members of a household is identity poison. Every family comes in contact with elements of poison, but left unchecked and unregulated, the results can be terminal.

Sometimes trace elements of toxins can actually prove helpful. The same principle found in the disciplines of biology and toxicology also apply in life. Dr. Joseph Mercola comments, "'What doesn't kill you makes you stronger' is a phrase that contains more than a grain of truth. It describes the theory of hormesis, the process whereby organisms exposed to low levels of stress or toxins become more resistant to tougher challenges."[27]

The principle of hormesis applies to the intentional family. There will be negativity, failure, and some form of toxic behavior in every family. There is no such thing as a perfectly sterile, healthy family environment. But there are households that keep toxins in check and under control. Those families may actually benefit from the strengthening process that comes from limited contact with relational poison.

The result of a toxic family culture is the rejection of it. In the absence of an inviting and meaningful family culture, children will seek to find identity elsewhere. They will look to peers, lovers, movements, pop figures—anyone or anything that will give them new marks of identity. Identity loss is one of the principal reasons for legacy failure.

You Need to Feast

Great family cultures feast. They spend lots of time eating together. They think about food and talk about it. They develop family rituals around food. They sit together often as a family. They use mealtime as a basis for showing hospitality to friends. They tell stories and laugh at the table. They learn to cultivate manners sitting around a dinner table. They pray at the table. They view mealtime as a daily ritual that not only feeds the body, but also refreshes the soul.

Many Latin American, Asian, and European cultures still make their family meal times prominent, and it shows in the success of their family cultures. The implications of a family culture that embraces lengthy, dynamic, flavorful meal times is significant. You see it in those cultures where meal times are carefully scheduled events. In his book *Seven Fires: Grilling the Argentinian Way*, the great chef Francis Mallmann offers a vision for a robust family mealtime as the centerpiece of family culture.[28] For Mallmann, Sunday is the traditional day many generations come together for a great family meal. Grilling begins on Saturday and is a lengthy process of preparation. Time, love, and thought go into creating the weekly feast. It brings the generations together.

There may be ten thousand factors that affect identity and legacy, but the decision to make meal times meaningful and regular may be one of the most important. God has designed a world in which all living creatures require refreshment. Sleeping and eating are two of the principal means of receiving refreshment. Sleeping is an individual experience; mealtime is not. The experience of eating together as a family is common to every civilization and epoch of time. More than any other expression of culture, the Bible identifies the family table as a place of blessing, encouragement, community, and legacy.

The importance of family mealtime may be lost on the present generation of Americans, with its emphasis on fast food dining and family fragmentation. Norman Rockwell's iconic Thanksgiving Day vision of the three generations gathered around the table has given way to a new model in which the home is more of a flophouse, and family mealtime is increasingly uncommon. Fewer than half of American families eat dinner together. Business is conducted 24/7, including at the table. Outside activities and demands on families make coordinated meal times more difficult.

Writing for *The Daily Press* in January of 2009, Pulitzer Prize-winning journalist and author Andrew Julien observed that, "If there is anything that tells the story of the American family over the past twenty years, it's the disappearance of dinnertime, a time when families used to set aside the demands of the moment to share their stories about the ups and downs of the day. It wasn't always calm, and depending on who was cooking, it wasn't always good. But it was always there."[29]

A 2010 study at Columbia University found that teenagers who frequently ate with their families tended to use drugs less often. A separate study conducted by the Organization for Economic Cooperation and Development found that students who ate less often with their loved ones were more likely to be truant at school. And research at Cornell has shown that children who eat group meals at home demonstrate fewer signs of depression.[30]

Mary-Catherine and I are lovers of food. Early in our marriage we determined that shared mealtime experience would become a defining ritual of our family culture. Now our children are food lovers as well, and food is the centerpiece of our family experience. We love everything about food—the process of growing it, selecting it, preparing it, serving it, and tasting it, the symbolism of food, and the role of food in family relationships. We love the smells and textures of food. We are fascinated by the seemingly endless food combinations available that show the brilliance and diversity of God's creation. Part of the joy of eating together is the company and conversation. Even talking about the experience enhances appreciation and wonder. Food is not to be viewed as mere fuel, but instead as a vehicle for relationship-building, artistic expression, and an experience reflective of God's goodness.

Preparing a great meal is like crafting a legacy. Both involve the intersection of science and artistry. Both are acts of love that involve discipline, study, experience, and intuition. Neither results from mere formula. In our kitchen, shelves are lined with jars containing our exotic spices and condiments we have collected from around the world. It is a laboratory for culinary experimentation, and everyone gets involved. That means developing the vocabulary that allows us to know the scope of what ingredients are available and the ability to describe their properties. Most importantly we want to discuss our shared experiences together as we eat the finished product.

Our family kitchen is an unending work in progress. New techniques in cooking require new tools, and experimentation leads to reorganization. More important than our pots and pans, however, is our Bible—in this case, *The Flavor Bible*. It is a book from which we have drawn great inspiration. The best chefs know that having a recipe is simply a starting point for cooking. Something more is needed. To cook well you need to understand balance and chemistry. It all matters—flavors, textures, and presentation. Eating a great meal is a total experience, one that engages all of the senses—taste, touch, smell, sight, and even sound. That is where *The Flavor Bible* comes into play. The book is a giant index that allows the reader to look up individual ingredients to find a happy match. From artichokes to zucchini blossoms—if it can be eaten, *The Flavor Bible* is there to assist.[31] Drawing from the collective wisdom of hundreds of chefs from around the world, authors Karen Page and Andrew Dorneburg have advanced culinary art and science by showing the potential for pleasing results through a fabulous array of food combinations. You know that chicken combines well with tarragon, but did you know that there is a "flavor affinity" when arugula, pears, and prosciutto are combined? But combinations are not enough. The authors remind us that great chefs not only understand the essence of the ingredients; they also understand the essence of the moment they are trying to create.

With our family meals we try to create an experience that engages every member of the family, no matter how young. Family meals may be as brief as forty-five minutes, or as long as three hours—usually they fall somewhere in the middle.

The best research and analysis on memory suggests that we retain and more easily access the past using multisensory cues. Food and wine can create memory landmarks, allowing us to recall conversations and experiences from the past. Our experience with friends and family around the table is punctuated by what we eat and drink.

A Beautiful Narrative

Your family is an unfolding story. Be aware of the narrative. Make it beautiful. Developing a robust family culture is one key to winning the heart of the next generation. Let your life be filled with stories borne out of the nobility of commonplace activities and the sweetness of family rituals.

Feast as a family. Climb rocks together. Create an atmosphere of delight. Nurture a community of people who enjoy the company of one another. You may never change Hollywood. You may have little influence on events in Washington, D.C. But every day you have a fresh opportunity to build a little civilization in your own home. Create your family culture. Love it. Embrace it.

Chapter 6

Treasure Hunts and the Legacy of the Heart: A Spiritual and Intellectual Journey

"For where your treasure is, there your heart will be also."
- Matthew 6:19-21

One of my favorite movies is a screwball historical fiction film named *Kelly's Heroes*. It's the story of a group of American GIs during World War II on a secret mission to pursue Nazi gold—lots of gold. It's an all-star cast, sort of a Who's Who of tough guys and comedians from the '60s and early '70s, including Clint Eastwood, Telly Savalas, Donald Sutherland, and Don Rickles.

The war is raging. There is chaos all over Europe. American soldiers are holding their positions. Then something happens that becomes a game changer for a ragtag collection of U.S. troops. A discovery is made of a secret hoard of Nazi gold. The story has all the elements of an ideal McAlvany guilty pleasure—tanks, guns, soldiers, good guys versus bad guys, extreme crisis resolved by ordinary blokes, and a treasure hunt for gold—lots and lots of gold.

In 1945 that gold was valued at only thirty-five dollars an ounce, but there was enough of it so that about fifty guys could split it and each walk away a millionaire. But first they needed to retrieve the gold. They had only three days to accomplish the mission.

The dilemma is set up by one of the protagonists named Oddball:

> We see our role as essentially defensive in nature.
> While our armies are advancing so fast, and every-

one's knocking themselves out to be heroes, we are
holding ourselves in reserve in case the Krauts mount
a counteroffensive which threatens Paris . . . or maybe
even New York. Then we can move in and stop them.
But for 1.6 million dollars, we could become heroes in
three days.

Their three-day quest concludes with an old west-style standoff in
front of the abandoned building housing the gold. A solo Panzer stands
between Kelly's heroes and the treasure trove. Out from the tank emerges
a black-jacketed Nazi—the sort of Nazi to end all Nazis—blonde-haired,
steel-jawed, smirking, indomitable.

Our heroes are faced with a problem. What to do? Their answer
reveals a bottom-line proposition in this chapter: when all is said and done,
you really know a man and his loyalties when he reveals the true desires
of his heart. And the way to understand a man's heart is to find out about
his treasure.

Crapgame: "Make a DEAL!"

Big Joe: "What kind of deal?"

Crapgame: "A DEAL, deal! Maybe the guy's a Republican. Business
is business, right?"

In the end, the Nazi and Kelly's team do cut that deal. They set aside
their differences and share the wealth. Self-interest and passion for treasure trumped political and military conflict.

Men love treasure. They love it so much that they will suspend other
priorities to search for it. The type of treasure they value reveals their true
priorities.

What is Your treasure?

The battle for your family's legacy is won or lost at the heart level. Get that
part right, and you will win the war. Everything else is secondary. It is all
about the heart—your heart and your children's hearts. The evidence that
you are engaged in a battle for the heart will be manifested in the spiritual,
intellectual, and ethical relationships you treasure.

This chapter investigates those issues in the context of our own personal family treasure hunts—our efforts to uncover the real jewels of

human flourishing. These treasure hunts are manifest in the values we communicate to our children, the spiritual realities that define our family, and the life of the mind. Spiritual nurture and ideas are the focus. But the centerpiece of our inquiry is the heart.

The Cornerstone of the Legacy Planner

In any great building, there must be a foundation stone that marks the beginning of construction. For intentional families hoping to build a legacy over the generations, there is a passage of Scripture which provides a potential foundation stone for the project—where your treasure is, that is where your heart will be.

Christ communicates this message to his disciples right after he has shared a panoramic perspective on virtue through the Beatitudes. The context of the Scripture makes it clear that His admonition about the heart is not an indictment on wealth or a rejection of financial steward-ship, but a serious reality check on personal priorities:

> Do not lay up for yourselves treasures on earth, where moth and rust destroy and where thieves break in and steal, but lay up for yourselves treasures in heaven, where neither moth nor rust destroys and where thieves do not break in and steal. For where your treasure is, there your heart will be also. (Matthew 6:19-21)

The point is that an individual's focus will be better invested in eternal treasure rather than earthly gain. Here we find a game changer for most modern families—one that stands in opposition to any theory of life focused on externals, personal performance, or even financial success. It focuses on the fundamental issue: the heart. If intentional families hope to be successful on this earth, they must first seek the kind of treasure that really matters.

Your observable treasure hunts will reveal the true state of your heart. If your children see you desperately seeking their best interests, fighting for them, loving them, and investing directly in their lives, there is reason to hope that they will discern that you have a heart of love. But if they see you speaking of love while prioritizing treasure hunts for corruptible, worthless junk, they will resent you.

Children need to understand that Mom and Dad are about something bigger than themselves—that you are treasure hunters for the transcendent. Children do not need or want perfect parents. The perception of perfection in a parent can be crushing to a child who can never attain that standard. What they need to experience is the reality of humility in relationships. They need to understand that their parents are flesh-and-blood people, highly imperfect, often failing, but with hearts directed to God, and committed to believing, thinking, and acting with integrity.

If your children know that—if they really get that, feel that, breathe that—they are more likely to wisely steward your earthly treasures. This "foundation stone" has immediate and practical implications. Your commitment to the heart precedes your ability to thoughtfully leave a financial legacy that will benefit your heirs. Most families capable of leaving a robust financial legacy have placed the cart before the horse. Their lives have been committed to wealth acquisition. They have defined success in terms of money rather than relationships, and their present energies are focused on intelligently passing on the wealth to their children. But in the process, they have allowed spiritual, intellectual, and ethical bankruptcy to fester like a disease within their ranks.

What Is the Heart?

In this context, the "heart" does not mean unbridled emotions or romantic intentions. Treasure is what you value. Your heart is the source of that value. If you want to understand why someone values A over B, look to their heart.

When modern songwriters and sloganeers tell you to "follow your heart," they rarely mean, "listen to the deepest and most thoughtful core of your inner being." In the modern context, the "heart" you are supposed to follow often refers to emotions. Young men and women are encouraged to follow their hearts—meaning their feelings—which may be little more than a translation for "follow your hormones."

Not so in the Hebraic and Hellenistic worlds. When the Greeks and Hebrews wrote about the heart they meant the soul or the mind. The "heart" was likened to a fountain from which flowed thoughts, passions, desires, and purposes. The heart is our core. When they spoke of the heart, they understood it to be a symbol of ultimate purpose and ultimate value. (The ancients associated the gastrointestinal organs with emotions and affections.) This was the intention of the word "heart" as found in the Bible. "Heart" was a concept that included intent.

The Greeks analogized the essence of man in terms of the geometry of three concentric circles. The first circle was an inner man; this is the location of the heart. Second, circling the heart was the mind, which was the source of decision-making. The body proper represented the third and most exterior circle. The body is the locus of human behavior.

To love God with all of your heart, therefore, is to love Him from the core of your being. To love Him with all of your mind is a decision of the will, which flows from your conscious mind. To love him with all of your strength is to manifest behavior that flows from your mind and your heart through your outward body (Mark 12:30-31).

The Heart of the Legacy Planner

The heart is at the core of Christian theology. The Gospel presents a universe in which God is said to have a "heart." He communicates as a father to his children in terms of the outpouring of his heart. Man, who is made in the image of God, has a heart because God does. David was a man "after God's own heart" (Acts 13:22). God blesses leaders who know and follow His heart. (1 Samuel 2:35; Jeremiah 3:15).

The vast majority of failed legacies stem from heart problems—problems that manifest in misguided treasure hunts: parents who have not decidedly given their hearts to their children, and children who have not given their hearts to their parents. The wisest legacy planner in history urged the prioritization of the heart: "Keep your heart with all vigilance, for from it flow the springs of life," (Proverbs 4:23). Because the heart is the centerpiece of decision-making, it is our fountain for human flourishing. The writer of Proverbs extends this bit of fatherly wisdom to his child: "My son, give me your heart, and let your eyes observe my ways," (Proverbs 23:26).

But how does it apply to legacy?

The first fruits of a commitment to the heart are the development of spiritual and intellectual traditions in your household. These serve as a foundation for the values and vision of the family. Without a solid spiritual and intellectual foundation, your best-laid plans for a financial legacy will have the worth of wood, hay, and stubble.

It is not an either/or proposition. Parents don't choose between investing in their children and advancing a financial legacy. Remember, the author of this book is a wealth manager with a combined fifty years in my family of also selling gold and silver. I have seen families self-destruct in the pursuit of treasure, and I have seen families prosper spiritually and economically as they have used earthly treasure as part of a treasure hunt for eternal rewards. It is not money, but "the love of money which is the root of all evil" (1 Timothy 6:10). Love God. Love your children. Use money, but don't give it your heart. Instead, invest your heart in your family, and you are far more likely to see your economic treasure preserved generationally.

It begins with a spiritual legacy.

The Nexus Between Our Spiritual and Physical Lives

Simeon the Stylite was a Syriac ascetic who is known throughout history as the man who lived for thirty-seven years on top of a pillar. Simeon was part of a movement known as the "pillar saints" or "stylites," a group of men who sought to diminish the physical component of their lives to focus on the spiritual. Their philosophy found its origin in part through an early heresy of the Christian church known as Gnosticism, a religious belief that tended to dramatically separate the physical life from the spiritual life. Opponents of Gnosticism rejected the radical dichotomy between the physical and the spiritual, pointing out that God cares for both, emphasizes both, and even speaks of the physical resurrection from the dead. In other words—life matters; the physical world matters, and the way we experience and live our lives in the material world is extremely important. It is an ancient argument that is well beyond the scope of this book, except for one important point: intentional families should not live in a dichotomous reality.

Rather than looking at the family life and legacy as a collection of radically separated disciplines, sacred and secular, consider a more holistic approach. The life of the mind, the spirit, and the body overlap. They are inextricably linked. The worship of God is not separated from the body; it comes in the context of living real life. God's presence is experienced through the daily rituals of life and work. Faith is not for Sunday, but for every day. It is not merely for prayer time, but for those moments when a man is joined sexually with his wife, when a family is enjoying God's provision around a family meal, when mother is training her children, or when a child is reading a book.

The Spiritual Legacy

Some of my earliest impressions are of my mother and father talking about the Bible. I never remember a time when prayer and faith in God were not present during those early days as a child. There was prayer at mealtimes and prayer before bed. There were Bible stories. There were conversations about God. There were stories about the work of God in the lives of my parents. These were not conversations relegated to Sunday, but part of the daily rituals of life. Looking back on my journey first as a happy son beside my father, then as an embittered rebel, and then as a man who rediscovered his father's heart, I realize now that the seeds of faith that were planted during those early years were sufficiently hearty— such that they weathered unrelenting storms, finally to blossom at a most unexpected time.

Powerful spiritual legacies often emerge in the course of real life. Watching people honestly live out their faith, however imperfect, can be more persuasive than a thousand sermons. That is one of the principal strengths of the family; it is a society based on blood or adoption and human experience that allows one generation to disciple the next on a daily basis. No institution has ever matched the family as an incubator of faith and learning. Those first impressionable years establish patterns, which sometimes perpetuate to a person's last breath. A happy, vibrant family life can inspire faith, even as a household filled with strife can wound it.

One of the most important gifts my father gave me as a boy was an integrated approach to faith. His faith inspired his worldview. His worldview influenced his analysis of everything from current events to economics. When I was a very young boy, it seemed like everything fit. It all connected nicely. Part of growing up, though, is testing theories and ideas and realizing that faith, philosophy, and ethics are not a LEGO set in which all the pieces can be neatly fitted together into a cohesive whole. (Or if they can, the ability to do so is somewhat elusive to mere mortals.) Things are just not that neat and tidy for a human race that has limited information and cognitive abilities and a predisposition towards selfishness. And yet the beauty of true faith is that when things get muddy, we have a rooted anchor that ties us to reality.

A Life of Little Conversations

People home educate their children for different reasons. Some do it because they don't like the teachings or influences in the government schools. Some want to give an education that reflects their faith and worldview. Some are persuaded that a one-on-one education, tailored to the individual student, produces the best academic results. Some prefer the flexibilities of a diverse academic and social life that home education offers. Some, despite the difficulties, just love the time with their children.

I find that each of these arguments have merits, but my own motivation is a little more nuanced. Through our own circuitous journey as a couple, Mary-Catherine and I have settled on a couple of core philosophic propositions that inform our choices for our children's education. First, we believe that there is a difference between knowledge and wisdom, and both are critical to a well-lived and properly educated life. Second, we believe that effective learning takes place through mentorship, direct hands-on experiences, and rigorous study that occurs in the context of meaningful relationships and real-world exposure. Third, we want to encourage our children to respond to learning situations not as parrots, but as individuals who must stand on their own reasoning and their own belief system.

Our inspiration comes from the people we know who, through deep curiosity and dedicated effort, continue to learn and grow, treating education as a lifelong pursuit. The more you know and understand, the more you realize you do not know and need deeper understanding. These men and women are fascinated by the complexity of the world God created and are constantly stirred by a sense of wonder and awe. There is a sense in which learning is interconnected with worship. Our teaching style draws first from the principle of walk-along, talk-along training modeled by the ancient Hebrew fathers who were required concerning God's precepts to "teach them diligently to your children, and shall talk of them when you sit in your house, and when you walk by the way, and when you lie down, and when you rise," (Deuteronomy 6:7). Second, we draw from the Socratic method the importance of questions, discussions, and individuals discovering things as if on their own.

For our family's lifestyle, Mary-Catherine and I know of no better way to facilitate all of these objectives than a relationship-driven approach to education. Home education helps us to accomplish this goal. It may not be the only way to do it, but it works for us. Whether you formally home educate your children or not, the fact is that you are home educating them in faith, the life of the mind, and ethics through your daily choices as a family. The choices may send a right message, or they may send a wrong message. But make no mistake, you are sending a message.

One of the disciplines that has changed my life comes in the form of a little conversation I have daily with each of my children individually. They expect it. I look forward to it. It is a ritual of life.

Me: "What was your glad, and what was your sad?"

Son #1: "Well, my glad was that I got to play with my LEGOs today."

Son #2: "I finished my book on the Roman legionnaires."

Daughter: "My glad was that I learned to do this [she pirouettes] in ballet class."

Son #3: "Gurgle . . . Gurgle . . . "

Me: "And what was your sad?"

Son #1: "I punched my brother and got into trouble."

Daughter: "I didn't get to see my cousin today."

Son #2: "I punched my brother and I got in trouble, too."

Son #3: "Gurgle . . . Gurgle . . . "

Asking about my children's "glads and sads" is more than just an emotional or spiritual temperature gauge; it's an opportunity for my own treasure hunt—to know my children as individuals and to discover new facets of their unique personalities.

When we practice the daily spiritual rituals of life—prayers, songs, "glads and sads," and readings at the breakfast table—Mary-Catherine and I feel as if we are the greatest beneficiaries. These spiritual disciplines ground us and remind us of our priorities. They extend sometimes into uncharted waters—like eventual honest conversations about sexuality and temptations hopefully dispensed with age-appropriate wisdom—and we must navigate these waters. They are ongoing family conversations that begin at an early age and carefully unfold over the years. We are determined that our children be comfortable talking with us, sharing their thoughts, emotions, and insecurities. That requires vulnerability on our own part with them.

The conversations at mealtime are like a multi-course sensation themselves where talking about school studies intertwines with personal experience and reflection, often followed by a principle that applies in the context. And each course receives comment (interruptions actually) from around the table. If we were to borrow from Hegel's dialectic, the breakfast and dinner table is the place where intellectual, emotional, and spiritual synthesis occurs. What does synthesis look like? For a few of our children, the issues of logic and evidence are at this age beyond their grasp, but discussing what something looks like in real terms and seeing if its livable, even our youngest have an awareness for what works or tips over into the absurd, the destructive, or the undesirable.

The Place of the Bible in the Home

My sister and her husband have a practice with their children that is really worthy of emulation. There are thirty-one chapters in the book of Proverbs and the same number of days in a typical month, so as a family they read the chapter that matches the day of the month every day of the year. By doing this over and over again for years in a row, some of them have memorized entire chapters. Their eldest daughter has memorized the entire book. It's a wonderful practice that merges the spiritual and the intellectual while often providing clear applications for life. In our own home, we prioritize similar daily reading of Scripture as a starting point in our spiritual and intellectual journey.

What are the marks of an educated person? What do we prioritize as a family? Perspectives differ on the marks of an educated person and the purposes of an intellectual journey. These perspectives tend to reflect the life of the person with the opinion. Some will emphasize practical skills, others science and technology because of their growing cultural importance. For our family, education is far more than catalogs of data to be dumped into young minds. Education includes the creation of a bridge connecting static information on a page to dynamic and life-giving action. What you learn either from life experience or the written word serves a purpose. Here is my reasoning: Knowledge is not an end in itself. Frankly, being educated is not either. But if you begin by asking the question, "What is a life well lived?" the purpose of education and the point of gaining knowledge begin to take shape.

A well-lived life is a collection of choices that reflect our greater purpose and demonstrate wisdom in action. To borrow from the Westminster Confession of Faith: What is the chief end of man? The answer presented in the catechism is to glorify God and to enjoy Him forever. I think it is fair to say that knowledge and education compliment the pursuit of our God-designed purposes. Other cultures have described this pursuit in terms of pursuing the greatest good. As much as we find wisdom and truth in Scripture, we find echoes of that truth as we study history, literature, philosophy, and the sciences as well. These fields provide the means for a comprehensive and winsome approach to life, rooted in our God-defined life purpose.

While there is a clear and understandable emphasis on the mind when considering what makes an educated person, there is a necessary complement. Sometimes neglected, this necessary complement is the development and strengthening of the heart. The heart informs how and when you use what has been put into your head. If you synthesize head knowledge with heart maturity you see a life that demonstrates compassion, justice, generosity, courage, and many other qualities. On paper these qualities are compelling, but in real life they are the essential to human flourishing—a life well lived.

In the evening, as I'm putting our children into bed, I will often express to them one of my deep desires: that they would always seek what is true, love what is true, and live differently in light of the truth. I equate the search for truth to going on an adventure—a quest of sorts. We know when we have begun the journey. Curiosity may compel some people farther along in this search. Curiosity often leads to greater learning, insight, and understanding. This particular quest is beyond the scope of what can be completed in the few short years a child is at home, so the search should continue throughout our lives. But it should continue with the same intensity with which we started.

I would note that the search itself, because it is a journey, has value regardless of the discoveries made. Searching for answers does not always include finding them. When you make a discovery however, it's like finding a priceless object. We value those things that come at a high cost. A discovery of truth—about ourselves, others, or some facet of the world—should fill us with a sense of gratitude for now knowing what we did not know before and humility as we recognize there are many things we still do not know or understand. Loving the truth is having an appreciation for the power it contains to inform and change our lives. This leads us to the last part of educational discovery, which is far beyond fact-collecting.

The educated person, in my opinion, integrates and lives a life informed by what they have discovered. Just as an encyclopedia has no soul, so a person must move beyond knowing to being and doing as expressions of all they have learned and discovered in their search for truth. All three elements—seeking, loving, and living—can be learned at home before a man or a woman goes to college, which is why it is so vital that intentional families passionately and critically appraise the resources they are drawing from to build their spiritual and intellectual legacy. Learning is one thing. Making choices and wisely integrating what you have learned—this takes us back to the original question informing our approach to education, "What is a well-lived life?" The purpose of knowledge is to inform the choices we make and enable a well-lived life. In our home there is simply no substitute for the discipline of extensive reading as a starting point.

Reading Broadly

President Harry S. Truman observed that "not all readers are leaders, but all leaders are readers." Spot on. Find a great leader, and more often than not, you have uncovered a bibliophile. There is simply no substitute for reading.

But reading alone is insufficient. Intentional families must cultivate a love for reading broadly. Thomas Aquinas warned against the potential for imbalance and excess that comes from a limited literary diet when he wrote, "Beware the man of a single book." The impact of reading broadly on the life of the great theologian Aquinas was noted by G.K. Chesterson, who observed that, "Thomas loved books and lived on books . . . When asked for what he thanked God most, he answered simply, 'I have understood every page I ever read.'"[32]

Why should intentional families read broadly? Your future depends on it. The principal purpose of reading broadly is to gain wisdom—the ability to apply transcendent truths and virtues to constantly changing facts and unique circumstances. You read broadly to help you understand the times. Don't limit your reading to a single genre, such as business or fiction; include books from a broad range of genres such as biography, philosophy, history, science, literature, and the social sciences. Different disciplines help leaders broaden their worldviews and become multidimensional thinkers. If you have traditionally read only business books, why not commit to read two or three books outside of your comfort zone this year?

Developing Your Intellectual Tradition Through Books

A family library should be a thing of awe to a child, a mysterious gateway into the world of the mind and past experiences that unlock secret stories and open the door to many conversations. In the family library, the child meets the thinkers who shaped his parents' lives. Family libraries are not meant to remain static. They grow with the priorities of the family. The introduction of new books reflects interests of the moment. Sometimes you can identify seasons in the life of a family, or even an individual in the family, by the dominant topic represented by the titles populating particular shelves.

A man with a great library has a thousand mentors. Books permit him to journey effortlessly through time, holding private conversations with those who physically walked with Moses and Alexander the Great. He may cross-examine Socrates, debate ethics with Aquinas, and ponder post-Newtonian physics with Einstein. There are few limitations. By the time a man marries he should have completed the most foundational reading of his life. His library is a chronicle of that journey. These are the books that his own father gave him; that brought him into outer space on futuristic rocket ships; that allowed him to march with Hannibal; that inspired him when he first fell in love; that caused him to imagine; that tormented him in his first year of college; that inspired him to love God more.

Our library is the physical manifestation of the intellectual and spiritual tradition Mary-Catherine and I hope to cultivate. It is a portal into the world of soul transformation and maturity. It is changing and growing as we change and grow. The shelves tell the story of our lives. Part of our personal story is the way our literary diets overlapped. When Mary-Catherine and I married, we enjoyed a happy discovery. Our libraries were largely duplicative. We had read the same authors, studied the same material, and collected many of the same books. We have one shelf that holds twentieth-century philosophy and another with Christian literary giants. Underneath that shelf is world history, and next to it our favorite painters, architects, and poets.

Profile of a Bibliophile

One of my mentors would rise every morning and devote the first three hours of his day to reading. Somewhere between 5:00 and 8:00 a.m., he digested chapters of interest, which might be anything from a theological text to the biography of a military leader or an author, to a work on astronomy, economics, physics, or horticulture. It was a practice he followed most of his life. His morning diet included Scripture. He would mark the date in the chapters so his children could see when and what he had read. He had a stack of Bibles in various translations and made it through multiple readings of the complete Bible each year. After finishing the sixty-six books of an individual Bible, he would switch to another translation. The Bibles, like all of the books, magazines, newspapers, and newsletters he read, were littered with scribblings and underlining from a thick black pen. In some cases, the specific Bibles, like other favorite books, would include a date in the back cover: "first reading 1982," "second reading 1991," etc. In future years, the children would be able to mark the commentary and emphasis points he left with specific events happening contemporaneously in the life of their father as additional insight into his commentaries.

After reading the Bible, he would digest at least three newspapers, including *The Washington Post, The New York Times*, and *The Wall Street Journal*. He read the A Section covering the news from beginning to end. Then he would skim the remainder, placing particular emphasis on the theatrical notices, sports headlines, human events stories, and business sections. He was especially fascinated by the obituaries in *The New York Times* because they were well researched and summarized the public accomplishments of noteworthy individuals.

Next came the books. His study was littered with them. Not just on shelves, but stacked four feet high on the ground. And he was a member of a dozen book clubs, which weekly sent him new additions to his already-voluminous library. The very existence of the library and the constant flow of books and information was an inspiration to his family— their dad was a reader. He could speak to any subject, and he required his children to do the same. On more than one occasion, I sat at his table and witnessed him quizzing his children.

Those were the days of paper information and before the rise of the Internet. Like my father, this man lived in a world of specialty newsletters and subscribed to no less than fifty, including the McAlvany Intelligence Advisor. He was also a subscriber to at least twenty magazines, including *Forbes*, *Kiplinger's*, *Consumer Reports*, and *The Economist*, just to name a few. Over the course of a month, he would work through these, picking and choosing articles of interest.

For each article that caught his attention, he would circle the headline, put the initials of his wife or a specific child in the circle, rip the article out of the original document, and place it in a manila folder to be handed to his secretary to reproduce and send to the intended recipient. A minimum of three days a week, twelve months a year, and over the course of twenty-five years, these clippings were sent to his six adult children. Most of the clippings had one-line personal notes from him to individual children with observations tailored for the interests of the specific child. For the first two years I was at college, I would receive one of those envelopes in the mail each week, usually the only mail I would receive. Over the course of his life, he sent more than 250,000 physical documents to his adult children.

The clipping packets filled with articles on diverse subjects provided common reference points, common wisdom passed down from their father, and facilitated a common cultural literacy. They were not only a means of ongoing education from father to adult children, but also of sharing his passions and interests. It was a connection that built family identity and reinforced the implicit bonds of loyalty between father and child.

But the process did not end with sending the packets. When he would meet with them or call them on the phone, he would ask specific questions to see if they were current in reading the documents. Life became a perpetual pop quiz, and yet, rather than being burdensome, it was fun—an expected part of the family culture. This man was one of the most articulate and informed men I have ever met, and I attribute it to the fact that he read much, and he read broadly.

Sharing and experiencing knowledge as a family is fundamental. In our home, we have found the emergence of a core common literacy, which is itself a core part of the intimacy Mary-Catherine and I share. It is essential to our daily communication. We share a familiar language, can translate similar code, and often finish each other's ideas on the basis of common reference points that allow us to seamlessly anticipate one another. Our children are gradually gaining a vocabulary that expresses both ideas and subjectively experienced feelings allowing us to better understand the state of their soul and offer guidance for maturing both heart and mind.

The Greatest Family Library in America

There are many great libraries in America. One thinks of the treasure trove of literature found in the Library of Congress, or even the literary artifacts housed down the street at the National Archives. The Boston Public Library stands out as one of the most distinctive and beautiful. The Hearst Castle Gothic Study in California is truly a modern Xanadu for the bibliophile. The more recent Skywalker Ranch Library is breathtaking. But for my money, nothing in America compares to a small rectangular building found adjacent to an eighteenth century home in Quincy, Massachusetts—The Stone Library of the John Adams Family.

It may be the finest example in American history of an intentional family establishing an enduring cultural, historical, and literary heritage in one simple space. The room is actually a small building with an open center and two stories of bookshelves that surround the premises, containing twelve thousand volumes. At first glance, the Stone Library is stunning for its simplicity and content. It smacks of the unassuming but inviting style of these anti-aristocratic American aristocrats. And it smells of old books.

In the middle of the room, is a great wood center table for reading. On the table are inkwells, massive leather bound tomes, and a table clock. The various nooks and crannies of the room reveal family artifacts that traverse more than a century-and-a-half of family life. There are busts of famous philosophers, patriots, and family members. There are wooden ladders that rise to the second story shelving. A painting from 1798 of the great family patriarch and founding father John Adams hangs on the wall opposite the entrance.

This family library is a window into the lives of four generations of Adams men and women, beginning in 1768 with John and Abigail Adams. The books and artifacts open to reveal insights into their personal histories, academic training, literary tastes, and diverse interests—from agronomy to Greek philosophy to political science. Only about 10 percent of the books belonged to America's second president. The bulk of the remainder came from his son, John Quincy Adams, the sixth president of the United States, his grandson, Charles Francis Adams, and great-grandson, Charles Francis Adams, Jr.

The library was not merely an evolving shrine to the intellectual history of the Adams family, but a working study, a sanctuary where generations of Adamses came to read, study, chronicle, and perpetuate the vision and life stories of their family. Adams children, grandchildren, and great-grandchildren could visit the library and read John Adams's personal copy of George Washington's "Farewell Address." They could hold the Mendi Bible, a gift presented to John Quincy Adams in 1841 by the captives he had successfully defended before the United States Supreme Court in the famous Amistad decision. Not only could children and grandchildren hold, read, and smell the artifacts of their family history, but they could also enjoy a unique experience of entering into the past with their ancestors by reading their private first-hand impressions of the volumes that shaped their thinking.

Despite the preciousness of books in the eighteenth and nineteenth centuries, John Adams established the family tradition of using them as tools. Consequently, he penned personal notes in them. The marginalia provided his children and grandchildren with precious insights into the thinking of their famous ancestor. Perhaps they were able to identify the argument, counter-arguments, evolving thoughts, and whimsy of the lawyer who defended the British after the Boston Massacre, helped to pen the "Declaration of Independence," and replaced George Washington as the premier statesman of a fledgling nation.

How Libraries Build Relationships and Family Identity

The Adams library represents not merely the intellectual and spiritual heritage of the Adams family, but also the ongoing vision of successive generations to perpetuate an intentional legacy. It was a rectangular world of relationships, a treasure chest of precious paper jewels and artifacts that tangibly connected the parents of the past with the children of the present and future. In the family library, they touched what their grandparents touched, read what they read, sat where they sat, and thought on the subjects their ancestors had thought on. They could effortlessly transport themselves to sit as observers of their ancestors during the early days preceding the American War for Independence to the Civil War, walking with brothers and sisters, cousins, nieces, nephews—all who were part of their family story. Although the vision for passing books to the next generation was cast by John Adams, it was his son, John Quincy, who made provision in his will for a permanent fireproof structure for the preservation and ongoing use of family books, maps, and documents. Wisely, he wanted the library separate from the main home. The house could burn, but not the library.

The Adams Stone Library became a symbol of identity, a tool for advancing the intellectual heritage of four generations, a record of family history, and the locus of many happy memories shared between parents and their children for nearly two centuries. There is nothing like it anywhere else. For this reason, it deserves to be ranked as the greatest family library in America, serving as a model for parents starting their own journey of intentionality.

Developing More Than Your Intellectual Tradition Through Books

Many ideas enter the mind but never travel to the core of a person's being (to their heart) and become transformative. Ideas can be ignored, disregarded, or remain ineffective if a heart is hardened or if preconceptions crowd out their consideration. Nevertheless, we as parents set the context for understanding and appreciating transformative truths and then pray those ideas come to life in the dispositions and actions of our family members. This is the essence of a well-lived life: By grace the life of the mind extends beyond a mere intellectual pursuit to heart regeneration and life transformation.

We consider our library to be the greatest resource in our home. Gold and silver have a specific market value. But, within our family, books are considered priceless because of the innumerable gems they contain. What is the value of an idea that can change the life of an individual, the health of a family, or the course of a nation? We practice a different kind of accounting, putting a higher value on books than on bonds, stocks, or gold and silver. We love treasure hunts and know that within the pages of the thousands of volumes in our home there is vast bounty to be unearthed.

The Rest of the Story

The great experimental musical composer, music theorist, and artist John Cage was once asked, "What is your favorite piece of music?"

"The piece I have not yet written," he answered.

Author Umberto Eco once observed that, "Books are not made to be believed, but to be subjected to inquiry. When we consider a book, we mustn't ask ourselves what it says, but what it means . . . "[33] When asked about the most important books in his own library of 30,000 volumes, he responded they were the 20,000 he had not read yet. He did not even know what he had not read, but he found greater value in what was not yet known. Ecco, like all who seek truth, was on a quest that will not be satisfied in this lifetime. And that is precisely what makes it so inspiring.

There it is. My philosophy on reading in a nutshell. The most important book I have in my library is the one I have not yet read. What treasure am I missing? What jewels do I need to discover? Will it be gold or a pyrite imitation? My search for treasure never ends. But it's a journey I want to share with my family. It is a journey of the heart, and it points us to an eternal treasure.

Chapter 7

The Financial Legacy

"Better is a little with righteousness than great revenues with injustice."
- Proverbs 18:8

The battle for your family's financial legacy is won at the dinner table, not in the board room. It is won in cigar boxes filled with quarters and silver coins, during long walks with Grandpa, and in the soup kitchen of your local community. It is won in hundreds of small conversations and thousands of prayers of thanksgiving. It is a battle that is fought from the earliest days of the life of a child to the parting words of blessing offered by an aged parent on his deathbed.

This is where most books on legacy begin and end. Typically, the discussion of money represents the totality of the discussion for wealth managers and legacy planners.

But it is not accidental that this chapter on the financial legacy appears closer to the end of the book than the beginning. Every ounce of counsel shared in this chapter proceeds from what you have read up to now. My recommendations presuppose the core theses of this book: families must be intentional about their vision for legacy. Families must have a holistic approach to legacy that focuses on culture, identity, history, and virtue. Families must have non-contingent relationships, sealed by a truly redemptive ethic that binds them to God and one another, allowing them to weather any storm.

This is a chapter about the relationship between family identity and financial planning. It is about the importance of building a financial legacy by starting young. It is about the relationship of your heart to your treasure. To be examined is the efficacy of hard and soft structures to your family's financial future, as well as the futility of both these important tools without forethought, virtues, and buy-in necessary for them to succeed. It is an inquiry into a problem that has resulted in spendthrift children, wasted family fortunes, and intra-family civil wars. The problem is generational wealth. How do you pass on a financial legacy without destroying your children? How do you see family wealth grow from generation to generation?

In this chapter, I intend to take you on a financial journey from early childhood to death. To get there, we will need to enter the inner sanctum of some philanthropic Chinese-American elders, go behind the scenes at a family council meeting, and examine the philosophy of one of the most significant orators since Cicero. But this story begins with a boy, a cow, and a cigar box.

The Boy, the Cow, and the Box

A financial legacy is birthed in the early days of a child's life when he or she begins to understand the meaning of value—why something has worth to an individual. Financial consciousness emerges in different ways with different children. For some it happens when they get their first ten-dollar bill from Grandma on their birthday. For others it is a bake sale or lemonade stand. Sometimes it comes through the care and sale of animals. Once upon a time, there was a boy and a cow. The cow's name was Angel. She was owned by a very precocious seven-year-old entrepreneur, who just happens to be my first-born son. Angel was a pretty cow, a nice cow, but none of that really mattered much to the boy because Angel was not a pet. She was the boy's first business.

Angel lives in a field owned by the boy's grandfather, where she spends most of her life eating grass and having babies. Angel is literally a "cash cow"—an ongoing business concern that generates a steady flow of cash for the boy. Every time Angel has a calf, the boy sells it, making between $700 and $1200 dollars. Overhead is very low because the boy's grandfather has offered his field as a home for Angel. Feed and medical care is negligible. In practical terms it means that 90 percent of the sale of Angel's calves is profit for the little boy. Two calves later, the boy is now ten and a bit wealthier. The greatest wealth he has received from the project is not measured in dollars and cents as much as it is in life experience gained.

Having a cow is a responsibility, but so is preparing a calf for sale and paying bills. Perhaps an even greater responsibility comes from financial success—What do you do with the profits? Reinvest? Tithe? Convert to gold and silver coins? Save? Start other businesses?

Buy a skateboard?

These are a lot of questions for a boy under ten, which is what I love. My goal is to do what my father attempted to do for me—to push the envelope of personal financial stewardship and obligation at a young age, while building the disciplines associated with wealth generation and wealth management. Which brings me to boxes.

If you are a boy, then you need a box. Not just any box will do. It can't be cardboard or paper. It can't be too small or too big. It needs to be the kind of box that you would find hidden away in an attic—the kind that contains old wheat pennies, cufflinks, pins, jack knives, and war medals. The box may look like a mini-wooden treasure chest, with leather straps, perfect for hoarding the artifacts of a boy's life. But more often than not, it takes a simpler form. Cigar boxes are perfect. Within the wooden walls of each cigar box is a tobacco-scented mystery—the nagging question of where the box has been and what adventures it has seen. Somewhere in the past, there were perfectly rolled sticks in color-ful bands lining the box. No doubt soldiers or adventurers passed them around before leaving on a quest. And now they are gone—the soldiers, the cigars, and the stories they shared. But the box now belongs to the boy. Why do boys need these kinds of boxes? (I'm sure I'll include my daughter in this, as she gets older.) If you were a boy once, you might remember that the accumulation of treasure is one of the unspoken objectives of life between age four and ten. And the box becomes a rect-angular storage unit he keeps in his room as a security vault for his most important prizes—stubs from baseball games, the Indian arrowhead he found, patches, and matchbox cars.

Watching my children, I came to realize that, at least for my family, these boxes were more than a private stash of childhood artifacts. They were the representation of my own children's steps towards financial stewardship. It was the first mile in a long journey to prepare them to receive, steward, and multiply family wealth—a physical tool for preparing a child to value a financial legacy.

It all came together one night when visitors came to our home. With fifteen people around the table for dinner, the conversation turned to gold, silver, and fiat currency. What is happening to the euro? Will Greece sink the EU? Thus begins a conversation about gold-to-silver ratios, the present undervaluation of the metals, the role of central banks in manipulating currencies, fluctuations with the euro, and finances in general. We discussed the multiplying effect over many years of working hard, saving money, and making investments. Light bulbs turned on. Every one of the eleven children at our table owned at least a few silver coins. Some had purchased silver with money earned. Others had received the coins as gifts. The conversation ceased to be academic. It became personal.

"How much will my coins be worth if the price of silver goes up by ten dollars?"

"Well, let's do the math."

"Is it possible that the price of silver will double?"

"Actually, I think it's possible that it will quadruple."

"How is that possible?"

"It has happened before."

And then something unexpected happened. The conversation turned to boxes. Treasure boxes. It turned out that all the boys age four and up had their own boxes at home. So did the girls. We learned that in each of their boxes were pennies, quarters, foreign currencies, and—the pièce de résistance—a small cache of silver coins.

It was more than my own boys could handle. They excused themselves, emerging minutes later with boxes in hand. The next hour was spent examining strange foreign coins, looking at the dates on American Silver Eagles, and performing simple mathematical calculations. The parents at the table all encouraged their children to give a portion of their earnings to help others. This conversation raised a new question: What if you could make even more money so you could give even more away? So the children talked about that. Growing a few dollars into a few more is personally rewarding, but also enables greater kindness and generosity to others. It is just part of life. Somehow this brought us to the subject of compound interest.

Compound Interest and Children

"If I save $100 every year for ten years, how much money will I have?"

"At a rate of six percent compounded interest, you would have $1,320. But if you saved $1,000 every year for forty years at the same rate of interest, you would actually have about $155,000."

A table of children sat with rapt attention. Why? Because they had a personal stake in the subject matter. The more we talked, the more these children loved mathematics.

Seeds were planted. There is just over a half a decade before most of them are eligible for business school, but they have already figured out a principle of financial success that most adults miss: it is the ant, not the grasshopper, that wins the day. Small consistent efforts accumulate over time to garner outsized achievements.

It was a point championed by founding father Ben Franklin, whose authorship of *Poor Richard's Almanac* earned him a reputation as the Solomon of the eighteenth century. In 1785 Franklin became the subject of a parody written by French mathematician Charles-Joseph Mathon de la Cour, who suggested that a small sum of money should be left in a will only after it had collected interest for 500 years.[34] Franklin loved the idea and adopted a variation for himself. At his death in 1790, he gifted about $5,000 to each of the cities of Boston and Philadelphia for the creation of a fund that would last for 200 years. The fund could not be touched for 100 years, at which time each city could withdraw $500,000, leaving the money remaining to grow for the next one hundred years. From the $500,000, each city could provide loans at 5 percent interest to young businessmen. The only conditions were that the young entrepreneurs had to be under twenty-five, married, have completed their apprenticeships, and obtained two co-signers to vouch for them. Had the fund grown at 6 percent per year, it had the potential to become $91,600,000—all from the original $10,000.

Franklin's goal was to disciple a young nation by teaching young people to understand the power of compounding interest and long-term thinking. As a founding father, he modeled for the nation the benefits of savings, the importance of investing in future generations, and the power of long-term thinking. Franklin understood his role as a father to a nation. More than one community of immigrants arriving in this new land of promise understood that they had their own role as fathers. They knew, for example, that if they could be successful, their efforts would pay off in the lives of children not yet born. That meant working hard now so their children's children could succeed later.

The Story of Carlton: A Profile in Generational Continuity

For more than one hundred years, Boston had been a hub for Chinese immigration and had become known for its thriving Chinatown. By seventeen, Carlton had demonstrated intelligence and an ethic for hard work as the son of a respected family in their Chinese-American community. His father was a businessman who earned a modest living, which he supplemented with the rental of the first floor of his duplex on Beacon Hill. Carlton and his family lived on the second floor where they maintained a tidy home for their family of four, replete with the decorations, ambience, and foods not uncommon for a first-generation immigrant family.

From 1840 to 1980 there were two great waves of immigrants to arrive in the United States from China. The first wave was driven by workforce opportunities opening up with railways and mines during the industrial boom and westward expansion of the nineteenth century. As they settled, they created communities known as Chinatowns, many of which exist in one form or another in some of America's larger port cities like San Francisco and New York. In order to build and safeguard their own community in America, often in the face of growing prejudice, Chinese immigrants built a series of district and clan associations that ultimately served as family-run councils for the purpose of dispute mediation, lending, health, education, and funeral service.

As an alternative to an American banking and lending system, the clan association and council provided Chinese-Americans with comparative ease of access to money. But to benefit from what they had to offer, an immigrant family had to reinforce the values of the clan and council. Family heads and community elders who placed a high premium on generational honor and continuity usually led these clan associations. In exchange for loyalty to the clan, immigrant families willing to develop a track record for hard work could avoid the American lending infrastructure. Immigrants' children were incentivized to honor their parents and identify with a distinctive culture. As a result, the Chinese-American community was able to make some headway towards some of the same objectives shared by intentional families—the ability to be self-perpetuating and self-sustaining, honoring the past while maintaining a compelling vision for the future. Carlton's family had arrived in the post-World War II "second wave" immigration and was now learning to find the optimal balance between maintaining a long-established Chinese heritage and embracing the modern culture of America. It was a difficult tightrope with its own unique challenges, but thus far they had made it work.

In 1982, Carlton's family had to make a decision that would affect them and their community for generations. What do they do with a highly intelligent, honoring, and hard-working son with bright prospects for academic success, but with insufficient funds to subsidize the journey? Carlton had been accepted into the highly prestigious Massachusetts Institute of Technology (MIT), but the family simply did not have the money to pay for the education. So they called for the family elders of the clan council.

What transpired, as reported to me by my friend whose family lived on the first floor of the duplex, goes to the very heart of my message on intentionality and financial legacy. The council of elders arrived at Carlton's home, where they were welcomed into the second floor apartment and served tea. There, they privately made their first impressions of the family's lifestyle. Then the meeting began. Carlton was presented by his father to the council. His father explained that he had been a hardworking son. He had honored his father and mother. He had proven himself faithful. He showed great promise, scoring exceptionally high on his tests and ultimately being invited to attend MIT. He had aspirations of earning a doctorate, but the family just did not have the means to cover the expenses associated with an undergraduate diploma. Would the council help? They had some questions for Carlton's father, which roughly boiled down to the following line of inquiry. Was he an honoring son? Answer: yes. Did he embrace the traditions of the community? Answer: yes.

Next, a question for Carlton: If we invest in you, will you someday do the same for someone else in our community? Will you invest in our children's children? Carlton agreed.

His tuition was covered. No other strings. No guilt trips. No burdens. No high-interest debt. No intense negotiations and surrendering of ownership. Carlton's down payment was made when he proved to his father and the elders that he had embraced his family's identity. It mattered that he had honored his mother and father. It mattered that he understood his culture. All that was required was a commitment to "pay it forward." And, of course, he agreed. The concept had been engraved on his mind and heart as part of his family culture.

More telling than Carlton's reputation, which had earned him a hearing before the council, was the philosophy of the council itself. It is reasonable to assume that at least some of these council members had been young Carltons themselves once. Somebody had believed in them and invested in them. Now it was time for them to "pay it forward" and prepare another generation to do the same. These men had achieved personal financial success and reputation. They were now in a position to be mentors and investors. Some of them were paying off an investment made in them twenty-five to fifty years earlier. These men were long-term thinkers. They understood their own philanthropic duties to give back to the community. They were willing to make a relatively small, but sacrificial, investment in the present for a potentially huge return in the future. Like all true legacy-minded thinkers, their goal was to set things in motion so their children would become beneficiaries in the future. Today, they help Carlton. Tomorrow, Carlton helps their children's children.

They were in it for the long haul. Their ROI (return on investment) might not be seen for twenty-five years or more. That did not matter. From an investor's perspective, the return has the potential to far exceed that of mutual funds and treasury bills. A PhD graduate from MIT from the Chinese American community would have a lifetime earning potential in the millions. And there would be a ripple effect with a potential to influence the entire Chinese-American community for good. Carlton would have the potential to become a businessman and investor himself, be a likely candidate to influence community policy, and someday sit on the same council. An investment in his life is an investment in their own clan and community. It is a smart move, but one that requires trust, generational thinking, and real buy-in. But this thinking works only if the battle for the hearts and minds of the next generation is already won in individual families.

A Generational Wealth Crisis

The idea of long-term thinking has been lost on many of the present generation. The examples of men like Benjamin Franklin and the elders of Carlton's local Chinese-American community are few. We have become a nation of radical individualists who live for the moment. In such a climate, what incentives are there to think in terms of financial legacy?

Actually, those incentives are all around us if we will only open our eyes. We may have more gadgets, but they do not equate to human flourishing. Our families are disconnected, and our safety nets are gone. Financial instability is all around us—within government and within the financial sector and private enterprise. In 2013, CNN Money reported that 76 percent of Americans are living paycheck to paycheck.[35] Fewer than one in four have enough money in their savings account to cover at least six months of expenses. These Americans have no retirement accounts and no emergency cash to cushion the blow of a job loss or emergency. The same report showed that only a little less than 50 percent of Americans have $500 in savings.

I am persuaded that the genesis of the problem is a fundamental cultural disregard for legacy and the ethical foundation upon which legacy rests. We are a nation of short-term-thinking pleasure-holics who prefer to "eat, drink, and be merry, for tomorrow we die." Many have never learned the disciplines of self-control and industry. Many more don't know how to be other-centric or plan for the future. The problem is not relegated to underprivileged, lower, or middle income wage earners. Lack of vision has no demographic boundaries. After more than fifty collective years as a family in the wealth-management business, one thing is clear: the vast majority of parents with resources in excess of $250,000 do not prepare their children for a financial legacy. Typically, they drop it on them. In some cases, they hide it from them. Precious few take the years necessary to bit by bit, conversation by conversation, example by example, prepare their children to inherit and manage family wealth.

In Chapter Two, this "shirtsleeves-to-shirtsleeves" phenomenon was examined and identified as a theme common to most civilizations. Years are spent building fortunes, but minutes are spent preparing children to receive them. I can probably count on two hands the number of young couples I have met who began their marriages thinking strategically about how to transfer wealth to their children. Resources are typically grown while children are growing up, and those wealth creators rarely feel able to speak with authority to a process or potential success that is a mere possibility at that time.

It should come as no surprise, therefore, that a whopping percentage of great fortunes are lost before great-grandchildren arrive.[36] The statistics are simply overwhelming. The most expensive and carefully executed legal and financial strategies to preserve family wealth generally fail within three generations. 70 percent of high-income families will lose the financial momentum created by the wealth visionary within about fifty years of his death. Some surveys indicate that the process is accelerating. Research from the Williams Group indicates that the 70 percent statistic now applies to the second generation, and that 90 percent of families will lose their wealth by the third.

Here is the reality: intentional families need to talk about things that do not yet exist. If they do exist, these families need to reinforce the collective memory of the family by saying and doing little things over a span of years. There must be constant reinforcement to ensure that there is an awareness of which direction the family is headed and what must be done. Take a look at four common indicators of family financial meltdown that can cause a generational wealth crisis.[37]

1. **Parents Don't Trust Their Children with Family Money:** U.S. Trust is one of the nation's most long-lived wealth-management organizations. Founded in 1853 as the United States Trust Company of New York, it operated independently until it was acquired by Charles Schwab in 2000 and later became a subsidiary of Bank of America. After a century and a half of watching client fortunes rise and fall, the company commissioned a survey of high-net-worth individuals. The recent survey focused on individuals with more than three million dollars in investable assets and their ability to pass on wealth generationally.

   Chris Heilmann, U.S. Trust's chief fiduciary executive, told *Money* magazine, "Looking at the numbers, 70 percent feel the next generation is not financially responsible enough to handle inheritance."[38] Often parents fear that their children, lacking discretion, will leak private information. In many cases, this distrust becomes a self-fulfilling prophecy. Heirs implicitly get the fact that their parents don't trust them and sometimes even try to live up to that reputation.

2. **Parents Don't Communicate with Their Children:** Another reason for the decline in generational wealth is the abysmal level of financial dialogue between parents and their children. Many parents have been taught not to talk to their children about

money. The idea is that discussions about money are unnecessary, perhaps even uncivilized. The U.S. Trust survey concluded that 64 percent of wealth generators acknowledge keeping their children in the dark concerning details of the family's wealth. One of the results of this code of silence is that the majority of heirs are incompetent at managing money.

3. **Parents Think Wealth Will Destroy Their Children:** Wealth creators had to work very hard for their resources. Some worry that their children will adopt an attitude of laziness and entitlement if they become beneficiaries of financial wealth. They would rather donate the money to charitable institutions than poison the family well. Of course, there is a lot of history and statistical data to support this concern. Nevertheless, children learn from parents' actions of generosity and other-centeredness, observing the way they handle wealth. The cure may be to combine the "caught" observations with the "taught" lessons on the purposes served with family wealth. Antidotes to selfishness and entitlement can be modeled by demonstrating generosity and gratefulness to your children from a young age.

4. **Parents Think Wealth Will Encourage Ingratitude:** Parents are not merely concerned that a large inheritance will turn their children into trust fund brats; they also have concerns over jealousy, greed, and infighting. How will heirs respond if they don't feel they got their "just" portion? Will they become embittered if a significant portion of the family wealth is given to charity?

Inheritance as an Act of Love and Provision

Parents have been leaving a financial inheritance to their children for as long as recorded history. Simply understood, inheritance was a gift of support, and possibly honor, given by parents to children. Parents gave their children an inheritance to help them as individuals and facilitate the ongoing provision for and status of the family.

For the Hebrews of the Old Testament, inheritance played a role that shaped their core understanding of life. They were a chosen people, a people set apart to receive an inheritance. They were willing to wait generations for that inheritance to become a complete reality. Many of the references to inheritance found in the Old Testament refer to the promises of God for His people—a Heavenly Father providing for His sons and daughters.

The message of God's love in giving an inheritance for His children is a central theme of the New Testament too. It is wonderful to receive an earthly inheritance, but an earthly inheritance is secondary to the inheritance God has prepared in heaven. How much better is it for men to store up treasures in heaven rather than simply storing them here on earth? (Matthew 6:19). First Corinthians 2:9 describes a promised inheritance, which is beyond any inheritance previously experienced because "no eye has seen, nor ear heard, nor the heart of man imagined, what God has prepared for those who love him." From their earliest days, family members were taught to think of themselves as heirs—heirs of spiritual promises and physical realities. Inheritance was the presumption of their hopes and dreams. Behind every inheritance promise was a two-fold message: first, you belong and therefore have a clear identity. Second, your Heavenly Father loves you, cares for you, and is providing for you. It is a message earthly moms and dads must replicate.

Principles of Inheritance—Who Gets What? Why?

The fact that principles of financial legacy management and inheritance are rooted in virtues such as honor, gratitude, love, and stewardship does not answer the really hard questions. We now come to the most controversial and complex part of the inquiry. Who gets what? Why? How?

It is a debate that has raged for millennia. Wars have been fought over inheritance, murders committed, and families divided. So don't be surprised if the entire discussion touches a nerve.

Each family is faced with unique facts and circumstances. That means there is no one-stop shopping approach to building a financial legacy and passing on an inheritance. You have to do the work. And you have to do it directly with your heirs. You can get help, but the process of the preparation, discussion, evaluations, and training of the next generation is primarily non-delegable.

Preparing your children to receive a financial legacy is actually one of the most important responsibilities of your life. It must be taken seriously. At the end of the day, your decisions could directly affect dozens, if not hundreds, in your own generational line, and the buck starts with you.

Equality Is Not a Ratio

The history of the world is the story of sibling rivalries emerging out of the perception of parental favoritism. Cain feels rejected and kills his brother Abel. Jacob deceives his father to claim a birthright from Esau. Joseph receives a coat of many colors and is despised by his brothers. The faithful brother is embittered by his father's warm reception of the prodigal brother. There are parallels in every civilization and every epoch of history from the dispute of Al Walid versus Sulayman in the eighth century to the Koch brothers in the United States and the Ambani brothers in India today.

There is a lesson here. Being treated well does not come down to a ratio of 1:1. Wise parents will attempt to walk a tightrope between benevolent proportionality and a donative intent based at least in part on the duties and responsibilities conferred on the beneficiary. Even so, children must understand that their value is not based on gifts being "even-steven." How a parent distributes assets has nothing to do with the dignity and value of the individual. Undergirding this lesson is an emphasis on responsibilities for others, versus the more common self-interested perspective on individual rights.

Families Should Care for Their Own

Loyalty and love for family members seem to be givens until an estate is being settled. Quite frequently this is when self-interest surfaces and relational rifts emerge. "But if anyone does not provide for his relatives, and especially for members of his household, he has denied the faith and is worse than an unbeliever," (1 Timothy 5:8). For the bulk of recorded human history, the care of family members was considered to be the responsibility of the family first and charitable organizations second. That perspective has largely been displaced in post-World War II welfare states throughout the world. In America, we experience politicians promising an ever-larger safety net based on the expectation of voters that their needs will be met by the state. But what happens when the state fails to deliver? What happens when dependence on the state changes the fundamental character of the citizenry or the family?

In the Bible, families, not the state, are presumed to be the principal providers and caregivers for the family. Although the ancient laws of primogeniture given to the nation of Israel are certainly not binding today, there are some relevant principles for twenty-first-century families. One principle is that with family money comes responsibility for the family. A key reason for assigning a double portion to a single individual was that that individual was responsible to care for remaining family members in the absence of the former caregiver.

Families take care of each other, and someone must be responsible for making sure that happens after the death of a parent. If the child directly in line to receive the double portion proved unfaithful, the legacy might pass to another child, even a trusted servant.

Consequently, one goal of a financial legacy transfer was to perpetuate the family through a form of self-insurance. The heir was not just the recipient of the legacy, but its trustee on behalf of the broader interest of the family. The implications of this principle for modern families are far-reaching and should be considered during estate planning. Note the focus of caring for others with family resources. Note the absence of "What's mine?," "What do I get?," and other worn-out expressions of self-centeredness. Who will care for others and carry forward a blessing to future generations?

Faithfulness Trumps Gender, Birth Order, and Even Blood

Children who break covenant with their family may lose some or all of their inheritance. Faithfulness to serving the broader family interest is, I believe, the common denominator. The Bible explains circumstances in which both sons and daughters may receive a greater portion of inheritance over an older, but unfaithful, child. It even provides for a faithful servant to receive an inheritance over an unfaithful son. Who can fill the role of trustee? Who will care for others before themselves? These are heart issues, but they are equally issues of training and maturity.

Somehow the centerpiece in our relationship with God, grace, is lacking in our family relationships when our expectations are not met. Conditionality of love is too often used as a means of manipulating behavioral outcomes and thus confuses the issue of inheritance with affection and relational commitment.

The story of the prodigal son has a self-centered boy receiving an inheritance without strings attached, a gift that is not used by the father to control or manipulate the behavior of his son. The son was immature. The son was selfish. The son had no vision for the future, just a base desire for pleasure in the present moment and an audacity to ask for his inheritance immediately. His older brother was equally selfish and immature, but also a self-righteous follower of the family rules. Both of them needed training and time to mature. Both of them had freedom. Only one of them ever did mature. Bankruptcy humbled the younger son and brought him to a point of gratitude and respect for what he had as a member of the family. The older son never learned these things. The older son remained hardened, ungrateful and uninterested in the care of others. Inferred in the story is the conclusion that failure is difficult to deal with, but by no means catastrophic. If we humble ourselves before our Father, there can be new beginnings. The lack of conditionality in the father/son relationship is a vital conclusion.

To Whom Much Is Given, Much Is Expected

The greater the bequest, the greater the responsibility. It is simply bad stewardship to give significant assets to someone who has a proven track record for wasting resources. It is therefore imperative to train, educate, and foster the development of maturity within your family. Teaching your children and grandchildren how to use their freedom should be modeled and mentored long before the reading of a will.

If you want to train someone to receive a larger inheritance, then part of that training involves gradually giving them responsibility and placing them in a situation where they have received something already—an incremental approach matching age with specific teaching opportunities. For example, when a child (or grandchild) turns eighteen, you might say, "I am giving you $20,000. I am an investor in you." Perhaps this investment is for college or a business startup, even a down payment on a home. If it ends up funding a sound system or a massive shopping spree, you have a few clues where remedial guidance ought to be directed. The beauty is that on a modest scale you don't think will be devastating to the family, you can begin a real-time experiment in preparation for taking on massive responsibility in the future. You might even consider it tuition in the school of hard knocks. After college, perhaps when they reach the age of twenty-five, you inform them you've set something aside for retirement, an IRA or Roth IRA which has been growing unbeknownst to them for years. It's a moment to reinforce the value and power of compounding interest and the necessity of taking action with a very long timeline in mind. Maybe in their late thirties to mid-forties, or after they've established a career path, you let them know that as a family member they have access to benefits that are funded by family wealth. Such benefits could be the use of the family ranch held in perpetuity or a means of financing a business venture through a no-interest loan from the "family bank." A parent wants to bless his children and not destroy them. Measured and modest steps are those that lead to maturity.

Is there is an allowance for failure? What if they try something and fail miserably? Are you or they in a position to figure out what went wrong and learn from it? They may be more ready for a larger bequest after having tried, failed, and reflected on what went wrong, gaining practical insight and wisdom from the experience. Recall the servant in the parable of the talents who is chastised for burying his gold instead of growing his gold talent. To grow is to put at risk, to put at risk is to take a chance with loss, and loss is a reality one needs to experience in order to fully appreciate what goes into success. Giving your children the freedom to fail is an absolute necessity. Seeing failure as preparation for success incorporates a redemptive ethic into the core of family finances. Coming alongside them and encouraging them to try again is equally important. Learn, grow, and move forward with the determination to do better the next time. When we fall down, we get back up again. We never quit. We try again and again. The Bible puts it this way, "for the righteous falls seven times and rises again, but the wicked stumble in times of calamity," (Proverbs 24:16).

The Battle Is Not Won Through Financial Instruments Alone

Most thoughtfully planned financial legacies can survive market fluctuations and social instability. They rarely survive legacy killers. Not surprisingly, there is growing skepticism about the efficacy of long-term planning on the part of wealth managers. With this skepticism comes the recognition that legal instruments and constructs do not win the day. Of course, that does not stop many in my industry from charging small fortunes to help their clients get these very legal instruments and structures in place. But honest wealth managers will tell you that, at best, instruments and structures simply slow the wealth deterioration process down. They cannot increase or generationally sustain wealth on their own.

Our analysis of the problem must be at a more foundational level, and our approach must be more holistic. Unlike many within my industry, I believe the principal reason for legacy deterioration is a heart disease. Issues like financial ignorance, lack of planning, mismanagement of resources, sloth, vice, greed, and jealousy all point to a more fundamental problem: What in the world is going on in the family relationship? The answer is that parents and children are disconnected at the heart level. Misplaced priorities lead to broken hearts and a lack of love between the generations. While love covers a multitude of sins, it is also true that a lack of love multiplies contentions. This "heart disease" tends to destroy. Here are four signs:

1. **Lack of Love:** The most famous chapter on love ever written is found in the thirteenth chapter of First Corinthians. It is perhaps the clearest statement on the primacy of love. It tells us that "faith" and "hope" are great, but "the greatest of these is love." This is the big one. The financial legacy is won or lost at the heart level. Children are motivated by hope, acceptance, and love. These are all matters of the heart. By the time most children are eighteen, they have resolved in their own hearts whether they can experience hope, acceptance, and love in a meaningful way through their family. This is one of the reasons why we can never separate the cultural legacy from the spiritual legacy or the financial legacy. They all tie in together. The heart is the common denominator. Where hearts are broken because there is a fundamental lack of love within the family, children want out. They simply don't care about the vision of the wealth creator. Recall the scandalous request of the prodigal for his inheritance while his father was still living. It reflected a heart that would prefer the father dead and resources accessible immediately. What is the backstory for the hardening of that heart?

2. **Lack of Identity:** Second, a healthy, clear family identity has not been established or appreciated. The search for identity is

inescapable. It is fundamental to life. Either you help to discern and define a unique family identity based on faith, ethics, and culture, or your children will seek their identity elsewhere. No vision for generational wealth can be sustained where the heirs do not know who they are or where they came from. It just won't happen.

3. **Lack of Training:** Third, there is a lack of continuing education to prepare heirs to understand the purpose of wealth and how to advance the family's wealth. It should always be kept in mind that multiplying the size of a family divides the scale of wealth proportionally unless the skills of wealth multiplication are inculcated in each future generation. If this is done properly, resources will continue to grow in each successive generation and not be constantly drawn down. It is simply unreasonable to expect that the next generation can advance a family's financial objectives without talking through those objectives and gaining the skills necessary to accomplish specific goals.

4. **Lack of Buy-In:** Finally, the heirs lack buy-in. They just don't care. Or they don't understand. In either case, they are unmotivated. If parents do not connect on the heart level, they can never expect buy-in. If they don't cultivate a desirable family identity, they cannot expect buy-in. If they don't train their children in the values and skills necessary to be successful as heirs, they should never expect buy-in. It's a progression of problems that combines to produce spendthrift, envious, lazy, or uninterested heirs who have little emotional, intellectual, and experiential connection to the vision of the wealth creator or any vision outside of direct self-interest. This requires time—lots and lots of time spent by parents with their children. It requires conversations, many conversations. It is a lifetime process of practical and relational discipleship, the basis of which was enshrined in a commandment (the Shema) given to the ancient Hebrews:

> Hear, O Israel: The Lord our God, the Lord is one. Love the Lord your God with all your heart and with all your soul and with all your strength. These commandments that I give you today are to be on your hearts. Impress them on your children. Talk about them when you sit at home and when you

walk along the road, when you lie down and when
you get up.

Buy-in comes from a lifetime of conversations bathed in love and
meaning. This walk-along, talk-along approach to life is one reason why Jews were able to maintain their unique identity through
millennia of dislocation and persecution. Children were often by
the sides of their parents, talking, working and gaining an appreciation for their cultural identity.

God is always after the heart. Parents should be too. Too often there is an
emotional disconnect between parent and child that results in confusion or
rejection on matters related to identity and values. Often ignored are those
virtues that build family identity and are necessary to manage and develop
wealth. The problem is compounded by an absence of the type of shared
family experiences that cultivate hard work, financial stewardship, and
philanthropy. Video games are no substitute for lemonade stands. Expensive
sneakers are not to be preferred over old cigar boxes filled with quarters.
The mall is a poor substitute for the family table. In the end, lack of love
results in lack of buy-in for a vibrant multigenerational vision to perpetuate
a sound financial legacy. If heirs lose the vision to build on the foundation of
the past, the problem can't be solved by a wealth manager.

Legacy killers always reduce to matters of the heart—self-righteousness,
a philosophy of entitlement, bitterness, envy. Here is a message to our children: It is not about you! It is not about your rights. It is not about what
you deserve. Legacy is about something much bigger than you. In the story
of the prodigal son, we see two sons suffering from entitlement issues. But
where the younger son had the spirit of intemperance and self-indulgence,
the older brother was a walking legacy killer. He followed the rules, but his
heart was not with his father. True, when the younger son demanded his
inheritance early, he was perhaps unintentionally sending a message: "I
can't wait for my father to die, so I am going to pressure him so I can access
the funds now." And it would seem as if the family legacy hangs in the balance as it is wasted on a wild and spendthrift lifestyle. Even so, the greatest
potential for legacy death was with the elder son, not the prodigal. As the
story continues, a self-righteous elder son makes it clear that he is embittered toward his father over the re-engrafting of the spendthrift son into
the family. Of course, we don't know the end of the story. Maybe his own

disappointments were used to humble him and restore his own heart.

Legacy killers usually take the form of institutionalized ethical chaos within the family. Every financial legacy killer can be understood in terms of a heart condition. Lack of love, misplaced identity, and the basic temptations for greed, sibling rivalry, sloth, bitterness, and insecurity can all fester in the petri dish of a misguided heart. Sun Tzu observed, "Know your enemy and know yourself, and you can fight a hundred battles without disaster."[39] There is nothing new under the sun. The same types of crises that affected the family of the prodigal son affect you and me. If we are honest about ourselves, we can admit that our hearts are often wandering and in need of repair. We can acknowledge that temptations for vice never disappear; this is why any construct designed to leave a financial legacy must address the heart and soul of the individual members of the family. Legacy cannot survive the death of virtue and family identity.

That being said, it is unreasonable to assume that virtue will win the day if it is not manifested in wise strategic planning. With this in mind, it is possible to have a meaningful strategic conversation about the hard and soft structures that safeguard generational wealth.

Wisdom in a Multitude of Counselors

At the end of the day, intentional families must call the shots. The big-picture vision is non-delegable. You have to own it. You have to understand it. You must be willing to execute a well-considered plan. But too much is at stake to approach your future without wise counsel. In our modern world, legal necessity requires intentional families to have, at a bare minimum, the counsel of an experienced attorney and input from a professional accountant. It is unrealistic and nearly impossible for family leaders to gain expertise in the constantly changing laws necessary to safeguard family assets. You are going to need to speak with professionals. Just keep in mind these advisors cannot cast your vision or call the shots. All they can do is advise. Get good advice. Apply it to your unique circumstances and personal objectives, and then act upon the best counsel. The best I can offer here are general principles that may inform your decision-making process when it comes to asset protection. With this in mind, there are two broad structural categories every intentional family should consider as they apply to asset protection and wealth management: hard structures and soft structures.

The Necessity of Hard Structures

Hard structures are legal constructs designed to advance financial objectives, preserve assets, and limit liability. The vast majority of asset-protection and wealth-management strategies focus on the creation of hard structures designed to help family money survive over generations.

Unless you are willing to convert your assets into gold, silver, and jewels and bury them on some uncharted island in the South Pacific in hopes that neither pirate nor government agency will stumble across the box, you are going to need hard structures. They are called "hard structures" because they are meant to withstand time like a foundation stone. Creating hard structures can be very expensive and time consuming, but their strength derives from their inflexibility and potential longevity. Hard structures typically involve legal techniques like estate planning, trust creation, and tax mitigation strategies.

At one level, there is something disturbing about a hard structure. They do not add value to the net worth of the family or multiply wealth. They are very expensive and time consuming to create. In a perfect world, we wouldn't waste a whit of time, money, or expense on the creation of hard structures. Their entire purpose is to prevent others from taking from you that which they have no right to in the first place. In one sense, the goal of a hard structure is to protect you from losing the value of your hard work through government confiscation and wealth redistribution programs, or sheer waste. Hard structures are like wall building and moat trenching; they provide a degree of protection from a limited number of threats. In another sense, they are critical to laying out boundaries and expectations. These become operating principles for a disparate group of people who will continue to make critical choices that affect the wealth you have stewarded, long after you are gone.

But even the best strategies for creating a hard structure can fall short. They are not infallible, and they cannot anticipate every potential future legal manipulation, political machination, or social trebuchet designed to separate you from your wealth. By employing some carefully devised hard structures, you have a realistic expectation that your wealth can withstand legal revisions of the next wave of politicians, or perhaps a generation of spendthrifts. Politicians have a history of using the law to plunder the private resources of citizens. Individuals, too, can operate in self-interest to plunder a family resource for personal gratification alone. This is why hard structures must exist. You don't know the "who" of tomorrow, but you can set in motion the "how," which are the rules of conduct and protocols a family abides by to keep peace and cultivate blessing for future generations.

Without a hard structure, you must assume that your family wealth will be depleted and marginalized over the course of time. There are very few successful businessmen and women who do not invest significant time, money, and attention in the creation of hard structures. But such structures are not just for the benefit of the wealthy. Every family with assets to pass on to the next generation needs to have hard structures in place. Because the process is arduous and complicated, many simply choose to avoid them all together and hope for the best. This is a formula for disaster.

It is not the purpose of this book to present an exhaustive overview of this very complicated subject. The fact is that even the "experts" have challenges because the rules are in a constant state of flux. I have had lawyers present comprehensive estate planning solutions that have had to be radically revised even after two years given the dynamic nature of the nation's legal situation. We pay them to stay on top of rules you and I find boring. My point is to make you aware of the big picture issues that must be resolved so that you can work with an expert on an approach tailored for your distinctive family needs.

The mission of hard structures can be reduced to the following dual aim: to maintain and pass wealth from one generation to the next without seeing that wealth dissipated by taxes, professional fees, and charges, and to put an organization in place with a distinctive tradition and vision that will make sure that the money is held, managed, and used for a very long period of time.

At a bare minimum, there are four basic hard structures that every family should consider:

1. **A Comprehensive Tax Strategy:** This is a vast and complex conversation, but with one clear objective: to develop an intelligent, legally-defensible strategy that connects your family's financial goals to your actual wealth in a manner that preserves assets by allowing you to pay as little in taxes as possible. This conversation can include the topics of annual gifting, lifetime gift allowances, step-up in cost basis, and use of a family foundation, just to mention a few.

2. **A Will and Estate Plan:** In a perfect world, you goal would be to have as little need for an estate plan as possible because you have organized your affairs such that you own as little as possible at the time of your death, having already passed it on inter vivos to individuals and trusts. Passing on inheritance during your life can have real benefits for your heirs, especially where the goal is to help them with education, business, and home ownership. This is a strategy that works nicely in the world of gold and silver. Under the present tax laws, you may gift each of your children $14,000 per year in gold, silver, currencies—anything—and do it without impacting your larger lifetime gift tax allowance. Families should also take advantage of the five million (5.43 million) dollar per tax-payer lifetime gift and estate tax exemptions. The numbers change with the political winds, requiring a routine reflection on the adequacy of the plan in place. Your estate plan should at a minimum have a will and/or trust, durable power of attorney, beneficiary designations for all financial accounts, and healthcare directives. You need these whether your estate is valued at $100,000 or $10 million.

3. **Investment and Bank Accounts:** You need reliable banks and financial service providers with access to tools that enable you to craft portfolios to weather the changes you will invariably see over the course of decades and generations. Dad and I felt so strongly on this point that we made it a matter of company policy to provide free safety ratings on banking institutions to our customers so they can make informed decisions. Here we are addressing publicly held assets: stocks, bonds, currencies, precious metals, and other commodities. When asset managers are required, integrity, professionalism, and competency are paramount. Establishing an investment advisory council amongst competent and interested family members is one way of delegating the oversight of the family's financial assets.

4. **A Family Trust:** Someone needs to own your family's money. Who should that person be? The ideal person is someone who never dies and never wastes money. Since that person does not exist, the family trust serves as a good alternative. Merely passing liquid cash down from one person to the next is the most sure-fire way to see your nest egg dissipated and perpetuate the "shirt-

sleeves-to-shirtsleeves" phenomenon. Simply put, cash burns a hole through the pockets of the best-intentioned recipient.

An interest in a privately held business or illiquid asset such as real estate should be held in trust for an agreed upon beneficial use. For that asset to be sold, unanimous consent might be required, or the trust documents could simply prohibit the sale altogether. Many cases I've seen have kept a lock-up period where the assets were of beneficial use, but not liquid until twenty, fifty, or even seventy-five years had passed.

In Durango I know of one heir in a fifth-generation ranching family. Their trust to a vast real estate holding in Wyoming requires that at least twenty-five heirs vote in agreement to liquidate the asset. But there is even more going on than trust restrictions. The family goes to great lengths to perpetuate the legacy vision for the property and promote buy-in. Great pride is taken in participation in something that has defined and continues to contribute to the ethos of that family. A first-generation recipient might have sold it off for a variety of reasons or fresh opportunities. The fifth generation can hardly imagine themselves as a family disassociated from the land. I spoke to one heir in her early twenties who explained that she feels her identity is linked to the land, and she intends to do her part to see her ancestor's vision passed on to her own children.

The Wyoming family estate illustrates the principle—trusts allow for the compelling argument of the moment to fade into the continuum of a multi-generational legacy. The trustees of a trust should learn to think like managers of pension or endowment assets, making decisions with long timeframes in mind and serving the interests of those in the present and those yet to be born.

There are many approaches to creating a trust. I am especially intrigued by the "dynasty" trust. In theory, this is a self-perpetuating trust that lives forever. Because it is not owned by an individual, nothing is passed from the dead to the living. This structure provides a means to minimize the inheritance tax problem for many generations to come. It is also a means for growth outside the estate when low-cost-basis, high-growth assets are contributed and then held over a generation or more. While it is not presently possible to avoid federal income tax or capital gains taxes by using a trust, you can get around the whopping inheritance tax problem, while allowing for specifically delineated benefits for family members. That is good news for your financial legacy.

So here is a review of hard structure strategy:

- **Strategy #1:** Get counsel.
- **Strategy #2:** Have a will and estate plan for the rest of your wealth.
- **Strategy #3:** Develop an intelligent tax strategy.
- **Strategy #4:** Create a family trust, probably a dynasty trust.
- **Strategy #5:** Find good banking and investment market partners.
- **Strategy #6:** Give much of your wealth away before you die either to a family trust, family foundation, family members, or towards philanthropic purposes.

The Primacy of Soft Structures

Financial survival in the modern world requires hard structures. Read any book on asset protection, and much time will be dedicated to how to strategically develop them. Even the best hard structure is insufficient to safeguard generations of wealth from internal family problems, though. The secret to preserving family wealth over the generations is the soft structure.

I have hundreds of books on the subject of wealth management, but one of the finest explanations of the soft structure comes from the father-and-son team of Bill and William Bonner. Here is how they explain in simple terms the concept of the soft structure:

> Our family has put in place our own system of soft structures. They are soft because they are not legal entities, but merely conventions and protocols the family sets up for itself. These provide a structure, a system, for managing wealth and harmonizing relationships between family members. Your family must sing together. These soft structures help get everyone on key. They provide instructions and rules for future generations of family members to follow.[40]

The soft structure is perhaps the clearest financial manifestation of the power and wisdom of the family as designed by God. The soft structure is the family at its very best—working together privately, with its own unique hierarchy, incentives, disincentives, and strategic planning to work for the best interest of the family and the individuals who make it up, including those yet to be born. Soft structures presuppose that there is something very special about the family that is not found in any other institution on earth. Blood is thicker than water, which is why families have a greater capacity to "fight it out" together than other relationships.

Recall that of the 70 percent of wealthy families who lose their wealth in three generations, most have hard structures in place. Few have implemented soft structures. Soft structures encourage buy-in. They have the potential to build family loyalty. Intelligent soft structures will build family identity. They will give every member of the family a stake in the overall success of the family.

The intentional family must be an institution, not a collection of people living in a flop house. It is a blood-tied community made up of many different personalities with individuals who each bring something unique to the table. The more developed the culture of the family, the more likely that soft structures will thrive. These soft structures can evolve and mature with the family members themselves. Adapting to changed circumstances and problem-solving as a family—and doing it self-consciously—is one of the benefits of the soft structure. Family members need to talk. They need to vent. They need to honor and respect each other. They need to listen to the concerns and needs of one another. Ideas need to be vetted. Rightly handled, the process can yield results in growth and unity.

Recently there was a special wine tasting week in Durango. Vintners came from around the country to present the best of their products to leading merchants. There were hundreds of vineyards represented. Of special note were those family companies that had been in the wine business for four to six generations. When asked about the key to their success and family unity, one vintner explained: "Our family has been in this business for five generations. Our founder started it from a little house on a property that we have kept in the family for one hundred years. Each year family members come from around the United States to meet there for a week to eat, drink, and talk a little business. It's part of our family history, and we connect with it."

Meeting once a year on a historic family property for wine, celebration, and a little business is a very compelling way to practice a soft structure. Who doesn't want to be part of that? Most families have nascent soft structures in place. They just don't call them soft structures. Soft structures can include protocols for conflict resolution, dealing with debt, financing, college education, and general survivability. They can include impromptu meetings around the dinner table or family reunions where memories are made that deepen connection and loyalty and cast vision for the future. The problem for most families is that their soft structures are inconsistent and undefined.

In a family, there are spoken and unspoken rules. There are traditions, patterns, even habits that inform what is acceptable and what is not. There is a social fabric of life, which binds individual members of the family tighter through the very faith, rituals, and culture that help define the intentional family. All of these are important and serve as the basis for soft structures, the existence of which could be the difference between success and failure for a financial legacy. These conventions are foundational to the family council.

Stage One: Casting a Vision for Your Soft Structure

Every soft structure begins with a commitment to intentionality. If you have started the process of casting a vision for your family's legacy future, then you have already completed stage one.

But when should you start? How about at the beginning? Right about the time a man and a woman decide they are going to spend the rest of their lives together in marriage is the perfect time to cast a vision for your soft structure—imagining what kind of a family you want, working together, living with one another, children, meals, work, life, and discussions. It's a time for lots and lots of discussions. This is the time to start sharing hopes, dreams, and problems. Where will the money come from? How do you as a couple plan to manage money? How many bank accounts? Who writes the checks? How do you handle savings? What about debt? Remember you are on the same team.

Mary-Catherine and I have created what we call our own "one-day rule." We avoid financial surprise by agreeing to a spending limit and a waiting period. If either of us intends to spend more than $200 on a personal item, we talk to the other person first. Somehow we have managed to stick by that rule throughout the entire course of our marriage. It has built trust and reminded both of us that we are accountable to each other for stewarding resources. This is one goal of a family council—to build the rapport and commitment between family members such that they keep the big picture before their eyes.

Agreement between a man and a woman on a financial vision starts day one—this is the family council in its embryonic form. It is the process that matters even more than the immediate conclusion. Conclusions will change. Circumstances will change. The process is what makes or breaks the family. If you can learn to work together, you will lay the foundations for a society of family members who thrive in a soft-structure environment.

The family council really begins the day your vision for legacy is communicated to other members of the family. It starts with casting the vision and opening up a conversation that will continue for the rest of your life. If you are that newlywed couple, the council may begin with a dialogue between you and your spouse, perhaps with input from your parents and in-laws, or perhaps just between the two of you. As children are added to your family, and as they mature and have children of their own, the shape and form of the family council may change and mature.

Ultimately, it should take the form of regular meetings, perhaps annually, in which the extended family is involved at one level, and representative heads meet with the family founders to understand and implement the long-term vision.

Stage Two: Preparing Your Children To Be Future Council Members

Remember Angel the cow and our community cigar box colloquy? That was a beautiful moment in my life as a father, but more was going on than wine, chicken, silver coins, cows, and children. It was one of those Deuteronomy 6, walk-along, talk-along moments of shared family experience, wisdom, and gratitude to God, in which two distinct families shared ideas and experiences about financial legacy. In other words, it was sort of a pre-soft structure experience—a training ground for future conversations. When those conversations come, the stakes will probably be higher than a treasure trove filled with a couple dozen quarters and a few silver dollars. Win the battle for ethical and financial wisdom with the eight-year-old at the dinner table, and you may not have to fight for it when he is forty and overseeing an empire.

In 2015 I was looking for resources that would bring both structure and creativity to our own dinner table discussions. Finding nothing readily available, I created my own materials and called them The Missing Chapter. The project developed into a full-blown online video curriculum, complete with downloadable questions and conversation points for the dinner table. It is my answer to the question: What does every man, woman, child, and future family board member need to know about money, economics, and financial freedom?

The family dinner table is the training ground for the family council meeting. I have seen it work. As soon as they are old enough to say "American Silver Eagle," children are capable of participating in family discussions about wealth management, asset development, and philanthropy. A six-year-old is absolutely capable of understanding the basics of wealth management. Here they are: (1) work hard; (2) save money; (3) be grateful and content; (4) share what you have with others. That is it in a nutshell. Learn this as a child. Stick with it. Then watch your family portfolio skyrocket.

Stage Three: Launching the Family Council

A family council is a bit like a mini-republic, where representatives of individual families in a generational line come together to enjoy each other's companionship and help manage and direct wealth. Each individual family must govern itself. The better its members do that, the more likely they are to make a strong contribution to the family council.

In this scenario, for example, Grandma and Grandpa were first generation wealth creators. They had six children, each of whom started their own families. Now their grandchildren are adults, with children of their own. Grandma and Grandpa were quite successful. They launched companies and amassed a small fortune, some of which they passed on to their children through gifts of lands and monies, and some of which they retain. But the bulk of their wealth has been placed in a dynasty trust. Grandma and Grandpa made the hard decision to create a family council and invite two people from each independent household in their family line to participate. It was a hard decision because it is always hard for a wealth creator to give up power to individuals who did not create the original wealth, but they did it because they wanted to benefit from the counsel of their children and encourage buy-in from the whole family for the vision they cast years ago. They also realized that time was working against them. There needed to be a new generation to lead. You can't have generational continuity without a new generation of capable decision-makers who outlive the original wealth creator. These individuals are not just born. They need practice and experience.

In our hypothetical example, the purpose of the family council is to make executive decisions for the family as a whole. If they make wise decisions, everyone will benefit. If not, the entire family will suffer financially. The family council has the responsibility for managing the trust and even making distributions of family assets. From this council, other necessary soft structures will be created.

Stage Four: The Family Mission Statement

The reason why the drafting of mission statements tends to intimidate is because too often the drafters think they need to recreate the Declaration of Independence. No need here. A family mission statement and possibly a constitution are evolving documents that outline objectives for the council and provide guidelines for how things should be handled.

Thanks again to Bonner and Bonner for suggesting some of the elements that might be included:

1. A simple statement of purpose—the macro objectives of a family financial council
2. Guidelines for resolving family conflicts
3. Guidelines for overseeing a family investment committee
4. Guidelines for decision-making and legal documents pertaining to estate planning
5. Policies for inclusion or exclusion of spouses and additions and removals of council members
6. Guidelines for managing the family enterprise and property
7. Guidelines for the organization of activities that build family identity and unity

Stage Five: The Family Bank and Continuing Education Program

Here is where the stories of Carlton and the inheritance principle of family self-insurance converge. Successful multi-generation legacies are sustainable because they develop self-perpetuating, internal economies that reward excellence and assist those family members in need of emergency help. Under this approach, the family, not the state or the banking institutions, is responsible for the care of its own.

None of these soft structures are designed to fund the lifestyle choices of family members. Those costs are directly born by each family member from current income. The point of a family bank is to assist family members with education, health care, financing a home purchase, and even entrepreneurial ventures. Whether the money comes in the form of a pure disbursement—as in the case of helping a widowed member of the family or someone with a health need—or as an interest-free loan, the goal is to encourage responsibility, excellence, and the financial stability of individuals. It is not a welfare system. It's a family-stability system that requires members to pay back loans and act responsibly as a precondition of the benefit. Throughout this process, education is vital. It can take place around the dinner table, through books, conferences, or distance learning, but it must happen.

Stage Six: Identifying Leadership

One of the most important objectives is a peaceful succession plan. Great leaders replace themselves. Most leaders are not great because they make themselves irreplaceable, refuse to relinquish power, or leave an organization in a state of chaos. Unless there is an agreed-upon process for succession, count on infighting and bitterness when the wealth creator dies. Here is another argument for no delay. Start now, before you are forced to make uninformed and pressured decisions.

The more an individual demonstrates buy-in, self-reliance, and commitment to a long-term family vision, the more influence and participation he or she should have in the family council. Wise families want each individual to be able to stand up on their own two feet. They should want to make significant contributions to the family itself. Of equal importance is a willingness to draw from the wisdom gleaned by other members. A family council member is one who respects education gained from outside opportunities and wisdom birthed from long-term experience.

Family councils require a division of labor in the context of an enduring system for leadership. It is not a bad idea to float the idea of different responsibilities to children while they are young. Let them know that the family needs different responsibilities filled. Those might include a wealth strategist, a legal mind, an efficiencies expert, perhaps even marketing guru depending on the nature of long-held family interests or enterprises.

Wealth strategists must understand asset allocation and risk management. Legal thinkers must understand the strengths and weaknesses of various instruments relevant to investments and be on guard for anything that could compromise the legal security of the family. Neither has to be an expert—you can hire the experts—but they need to have some experience, a working vocabulary of the issues, and good judgment.

Patrick Henry on Inheritance

He was perhaps the greatest orator in American history since Cicero. Once described as the "Trumpet of the Revolution," it is not unreasonable to conclude that without Patrick Henry beating the theme of freedom in the town halls and public squares for more than a decade, the leadership base for the American War for Independence might never have been organized.

By the end of his life, Henry's many successes as a businessman and attorney had helped him become one of the largest landowners in the Commonwealth of Virginia, yet he always remained humble and close to home. His family was his priority, and his actions proved it. He turned down an appointment as Justice in the United States Supreme Court, a minister to Spain and France, and Secretary of State so he could stay at home with his children—all seventeen of them.

Henry would die in 1799, the same year as George Washington—both men closing the eighteenth century and a unique era in world history. But as Patrick Henry reached the twilight of his life, his thoughts turned to a lasting legacy. What would be the true inheritance he bequeathed to his children? He realized that the vast holdings in lands would make them wealthy, but land holdings were insufficient as the ultimate objective of his legacy. Land and estates could even be a distraction away from the one thing capable of making his progeny truly rich—a sustainable faith in God. And so, he penned his last will and testament, including the following words: "This is all the inheritance I give to my dear family. The religion of Christ will give them one which will make them rich indeed."[41]

Patrick Henry's comment brings me to the single most important observation ever made on the issue of the objective of an intentional family. It is the core message that brings legitimacy to the concept of legacy. At the height of his earthly ministry, Christ posed the following question about value, "For what will it profit a man if he gains the whole world and forfeits his soul? Or what shall a man give in return for his soul?" (Matthew 16:26). This is a spiritual question presented in an economic context. Profit, assets, and value are the three elements in the equation. At one level, it is a question about rates of exchange—the value of an asset you are willing to exchange for another asset in order to make a profit. The asset is your soul. Value is the worth you ascribe to your soul vis à vis the treasures of the world.

But the question appears rhetorical, as if to say, "Isn't it obvious that an eternal asset is of greater value than a temporal one?" The soul is the ultimate benchmark of asset value; it is the only thing you have that uniquely belongs to you and survives your death. Its value is inestimable. It cannot be depreciated by market trends, war, or famine. It is eternal. All other possessions are temporal.

So why the question? Because the history of man is the story of bad decision-making on matters of value. Men lose perspective. They think short term. They panic. They become prideful or greedy, and they under-value assets. Like Esau, they exchange a valuable birthright for a mess of pottage.

Your greatest asset is your soul. Tend to it. Don't lose it. Value it. There is a corollary for intentional families. What shall it profit a family to amass a fortune in wealth but to lose their children? To lose their souls? What good is a robust financial legacy?

Fight for the hearts of your children. Let them know you value their souls more than family wealth. And when you do, don't be surprised if you end up seeing that the battle for the soul and the stewardship of resources are not mutually exclusive. You may discover grateful heirs who want to preserve and use their financial legacy for a greater purpose.

Chapter 8

A Strategy for Charting the Generations: Practical Tips

"The most effective way to destroy people is to deny and obliterate their own under-standing of their history."
- George Orwell[42]

Having planted the seeds of intentionality in the life of your family, you may find fruit in unexpected places, even a ski slope. That was my own dis-covery . . . My daughter is a little sprite of a thing, but a 100% all-Ameri-can power-packed girl. One moment she is a ballerina, the next a princess, and the next, a Jedi fighter taking on the Death Star. When she was a baby, she was swooping down the ski slopes of Colorado in my backpack, but by the age of three, she was negotiating turns on her own. Early on she learned that the privilege of skiing came with certain expectations which reflect our values as a family:

"Everyone falls down. But what do you do next?"

"I get back up?"

"That's right, you get back up. No whining, no complaining. No quitting. Just get back up." That had been my mantra. She heard it a thousand times. "Okay, it's cold, and it felt bad, but what are you going to do now, Darling?"

"I'm going to get back up again, and I'm not going to whine."

It was a conversation similar to the ones I had hundreds of times with her brothers during our bouldering jaunts. "One step at a time. You can do this. Finish what you start. I will help you find a way to the summit. No turning back now."

Then one day, when my little girl was about five years old, I overheard her make the following declaration to her brothers: "We are McAlvanys. We don't quit."

Music to my ears. But where did it come from?

Perhaps part of it was family code, but I am convinced that a major component was cultural osmosis. Over the course of her brief life, she has heard permutations on the same message over and over again. She has seen it lived out in the lives of her grandparents, uncles, and aunts. She has heard it from her parents, and even her brothers. There are ten thousand mistakes McAlvanys make, but one mistake we try to avoid is giving up in the midst of a crisis. And when we get together as an extended family, there are three generations who agree. No quitting!

What is your intended destination? What message would be music to your ears? It may take some time to arrive there. Every voyage begins with a map. You need to see where you are located, identify your destination, and then chart your course. As a mentor of mine once observed, "If you don't know where you are going, any train will get you there." The problem with building a legacy is that the process is organic. More is involved than reaching a destination or going from point A to point B.

Reverse Engineering

Intentional families want a particular legacy outcome, which requires a process of reverse engineering your ultimate objectives. When people speak of reverse engineering, they are usually referring to the act of extracting design from something manmade in order to reproduce it.

For example, you like Coke, and you want to make a drink that looks, smells, and tastes like Coke. Your problem is that the formula for Coke is a carefully guarded secret. So you do your best to reverse engineer the product, identifying its ingredients and the process of producing it. The reverse engineering experiment requires study, analysis, and time, but the closer you get to the right formula, the more pleasing the results.

Reverse engineering the legacy you want to create means understanding what you want the finished product to look like, breaking it down into component parts, and seeking to better understand how the pieces fit together. It involves both analyses and predictions. Clear legacy objectives combined with reasonable assumptions provide a platform to prayerfully approach the process of reverse engineering your legacy.

Making Predictions

What if you could predict the future? Would it change the decisions you make today? It is easy to say, "If only I had invested in Microsoft in 1980, I would be a billionaire today. Then all my problems would be solved." Behind the fallacy that great wealth solves life problems is a more fundamental issue: even if you could predict financial success, that is not the basis for reverse engineering your legacy. Legacies —even the most far-reaching and successful—are built upon family identity, not bank accounts. But there is a way to humbly reverse engineer your life—I say humbly because you cannot know the future. What you can do is make reasonable predictions based on a careful study of available information.

Intentional families are looking for different types of predictors. They are asking the question: What are the vital ingredients necessary for building the identity of my family such that future generations will want to live wisely? They want to understand the impact of the spiritual, intellectual, social, cultural, relational, and even day-to-day financial life of the family on building the identity of the individual. Some predictions are reasonable. Others, less so. Predicting who will be the president of the United States in twenty years is unreasonable. Predicting the likelihood that at least one member of your family will suffer a medical crisis in the next twenty years is reasonable. Reverse engineering your legacy requires that you understand the difference between the two approaches and that you are willing to chart your course based on the best available information and analysis.

You can, for example, predict physiological changes that come with age and will affect your productivity. You can predict the impact of forgiveness in a family. Families who really forgive one another are more likely to stick together over time. You can predict the impact of an honest and robust spiritual life on future generations. The old saying that, "The family that prays together, stays together" is not far from the truth. Most importantly, you can predict that the overall impact of a vibrant family life on the hearts and minds of children is more likely to produce children who identify with that family.

It is reasonable to conclude that neither you nor any of your children will live to the age of one-hundred-and-twenty-five. It is far more likely that even in the best-case scenario you will live into your nineties. Sure, science, nutrition, health, and environmental factors appear to be extending human life expectancy. The numbers might continue to rise, but there is nothing in our present paradigm of longevity that supports the idea that you will survive for a century and a quarter.

Knowing the limitations of the best-case scenario of your window of life gives you an identifiable maximum available time to execute life objectives. Of course, you might not live to your next birthday. Anything can happen. Something as dramatic as a meteorite could fall from the sky and kill you and everyone in your home, or something as common as a car accident could end your life prematurely. We are in the hands of God. And yet, we must prepare, plan, and act. We do it every day. Our lives are built on assumptions of the future. Daily we make decisions based on reasonable assumptions of cause and effect. We go to work believing that the contract we have negotiated with our employer to compensate us for our time will be honored. We approach education with the objective that the training and certification we receive will help us to accomplish specific goals in the future. We adopt a diet and health program based on the assumption that choices have consequences for our personal well-being.

Ask yourself the following:

- Are children who can articulate and understand the values and worldview of their family more likely to identify with those values and with that worldview and then pass them on to the next generation than those who cannot?
- Are children who are aware of the dominant themes impacting their family over the generations in a better position to embrace generational strengths and overcome generational weaknesses than those who know little about their family history?
- If, as a parent, you who are keenly aware of the milestone events in your children's lives—past, present, and future—and can predict how these landmarks overlap with landmarks in the lives of other family members, are you more capable of reverse engineering a legacy?

Reinforcing Your Family Identity

This book makes the case for the primacy of identity to the cohesion of the intentional family. This identity is shaped through four overlapping elements of family life: The faith, culture, ethics, and history of the family. In the real world, these areas converge. They overlap through their expressions in the intellectual and literary life of a family, the family table, celebration, athletic experience, aesthetic expression, worship, business, community, and even through unique family idiosyncrasies.

In previous chapters, we saw how these basic categories serve as the umbrellas of experience for the life of the family. We concluded that to build a healthy family identity you need love, life together, and training. Love is the unqualified outpouring of the heart from one family member to another. Life is the world you build, complete with culture, history, ethics, and faith. Training is the philosophical reinforcement and practical preparation that allows families to accomplish legacy-oriented goals—the most important of which is the ability to help the next generation articulate and live the faith, philosophy, and vision of the family who helped shape identity.

We must answer basic questions: Why is our family our family? What makes us tick? How are we different? How are we the same? What do we believe? What is our history? What do we love? What do we hate? How has it shaped our identity? What are our dreams and aspirations? What are our philosophies of success, failure, money, and work? All of these things guide our actions.

One way to define family identity is to talk about it. Identity emerges through ten thousand undefined actions and experiences, but it is also shaped and formalized through conversation about identity. Never assume from one generation to the next that a single conversation is sufficient. We repeat, so we remember. We too easily forget the vital elements of the past, being absorbed into the intrigue and urgency of the present. These conversations may take a hundred forms, but the goal is to answer the question, *Who are we?* The success of any organization or society hinges on the ability to answer this question.

Family Codes and Mottos

How do you capture the essence of family identity and transfer that message to generations you may never know? The family is not a military unit, but there are things we can learn from the military. As an individual organization, each branch of the military is keenly focused on the question of identity. This identity—and group cohesion—is advanced when every member is able to reduce the core values of that group to simple expressions of belief and commitment. Ask any United States Marine to explain the basic values of his branch of the military, and he or she will summarize the complete code of conduct with this short three-word motto: "Honor, courage, and commitment." Mottos are pithy expressions that encapsulate the core principles of a code. Ask that same Marine to tell you his code of conduct, and he will repeat the following:

> I am an American, fighting in the forces which guard my country and our way of life. I am prepared to give my life in their defense. I will never surrender of my own free will. If in command, I will never surrender the members of my command while they still have the means to resist. If I am captured, I will continue to resist by all means available. I will make every effort to escape and to aid others to escape. I will accept neither parole nor special favors from the enemy. If I become a prisoner of war, I will keep faith with my fellow prisoners. I will give no information nor take part in any action which might be harmful to my comrades. If I am senior, I will take command. If not, I will obey lawful orders of those appointed over me and will back them in every way. When questioned, should I become a prisoner of war, I am required to give name, rank, service number, and date of birth. I will evade answering further questions to the utmost of my ability. I will make no oral or written statements disloyal to my country or its allies or harmful to their cause. I will never forget that I am an American, fighting for freedom, responsible for my actions, and dedicated to the principles which made my country free. I will trust in my God and in the UNITED STATES OF AMERICA.[43]

Love it or hate it, those are words of power and conviction. And they are memorized by every member of the United States Marine Corps. This code does more than enforce a set of values; it inspires the men and women who advocate it.

Do you have a family code that governs how you will handle conflict or how you will represent your family to others? Maybe you have concerns about buy-in: Will my children rally around a new vision? The sooner you begin in their lives, the more likely there will be buy-in. But even if you feel that you are late to the game, remember that families follow courage. When children see that their parents really mean what they say—when they sense sincerity and courage—they follow.

I know of a man, I'll call him Smith, who has a three-sentence motto he often repeats to his family at the dinner table, during the family time, and on car trips. It is simple, but it's powerful: "We are Smiths. Smiths fear no man. Smiths fear God."

His children have heard it a thousand times, and they say it right back to him. Maybe one day that brief confessional motto will really pay off. There may come a time when a child, perhaps then an adult, is faced with a tough choice between fear and courage. If that day comes, it is reasonable to predict that his father's oft-repeated words will echo in his or her mind. "We are Smiths. Smiths fear no man. Smiths fear God."

Sometimes family mottos and codes emerge, not so much as a result of formalization, but through a form of cultural osmosis. These are some of the best moments of parenthood. Out of the blue, little Susie says something that reflects a core value. You can't remember teaching it to Susie the way she is now expressing it. She sort-of gathered the component parts of that value proposition through a series of experiences and then assembled them in her mind. Then, at just the right moment, she expresses the family motto in her own words. It is especially satisfying because when a child personalizes a family code, it usually means that he or she owns it.

A motto is only as meaningful as the scope of its acceptance in the group. Where it is internalized by individuals, it can be a rallying cry for self-discipline, action, or focus. The power of mottos to motivate and build cohesion in a group was modeled by Lord Badon Powell's decision in 1907 to build what would become an international scouting movement around a phrase: "Be prepared." If you were ever a Boy Scout or a Girl Scout, you know that phrase. It was the code of your childhood. It meant that you thought in advance. It meant that you brought your tools with you. Powell successfully launched a group that has lasted more than a century, rallying one generation of boys and girls to the next and teaching them to contribute to the safety and needs of others in the community.

Historically, mottos have played an important role in heraldry and on family crests. They have been used in Western civilization for at least a millennium. Family mottos are passed from one generation to the next and often become a vehicle for motivating the up-and-coming generation to remember the victories and losses of past generations. There are thousands of examples, but three famous long-standing family mottos include: "To a valiant heart, nothing is impossible." "He conquers twice who conquers himself." And, "To be, rather than to seem."

For three centuries, the Florentine banking family of the Medicis exerted powerful influence over Europe. One of the most famous families in history, they produced four Popes and numerous political and military leaders. The Medici family advanced the science of accounting by introducing the world to the general ledger system, and they tracked credits and debits using a double-entry bookkeeping system. By reputation, however, they were heavy-handed and greedy, a description they reinforced by adopting as their family motto: "Money to get power, and power to guard the money." It was the summation of their family identity.

Queen Elizabeth II of England comes from the House of Windsor, which traces its origins to the Norman Conquest of England. Hearkening back to its Norman roots, the Windsor family motto is written in French and reads, "Je me fie en Dieu," which means, "I put my trust in God." Some believe that it originated as a battle cry reflective of the Windsor confidence in Divine Providence to vindicate.

If your family does not have a motto, take the time to develop one. Here is one approach to developing a motto that expresses your family identity:

- **Schedule a Meeting:** Schedule a meeting where three generations from your family can attend. You want as many members of your family to be present as possible. The grandparents will bring wisdom and experience. The parents should communicate vision. Because the children will be the heirs to the motto, they not only need to be part of the process, but also to engage in it.

- **Appoint a Family Secretary:** The job of the family secretary is to keep the minutes of the meeting and record the ideas presented by everyone, from the youngest to the oldest. In the future, this process of vetting ideas and sharing stories could play an important role in your family story. Imagine fifty years from now when little Johnny, now a grandpa in his own right, gathers his grandchildren around the table and reads from the notes of that meeting.

- **Establish Ground Rules:** The vision needs to be explained. Why are mottos important? What will a motto mean to the life of your family? Where might it be used—on holiday cards? A family crest? As an encouragement in daily life? Everyone gets to participate. All ideas will be heard, but the goal is to keep things simple. Mottos must be short.

- **Share Examples:** To help everyone visualize the objective it might be helpful to share some examples of mottos families have used historically. You might even offer examples from modern advertising. KFC's motto used to be "finger-licking good," but today it is "We do chicken right." Millions of people know the motto and identify the expressions with the company made famous by Colonel Sanders.

- **Identify Core Family Values:** Developing a family motto is a wonderful way to start a conversation on the values you most highly prize as a family. Sometimes these values are informed by significant experiences—great victories, losses, betrayals, and hopes— all of which form the backdrop for the values you embrace. The Neary clan adopted the maxim "nunc et nunquam," which means "now or never" apparently because of the tumultuous political events surrounding them at the time. The Ogilvey family motto is "Nil desperandum," which means "never despair." Identify Your Words: Mottos are often found written in Latin, but yours need not be. Just make sure that your language choice is backed by good reasoning that will stand the test of time. I like Latin because it speaks to scholarship, permanence, and is consistent with a millennia-old Western tradition, but that is my preference. The problem with Latin is that, by and large, we live in a Latin-illiterate society today, which means the phrase must be translated when used. After selecting the language, start identifying adjectives that communicate the values under consideration. Examples could include "faith," "perseverance," "hope," or even "frugality." Or you could take a different approach altogether. It is up to you.

- **Application:** It might take several meetings over many months before your family agrees upon just the right motto for you. But once identified, make sure to use it. Incorporate your motto into your conversation. Include it on holiday letters and cards. Put it on the walls of your home.

The Case for the Family Catechism

Another way to reinforce your family identity is through family catechisms—a series of short questions and short answers you craft together as
a family that remind you of your core values and express your worldview.
A catechism is a summary of beliefs in question-and-answer format. One
of the most famous catechetical questions ever asked is found in the first
question of the Westminster Shorter Catechism:

Question: What is the chief end of man?
Answer: Man's chief end is to glorify God and to enjoy Him forever.

The purpose of a catechism is to distill complex ideas and beliefs into
concise, simple statements that can be memorized and repeated and that
constitute a summary statement. Children are taught this question early
in life, less because a five-year-old is expected to understand the complex
points of theology, and more because the most important values must be
understood in terms of simplicity. As Oliver Wendell Holmes Sr. has said,
"For the simplicity on this side of complexity, I wouldn't give you a fig.
But for the simplicity on the other side of complexity, for that I would give
you anything I have." Simple expressions of truth last. Concepts that are
reducible to maxim stick. I know grown adults who will never remember
their trigonometry equations and have long forgotten who was the tenth
president of the United States but who will be able to recite the first question of the Westminster Catechism on their death bed. For intentional
families, these "truth sessions" are more than just imprinting. They constitute a handshake from one generation to the next concerning the core
faith of the family.

Hebrew families followed a form of "inverse" catechism, where the
children would quiz their parents on fundamentals of history and doctrine. For millennia Jews have done this on the Passover, as the eldest son
asks, "Father, why is this night different from all others?" And the father
would state the answer. Although most people think of catechisms in terms
of Christian doctrine, the idea of a catechism format is part of daily life
for many people. When a mother asks her son, "Bobby, why do I expect
you to wash your hands before dinner?" and the son responds, "because
cleanliness is next to godliness," a catechetical life ritual is taking place.
The parent is asking a question, the answer for which has been ingrained

in the mind of the child through repetition. We don't tend to think of these interactions as life catechisms, but in effect, that is exactly what they are.

Some people object to catechisms on the basis of the fear that they tend to promote a cold, austere, legalistic formalism, one in which the student learns the answers, but hates them in his heart. That is a real possibility. But the issue is usually not with the catechism, but with the spiritual love life of the family in which the catechism is transmitted. At the end of the day, most people find it extremely helpful to be able to reduce big ideas to simple, bite-sized statements that tend to stick. These statements become part of the arsenal of tools that equip individual family members not only to better understand the value system their family embraces, but also to defend it if and when it becomes necessary. The next generation may choose to reject those beliefs, but at least they do so after being exposed to the values in a manner that was coherent and meaningful.

Here are some examples of possible catechism categories around which you might build questions and answers:

- Foundational beliefs you share as a family
- Important facts pertaining to your family history
- Important lifetime directives you have for your children
- The meaning of names given to the children.
- Great dates and events in the life of your family that remind your children of the special mercies and blessings of God.

With these broad categories as a foundation, here are a few specific examples of how they might be applied. Remember, your answers to these questions will be different from mine. You can have a few questions or many questions.

Question: What is the strategic mission of the McAlvany family?
Answer: To be salt and light in the world around us.

Question: What do McAlvanys believe is the greatest book ever written?
Answer: The Bible, for it is the only book ever written by God.

Question: What lifetime goal has your father set before you?
Answer: To seek the truth, to love the truth, and to live the truth.

Question: Why is February 1990 important to our family?
Answer: It is when David and Don were reconciled at a Waffle House.

Question: What is the significance of each of the names of the McAlvany children?
Answer: Each name carries a spiritual meaning, carefully chosen by our parents to encourage us throughout our lives.

Question: Why is September 3, 1970 a special day to our family?
Answer: Because it is the day that Don and Molly McAlvany were wed.

Question: What do McAlvanys believe is the most important purpose in life?
Answer: To glorify God and enjoy Him.

Question: What are the highest aspirations that McAlvany parents have for their children?
Answer: That each flourish as individuals pursuing their highest potential as men and women who love and serve God.

There is an endless number of potential questions and answers, but just start simply. Write them down. Adjust them. Take your time. Develop them over the years. View your catechism as a working document, and don't be afraid to make improvements. As your list grows, repeat the questions at least once a month with your family at dinnertime, or in the car during road trips, or on special family gatherings and holidays. Use them as starting points to discuss your philosophy and lifestyle as a family. Let your children interact with you on each point. Eventually, you can put your family catechism into your own book and give one to each of your children.

Children tend to be creatures of ritual. There is satisfaction in the recurring themes and practices of life. These family dialogues become more meaningful over the years, like stones of remembrance that are laid in a garden and frequently visited as a reminder of why the flowers were planted in the first place.

To be clear, simple codes, mottos, and catechisms will become worse than useless if they do not reflect a heart commitment that flows from the parents and grows in the lives of each of the children. Success is a function of healthy relationships that must be nurtured. Where parents are passionate about their beliefs and fight to have a redemptive family life, family catechisms offer practical reinforcement as you shape your family identity.

Predicting Landmarks and Disturbance Events

Catechisms and codes will help reinforce your family identity, but what of strategic planning? What if you could trace past events to identify re-oc-curring themes within your family? What if you could predict realistic outcomes by anticipating key events? What if a solid grasp of the past and realistic anticipation of the future could assist you in reverse engineering life decisions?

How old will your children be when the time comes for them to go to college? Can you predict the type of work you will be doing at that time? The income you are making? Your mental, physical, and spiritual health? None of us can predict the future with certainty. We are actually warned in Proverbs 27:1 against "boasting about tomorrow." And yet, all of us make daily decisions based on reasonable expectations of future outcomes. We assume the sun will rise again. We expect that our employers will want us to show up for work. We anticipate the birth of children. We reasonably believe that hard work in college will eventually result in a diploma. We also take precautions to mitigate risk by purchasing insurance, wearing seat belts, and getting counsel on important decisions. We go to the doctor for routine check-ups. While we hope for positive outcomes, we continue to prepare for disturbances.

However, the truth is that few of us take the time to evaluate our own lives and our own "legacy portfolio." Family histories make up part of the lore of the household. Here I am making the case for you to document the landmarks in the life of your family, looking back into the past and casting vision for those landmarks of the future. Essentially, I am arguing that you perform your own socio-economic historical study on your family as a tool to help you make rational predictions about your future.

This could be a completely daunting task, one that involves charting everything from the genetic history of your family going back generations, to their personal proclivities, to your family's financial track record. What I am suggesting is a very simple approach: creating a very basic timeline chart of the past and the future, going at least two generations in both directions. The chart provides you with a timeline of accomplished and anticipated life landmarks for every member of your immediate family and allows you to better plan for your future by anticipating the ups and downs of the various seasons in each of your lives.

You need to build your own, prioritizing those issues that are important and most helpful to you. In my experience, the process of asking the questions and filling out the timeline is revelatory. It forces one to consider the brevity of life and the urgency for each of us to take seriously the choices we make.

Past History

- **Life Landmarks:** Significant events and dates in the lives of your ancestors going back at least one generation—further if you can trace the information
- **Disturbance Events:** When did your parents and grandparents experience disturbance? What was happening in their lives at the time? How did they respond? How did the disturbance, and their response to it, affect the generational history of your family?

Future History

- **Predictable Life Landmarks:** From birthdays to college graduations, to home purchases, to the arrival of children, their eventual marriages, and grandchildren
- **Predictable Disturbance Events:** Most disturbance events fall into one of ten categories (which I will list shortly). You don't know which disturbance will strike, or when, but you can chart a course that takes into consideration their arrival and your response.

Anticipating Life Landmarks

There are two tools you will need to chart your generational legacy trajectory—a journal and a timeline.

The purpose of the journal is for you to have an ever-expanding document that allows you to collect ideas and data. The journal is where you mark down the answers to key questions and note significant anticipated legacy dates. Because legacies are in flux, your journal can be a place to update with new ideas and events, or even scratch out information that has proven unhelpful.

The timeline you will need can be very simple or elaborate, depending on your preference. Essentially it is a horizontally expandable document with layers of lines going from right to left, with each line representing a different life within your immediate family tree. By assigning fixed dates to the lines and layering them, you can have the foundation for a chart that will allow you to see the ages and anticipated dates of key events in the life of your family members. But the real benefit of this chart is the margins. In the margins, you can include ideas, comments, and observations that speak to your legacy prospectus. You can also mark anticipated life landmarks or potential disturbance events based on their respective likelihood or vulnerability.

I keep a very simple journal in my home in which I jot down my own lifetime landmarks—from birthdays to education events. In my journal, I sketch out a chronology of my life. I note where I think these events will occur. Of special interest are those events that overlap. For example, my first-born son will be eligible for college at about the same time I turn fifty. Both of us may be going through significant professional and personal transitions at that time. Can I anticipate those transitions and better prepare to make intelligent strategic choices about the future? What will my son need at this season of his life, and how will I provide for that? It is a question that could take me by surprise. I don't want the tyranny of the urgent to override the wonderful opportunity of being aware of his needs. I want to be prepared when these moments arrive so that I can engage meaningfully with him.

Lifetime Landmarks include some of the following categories:

- Birthdays
- Educational accomplishments (graduations, licenses, degrees)
- Professional accomplishments
- Health and fitness accomplishments
- Financial accomplishments (house purchase, salary objectives)

The Questions of Your Life

An approach to identifying lifetime landmarks is to begin by answering "the questions of your life." These are the big questions that outline the choices you will make in life. You already know the most important ones; these are the questions a father once presented to a prospective suitor when he came to ask for his daughter's hand. They are the basics that must be answered. These questions serve as an informative backdrop to your legacy chart. Depending on your age and place in life, these questions might already be answered for you. If so, then they need to be answered for your children. The answers to these questions might change over time, but begin the process of writing down your answers in the legacy journal.

- What is my skill set and my educational trajectory?
- What kind of a person do I hope to marry?
- Will I have children? How many do I hope to have?
- What communities will I be a part of?
- How will I provide for my family?
- How will I educate my children?

Anticipating Personal Disturbance Events

Beginning today, you can start a conversation with your family that will allow you to start the process of reverse engineering your family legacy as to critical points where even the best legacy planners fall short—the anticipation and mitigation of predictable disturbance.

Chapter Four examined the inescapable presence of disturbance in our lives and the need for clear thinking during times of crisis. Here, I want to suggest that intentional families take a proactive approach to disturbance anticipation. Challenges are coming whether we like them or not. Though they come in different shapes and sizes, few people escape tragedy, heartache, and loss. What life tragedies are reasonable for you to anticipate in your life or the lives of any of your children and extended family? Are you prepared to respond to them if they come? How would any of these disturbances impact your response to a vision of intentionality, or alter your vision for intentional legacy?

I want to argue against paranoia and fear. Many people prefer ignorance over knowledge because knowledge of potential problems can feel overwhelming. Perspective is everything. I know of people who are incapacitated by the fear of rogue terrorist groups placing anthrax in their water supply, or a bomb emitting an electromagnetic pulse (EMP) over their city, wiping out cars and computers. In some cases, fear of germs and disease results in social paralysis. The great Howard Hughes was an example of someone who was so affected by a fear of germs that he, despite his vast fortune, felt the need to retreat from virtually all human contact.

Take comfort to remember that the same Bible that declares, "The prudent sees danger and hides himself, but the simple go on and suffer for it," (Proverbs 22:3) also clarifies, "for God gave us a spirit not of fear but of power and love and self-control," (2 Timothy 1:7).

Ten Categories of Disturbance

There are ten leading categories of personal disturbance that should be considered in the reverse-engineering process. You may be that one-in-a-million person who is never affected by disturbance, but don't count on it. It is far more realistic to take an honest look at life and assume that any or all of these disturbances will affect you during your lifetime, possibly on more than one occasion. They are coming. You know they are coming. You are not sure which ones are going to hit or when, but crisis and calamity are part of life. Your family is not exempt.

Consider these key categories of disturbance that impact legacy outcomes:

- **Health Crisis:** At some point in the life of your family, one or more individuals may suffer a significant health crisis that impacts both the individual and the family as a whole.
- **Moral Failure:** If you are a human, then you have both been tempted and also succumbed to moral failure at different moments in your life. Moral failure can range from business impropriety to infidelity to dishonesty; it is any action of a moral nature that represents a compromise of integrity.
- **Criminal Assault:** From cyber-attacks to pick-pocketing to old fashioned stick-ups, there is always the real possibility that you or someone in your family could become a victim of a criminal assault.
- **Natural Disaster:** Hurricanes, floods, lightning, and other natural disasters might seem like a remote possibility until one of them

has happened to you or a member of your family.

- **Employment Crisis:** One family member's loss of employment can impact the whole. What happens when a member of the family loses his or her job?
- **Debilitating Debt:** In the same way that compounding interest over time works to the benefit of a family, compound debt can throw a monkey wrench into the strategic plans of an intentional family.
- **Death:** This one is inescapable, but it can hit unexpectedly and strike at any age.
- Relational Crisis: Broken hearts, broken friendships, and relational rifts can be life-altering.
- **Divorce:** It is possible that your family will be the exception and remain untouched by divorce, but the statistics are working against you.
- **Accidents:** From car wrecks to unintended fires, most members of your family will experience a few significant accidents in the course of their lives.

Once you have identified each of the areas, consider if there are unique vulnerabilities that make your family susceptible to particular categories of disturbance. Do you have a genetic predisposition to cancer? Is there a history of divorce in your family? Do you live within ten miles of an active volcano? Is there a high crime rate in your community?

Every day the president of United States gets what is called a "matrix" report. It is a summary of the top threats to United States of America ranked by security specialist. And our family, we have our own version of a "matrix report." Mary Catherine and I meet weekly for our date nights and discuss the top challenges facing our family. In your journal, create a chapter to help you develop your own personal "matrix report"—a list of potential disturbance threats in order of concern, along with your ideas on how to mitigate the risk of their occurrence long before they become a reality. A simple example would be this: "Note—five members of my immediate family have diabetes. My goal is to develop lifestyle habits that will prevent my own family from becoming numbers six through ten. Towards this end, we must dramatically reduce the sugar intake in my household, get regular check-ups with physicians, and embrace a regimen of exercise. We will pay now, or we will really pay later."

Basic Life Facts about Your Parents and Grandparents

One benefit of your journal and legacy chart is that they are works in progress. They change and grow as you assess issues and gather more information. They are also expandable. My recommendation is to take the time to gather as much information as you can about your own parents and grandparents, even adding their lines to your chart. In some cases, you can take your children and make it an event—videotaping the life story of Grandma and Grandpa. In other cases, these questions are best asked during a long walk. The approach you take is family-specific. Just make sure to take the time to understand the life story of those who came before you. Here is a simple guideline:

Life Chronology

How old were your parents when they were married; they completed their formal education; you were born; their other children were born; their parents died; they retired?

How old was your father when he was married? How about when he had you as his child? Have there been any similarities of experience between your personal history and the chronology of events of his life?

Disturbance

What types of disturbances have your parents experienced in their lives? Do you know when? How often? How many of the ten key types of disturbance are you aware affected their lives? To what extent were they able to overcome the disturbances?

Are there lessons that can be learned from the way they responded to these disturbances? Can you see any trends in your family lineage? Are you struggling with the same types of disturbances your parents suffered from? Do the answers to these questions provide any insights into generational baggage?

As you flesh out information in your journal and add data points to your legacy chart, you will be able to answer questions like these:

How old will the following people be on your 40th birthday?

- each of your children?

- your wife?
- your own father and mother?

What critical issues can you anticipate when you turn 50?

- your career?
- finances?
- your children's higher education?
- what are the most likely disturbances?
- what life goals do you hope to have accomplished?

How old will the following people be on your 75th birthday?

- your wife?
- your children?
- your grandchildren?
- your own father and mother?

Building a Sense of Historical and Cultural Perspective

Perspective is everything. From the vantage point of walking on the earth, everything seems flat. Cars, houses, and other manmade objects seem large. Look down from the window of a plane at 40,000 feet, though, and those objects disappear, giving way to a grander view. One of the macro goals of a life journal and legacy chart is to grant perspective—to allow you to see the story of your life from 40,000 feet.

But how do you translate a 40,000-foot perspective to young children? There is really no substitute for talking to them and engaging in perspective-building conversations.

A practical approach is through storytelling and quizzes. By telling the stories of past generations, children learn to think beyond the present. By quizzing them on the details of your family's generational story, you promote emotional investment in those stories. Here are a few sample questions designed to encourage buy-in to your own family's story and challenge your children to think in terms of generational history:

Who were President and Vice President of the United States when:

- you were born?
- dad was born?
- grandma was born?
- mom voted for the first time?
- grandpa voted for the very first time?
- mom and Dad were married?

How many generations has it been since:

- your mother's ancestors came to the United States?
- your father's ancestors came to the United States?
- World War II?
- man landed on the moon?
- the War of American Independence?
- your family started going to church?

Which of our family ancestors:

- was the first to buy an automobile?
- was the first to get rich?
- was the first to go bankrupt?
- was the first to write a book?
- was the first to graduate from college?
- was the first to fly in an airplane?

How many:

- descendants have come from my mother's patrilineal line?
- descendants have come from my mother's matrilineal line?
- descendants have come from my father's patrilineal line?
- descendants have come from my father's matrilineal line?
- descendants will I have if I have six children, each of whom have six children, and each of their children have six children?
- descendants will I have if I have two children, each of whom have two children, and each of their children have six children?

Can you name:

- three of Grandpa's favorite movies?
- three of Grandma's favorite books?
- three of Dad's favorite poems?
- three of Mom's favorite musicians?
- every city where your family has lived for the last fifty years?
- every country

Charting Unspoken Objectives

Not every element of our intentional legacy strategy is a matter for discussion with our younger children at a given point in time. Some things emerge. Others are best discussed as we gain greater personal clarity. As Mary-Catherine and I have our weekly date night and informally review our "matrix report," there are objectives we have in the parenting process that fall into this unspoken-to-our-children-for-the-present category, yet play a vital role in the process of helping them grow and mature towards a certain goal.

Several of these objectives emerged out of reflection, discussion, and prayer between us. By having long-range goals in the back of our minds, we find our daily decisions more consistently aligned and in tune with our ideals and intentions. In many cases, these objectives are more likely to succeed if they are "caught," than just verbally "taught." In other words, my children need to see me model the principles. The burden is on me to create an environment in which these values thrive.

In my journal I include a life-preparation list exactly as follows. These are questions for myself, each of which begins with the following query: Will I prepare my children to . . .

- handle conflict with strength and grace?
- make decisions in challenging or new circumstances?
- overcome fears?
- recognize right behavior in particular circumstances?
- see others as they are?
- see others as they could be (i.e. through the lens of a visional ethic)?
- think well of themselves (accurately, deeply, critically, generously)?

- give when a need is obvious?
- discern when a need is disingenuous?
- listen well?
- love well?
- be a dedicated friend?
- remain flexible?
- be persistent?
- think well?
- imagine well beyond their immediate circumstance or experience?
- walk in faith?
- savor all of life at its right time and place?
- love God and fear Him only (irrespective of the inclination to please others)?

There are other categories in my journal applicable to the reverse-engineering principle. Some appear as strategic business plans for enterprises yet to be birthed. Others are reflections on areas of needed improvement as a husband or lists of adventures I intend to take individual family members on. The adventures and activities tie into the life-preparation list and remind me that certain character qualities can be underscored and explored through unique activities.

For example, to practice persistence and overcoming fears, we may find ourselves trekking the Grand Canyon or climbing one of Colorado's many 14,000-foot peaks. Knowing what I want to teach allows life events to become far more instructional when they occur.

Time To Get Busy

The great inspirational author Zig Ziglar observed, "Many people spend more time in planning the wedding than they do in planning the marriage." It's a point that is worth considering. Tremendous energy is applied to the bells and whistles of life—the car I want and the vacation I must have—but what would happen if greater preparatory effort was applied to the biggest moments of our lives? What if we anticipated those events and reinforced the values and virtues necessary to attack our future as a family with zest?

We spend much of our lives being busy. I want to suggest that more is required than mere busyness. Intentional families must draw from a life of careful thought, reinforcement of core values, and regular communication of vision. Thomas Edison put it this way: "Being busy does not always mean real work. The object of all work is production or accomplishment, and to either of these ends there must be forethought, system, planning, intelligence, and honest purpose, as well as perspiration. Seeming to do is not doing."

Paul J. Meyer, the founder of Success Motivation Institute and author of countless books, observed that "Productivity is never an accident. It is always the result of a commitment to excellence, intelligent planning, and focused effort." Communicating a family code, crafting mottos and catechisms, and launching a life journal and legacy chart are tools in the process. But they must be aimed towards a worthy goal and sealed with the heart.

Chapter 9

Back to the Beginning

"Any resolution which is made today must be made again tomorrow."
- Albert Grey[44]

December 30, 2014, was a very cold day in Durango, though I never experienced it. As the last moments of the year came to a close, I found myself in a warm and inviting world of beauty, but not just because of the idyllic weather or the magical surroundings. Years of planning, discussions, failures, victories, hopes, dreams, confessions, and redemptions—in short, the stuff of intentionality—had resulted in an epiphany: It was time to go back to the beginning. And yet not really the beginning. Rather, it was a renewal of purpose.

It happened on an island.

Somewhere about a third of the way between Trinidad, Tobago, and Puerto Rico is the volcanic island of Nevis—to be precise, that somewhere is latitude 17.11 N and longitude 62.35 W, smack dab in the West Indies. With a combined total of 104 square miles between Nevis and its sister island of St. Kitts, these two bumps in the ocean combine to form the seventh smallest nation in the world. Birthplace of Alexander Hamilton and once the haunt of pirates and slave traders, Nevis is a surprisingly quiet world of sunshine, coral reefs, and Caribbean beauty. I will always think of it as my personal Ebenezer of hope in a journey of life, love, and legacy.

It had been thirty-five years since I donned my three-piece suit to confidently deliver my father's message on inflation to an audience of friends. Close to twenty-five years had passed since I left my job slopping pigs and reconciled with my father in a Waffle House. The personal, spiritual, and intellectual journey that took me from South America to Oxford to Israel to California, and back to Durango was close to two decades in the past. And it was fifteen years since I had met and married the love of my life.

And for one special moment they came together—the men, women, and children who represent the heart of my own legacy journey—the fellowship of the hopeful. They were all there. They came because of the power of confession. Not just the confession one thinks of when revealing a secret or admitting to a fault, but the creedal variety that Christians sometimes profess like a "confession of faith." My family traveled to witness and affirm a family confession of faith between Mary-Catherine and myself—the rededication of our marriage vows.

There on that tiny island beside the remains of the Cottle Church, my family and close friends assembled to affirm our status as bondservants to the living God and speak of the covenant of marriage that seals a vision of legacy for Mary-Catherine and me.

For one special moment, time stands still. A lifetime of experiences flash before me, along with memories of my parents and mentors—those who patiently endured me and held my hand.

***

Standing with me on this day is my father, whose own journey served as an inspiration for mine. Dad the indefatigable. Dad the passionate. Optimistic, pessimistic, often paranoid, devout, intense, relentless, compassionate—the man who would travel around the world to sit in a hotel room to talk with his son about life. My father.

I look at him and realize that this man has raised the bar on what it means to "not go gentle into that good night." At seventy-five years of age, he has embraced a new career, lives in a nation that is far removed from his former world, and, to boot, Don McAlvany can lift more weight than most men half his age. He reminds me of the biblical figure Caleb who, during the same season in life, declared that he was as strong as he had ever been. That is Dad—the object of my youthful angst and the man who became as a redeemer to me because he simply forgave.

There is my patient and tender mother. She is holding a baby in her arms, a reminder to me of life. Now she is beside my father, as she has been for near half of a century. She looks at Mary-Catherine and me with that same affirming look she gave me when I was lost in the wilderness of despair—as if to say, "I always knew it would turn out this way. I always knew."

Molly McAlvany believes in me and lets me know that fact—not so much through words, but in the way that only a mother can communicate. As we gather under the bowers of our island chapel, her presence brings stillness, peace, and favor to my soul. This is now the third time I have said my vows—first after an elopement, then a formal wedding, and now fifteen years later, and the reality of my mother's blessing on the legacy Mary-Catherine and I aspire to build continues to inspire. There is a Scripture that puts it nicely: "When I was a son with my father, tender, the only one in the sight of my mother," (Proverbs 4:3). That's it—"tender and precious to my mother." Mothers endure much. Molly McAlvany has endured much. But you would never know it because she has chosen to be a woman of discretion, equanimity, and affirmation.

There are my sisters and brothers—each real men and women with their own remarkable journeys. There is Lauren who, alongside my brother-in-law Curtis and their nine children, are changing the world with their own family in their own big and small ways. Today we love each other. We have found synchronicity as part of a broader family legacy, but it was not always so. There are pieces of our lives as brother and sister that I can no longer remember—memories that have faded or disappeared, a blank-slate testimony to a season of my own self-absorption. There were days I do remember during our youth where Lauren and I found each other intolerable. All that began to change when my father extended to me the hand of redemption; I found my family again. I even began to work with them. My season working in the restaurant business with Curtis sealed our mutual respect for each other and commitment to family legacy as brothers.

There are my children. Four little bodies that carry our best aspirations for the future. Thousands of collective meal-time conversations, prayers before bed, business trips together, daily dialogues on their "happy" and their "sad," the classroom in our home, walks in the Colorado outback— all of this converges at this precise moment as we come together before the Lord to recommit a marriage and refresh our vision of legacy as an intentional family.

Most importantly, there is my wife—my own personal angel. She who has forgiven much and loved well. There on the grass we repeat the same vows we'd declared fifteen years earlier.

***

Imagine a scene like this in heaven—loved ones and friends, joined together in perfect communion with each other—forgiven, radiant, and bound by a common love in the presence of their God. There at the end of the earth we gathered to form our own private band of brothers, a cadre of souls dedicated to a cause more meaningful to my family than all the gold in the world—legacy.

The Legacy Vision of the Man Who Loves God

There are moments in time when everything converges—brief windows that allow you to rise to 40,000 feet and look down with fresh perspective on the panorama of life. From that altitude I am reminded of some of the details of my personal legacy, beginning with the name I was given at birth—David—and the person for whom I was given it. Here was the boy who fought a lion and won, healed the spirit of a king with his music, stood before a giant and invoked the name of the God he loved, toppled his opponent, and took his head. Here is the mighty warrior who defeated army after army and built a kingdom. And here is the failing man of sin who committed adultery and then had the husband of the woman with whom he committed adultery placed in harm's way of death to cover for his sin. Here is a man who kept commitments and broke them, who acted with humility and pride. He was a whole man, a sinful man, but of him Christ said, "He was a man after God's own heart," (Acts 13:22).

King David's defining vision of legacy is instructive. Because he was a bloody man of war, God did not allow him to complete the mission of building a temple, but David's son would. Now his hopes and dreams of legacy are passed on to Solomon. As David approaches the end of his life, he offers perhaps the greatest recorded prayer of legacy in history.

> Then he called for Solomon his son, and charged him to build an house for the Lord God of Israel. And David said to Solomon, 'My son, as for me, it was in my mind to build an house unto the name of the

Lord my God:' But the word of the Lord came to me, saying, 'Thou hast shed blood abundantly, and hast made great wars: thou shalt not build an house unto my name, because thou hast shed much blood upon the earth in my sight. (1 Chronicles 22:6-8).

Having acknowledged the limitations placed on his own life, David reflects on the promises of God for the next generation:

Behold, a son shall be born to thee, who shall be a man of rest; and I will give him rest from all his enemies round about: for his name shall be Solomon, and I will give peace and quietness unto Israel in his days. He shall build an house for my name; and he shall be my son, and I will be his father; and I will establish the throne of his kingdom over Israel for ever. (1 Chronicles 22:9-10)

And now David charges his son with the hope and vision of legacy fulfillment:

Now, my son, the Lord be with you, so that you may succeed in building the house of the Lord your God, as he has spoken concerning you. Only, may the Lord grant you discretion and understanding, that when he gives you charge over Israel you may keep the law of the Lord your God. Then you will prosper if you are careful to observe the statutes and the rules that the Lord commanded Moses for Israel. Be strong and courageous. Fear not; do not be dismayed. (1 Chronicles 22:11-13)

David was a man deeply concerned about legacy. He wrote about it. He made provision for it. He sometimes acted contrary to it. But he always returned to the desire of his heart—to fulfill his role in an unfolding legacy.

And God gave it to him.

Again the words of King David inspire. Here are the legacy objectives of this entire book summed up in a simple declaration of legacy from the man of blood, war, sin, who had a heart that yearned for God:

Praise the Lord!
Blessed is the man who fears the Lord,
who greatly delights in his commandments!
His offspring will be mighty in the land;
the generation of the upright will be blessed.
Wealth and riches are in his house,
and his righteousness endures forever.
Light dawns in the darkness for the upright;
he is gracious, merciful, and righteous.
It is well with the man who deals generously and lends;
who conducts his affairs with justice.
For the righteous will never be moved;
he will be remembered forever.
He is not afraid of bad news;
his heart is firm, trusting in the Lord.
His heart is steady;[b] he will not be afraid,
until he looks in triumph on his adversaries.
He has distributed freely; he has given to the poor;
his righteousness endures forever;
his horn is exalted in honor.
The wicked man sees it and is angry;
he gnashes his teeth and melts away;
the desire of the wicked will perish!

It is all there in Psalm 112—the intentional journey of the man of faith. He loves his God and delights in the words of his God. The hearts of his children embrace this love as well. The result is that they become "mighty in the land." Their lives are blessed. Their homes are happy and filled with the treasures of blessing. Good comes to them, and blessing is multiplied as a result of their generosity to others. They model an ethic of virtue, which is exemplified in the fairness of their personal and business affairs. And they understand the right response to disturbance. When crisis emerges, they are calm. They don't fear bad news. They have steadfast hearts capable of overcoming obstacles and external attacks. They may be hated by others, but that does not matter because they have a legacy of immovable faith before their God.

Rebooting Our Vision

The best efforts at intentionality require recalibration and recommitment. There are reasons why the best music is often composed in the fields of supreme joy or the most painful, gut-wrenching emotional experiences. Both pain and joy inspire. They teach and mold. They prepare us for the next step of the journey. All of our experiences—good and bad—are part of our progress as pilgrims in life.

Fifteen years ago, Mary-Catherine and I only thought we knew what we were committing to. Now the picture is far more clear. Tomorrow it will be even more so. That clarity comes at a price—the many experiences of life, running the spectrum from joy and bliss to sadness, disappointment, and grief. It is the beautiful and painful journey of intentionality.

Within the context of a deep and transparent relationship, there is the possibility of the greatest intimacy and relational connection and the worst imaginable pain and disappointment. And so, we came to once again restate our covenant before God and man. Restating our vows was with full knowledge of our frailty and devotion, bathed in love and forgiveness not entirely our own. On this day we were celebrating God's goodness and grace, grateful for the past and for having a clearer vision for the future.

Mary-Catherine, the children, and I came into the venue singing together as a family. It was a moment of exultation—the gift of song becoming an ornament on the works of grace in the heart. Music as a declaration of deep satisfaction and worship. Later, my brother, along with a friend I have known from birth, led us in worship and praise, which set the tone of gratefulness and joy.

We have made a commitment to each other, before God, and reaffirmed it. We have made a commitment to friends and family and reaffirmed it as well, reminding them of their roles in our life.

The Fellowship of Grace at Our Wedding

There are many graces from God. One is the experience of the fellowship of our friends. The grace that comes with friendship is one that implies a lot for us. Integrating our friends and family into the service was for us a way to say again, fifteen years later, "we entreat you, we implore you, we invite you to reflect back to us what you see in our relationship, provide insight to what you hear, help us grow in maturity, and invest in us toward the success of our relationship." Accountability is not precisely what comes to mind. That idea inheres to a larger picture of grace in community.

Our children were a cornerstone of the gathering. A part of the reason we chose year fifteen instead of a more auspicious anniversary was to bring our kids into the promise-making so that in our daily lives, as they continue to grow in our care, they know, and we know, what it looks like to live out the vows made.

There is a degree to which we raised the stakes by including our kids in the promise. Our hope is that they, in time, reflect on marriage more winsomely, having begun to think about it while still children—not merely as a romantic fairytale, but as the heart of legacy. We want them to understand that grace and forgiveness are the foundations for a successful relationship that stands the test of time.

The Summation

I cannot think of a more fitting way to conclude this book on legacy than by sharing with you something so personal—the very renewal of our vows as an intentional family. On the one hand, both Mary-Catherine and I feel a level of vulnerability opening this moment of our lives to you. It is private and personal. On the other hand, it is the summation of our journey up until now and the convergence of each of the themes I have communicated through the chapters of this book:

1. Legacy is a defining issue in the life of every man and woman.
2. You were created to serve, love, and enjoy God forever, and one expression of this service, love, and enjoyment is the legacy you leave behind.
3. Legacy is inescapable. The question is not *if* you will leave one, but what legacy will you leave? What are you creating today to leave for tomorrow?
4. A proper understanding of legacy is holistic—it involves the legacy of family history, culture, faith, business, and wealth.
5. Successful legacy planners are intentional. They seek to reverse-engineer their legacy by looking at the journey of their lives from end to beginning and then making choices that help them achieve

the wisest and most noble results. Intentional families make plans, revise plans, adapt plans. They are constantly about the business of planning, evaluating, and executing.

6. Even the best-laid plans of mice and men go awry, which is why intentional families not only expect disturbance, but they also prepare for it—mentally and practically.

7. Each element of legacy planning is important: the way a family preserves and cultivates family histories that reinforce the identity of the individuals; faith as the centerpiece, glue, and the hope for divine blessing in the household; a dynamic and robust family culture, which includes reading, mealtime shared with the entire family, and unique expressions of family identity; the family's approach to business and labor, which not only produces wealth, but also shapes family reputation in the community; and an intelligent strategy of wealth development and transfer, especially in economically uncertain times.

8. Intentional families are aware of the legacy baggage they have inherited and make it a point to identify past errors, break cycles of sin and selfishness, and jettison the baggage.

9. Generosity is a foundation for blessing. Intentional families give generously, investing time and resources into the lives of others.

10. Most importantly, intentional families look at the individual members of the family through the grid of redemption and hope. Their relationships are non-contingent, and their view of each other is visional. Looking past present shortcomings, they see their potential as men and women of inestimable value made in the image of God.

Rocks of Remembrance

Why did we do it? Why did we come together to once again "pledge our troth"?

The simple answer is that we felt compelled to do it. God had placed a burden on our hearts to declare His goodness and the beauty of His holiness as it has been made manifest in our lives—one needy family on the road to building a lasting legacy.

But there were other reasons: because any resolution made today must be made again tomorrow; because our personal journey as husband and wife includes victories and failures and redemptions that speak to the deepest part of our journey as an intentional family in need of regular acts of redemption and rededication; because speaking vows again is an acknowledgment of both the sacredness of the vows and the beauty of the journey; because we crave the ongoing involvement of our children, family, and friends and long for their ongoing witness in our lives.

On the issue of marriage rededication, I have no recommendation to make to another family other than this—your path is unique. Your needs are particular to your family. Legacy rededication will look different for everyone. But one thing you must do is remember your vows and from time to time set them before your family and friends as a rock of remembrance.

The great author Carl Sandburg once penned a book called *Remembrance Rock*, which he described as "an epic weaving the mystery of the American Dream with the costly toil and bloody struggles that have gone to keep alive and carry further that Dream."[45] To put it another way, epic struggles and mercies must be remembered in order to realize the greatest dreams. Rocks of remembrance are placed for two principal reasons: first, so that that those who have personally experienced mercy can communicate honor, gratitude, and thanksgiving, and second, so that long after the original fathers have placed the rock of remembrance, their heirs will remember the journey and become grateful recipients of the legacy inherited.

The principle of the rock of remembrance finds its origin in Holy Scripture. The act of placing a stone, marking it, and ascribing commemorative meaning to it is associated with gratitude for the mercies of God. The prophet Samuel, whose name means "heard of God," is one example of a man of faith who set up a stone as a marker of remembrance. After a great battle, he stood between Mizpeh and Shem and placed a large stone, which he named "Ebenezer," meaning Stone of Help. After placing the stone, he declared: "Up to this point the LORD has helped us" (1 Samuel 7:12).

These rocks are representative of one of the most defining themes of the Scripture—"remember." It is a message that cannot be emphasized enough—remember. Remember God's deliverance in your life (Exodus 13:3); remember the day of rest (Exodus 20:8); remember your fathers (Exodus 23:13); remember when you provoked God to anger by forgetting your promises (Deuteronomy 9:7); remember the marvelous works of God (1 Chronicles 16:12); remember the brevity of life (Psalm 89:47). Without the physical marker, it is too easy to forget. The imperative to "remember" and the principle of the rock of remembrance finds expression in hundreds of rituals and acts of dedication and remembrance in the life of the intentional family. As Mary-Catherine and I gathered to rededicate our life together, we stood on hundreds of pebbles and stones of remembrance, which have become part of our journey forward.

The Legacy of the Son of Prayer

What do our children really see? How deeply do they feel about what they witness in the life of family—both the good and the bad?

Perhaps more than we might ever imagine.

When do the seeds of legacy begin to sprout? On this special day on our island at the end of the world, I watched as the process of legacy germination took root, producing a special bud of encouragement—this time an affirmation of a mother and father by their child. It was one of the greatest moments of our rededication, and it came directly after the close of the formal ceremony. The most meaningful part of the service was when my son owned his name. He approached Mary-Catherine and me to make a special request: "Can I pray a blessing over you and Mom?"

God was moving his heart. In his youthful earnestness I witnessed an inspired maturity.

My son was not wearing a three-piece suit and certainly was not giving a memorized message to an audience of family friends. He just wanted to pray. Privately. He was responding to the grace and mercy of God in his parents' lives. Seeing them reaffirm their commitment and love for one another, he was grateful for his eight years with us and wanted to bless all our future years together. So he began to pray—not the prayer of a preacher, and not the prayer of an adult. The prayer of a little boy who is a man-in-the-making.

As my own name of David has served as a reminder of God's grace in the life of a sinful man who had a heart after God, the name of my firstborn carries its own unique message. We had given our boy a name that speaks to the power of prayer. A legacy prayer said when he was still a child in the womb was now a reality. He was living from head to toe into the meaning of his name, "God hears the man of prayer."

***

My son is not only giving me a blessing, but also a prayer that constitutes his own unique rock of remembrance in our family life—an event as part of a larger story that marks the past and points to the future. As he prays, I feel the summation of our life together embodied in those boyish, but pristine, words. In my mind I see our many walks in the Colorado mountains, hundreds of hours around the dinner table walking through the Word of God, late-night conversations talking about the battles of Roman legionaries, business trips where he participates in discussions on gold and global currency, gatherings as a family to rejoice before the Lord in song . . . they all take form right now in a simple expression of filial honor, of devotion to God, and love for his parents. He speaks with the virtue of simplicity Christ declares precious—the faith of one of these "little ones."

I also see the painful discussions—the transparent ones we have had, where I have had to confess my own sins to my son, and he has forgiven me, as well as those where I have had to act as a father, walking him through the consequences of his own shortcomings. I see the fruits of confession and forgiveness birthed in the freedom my son now has to share a blessing.

My Waffle-House conversation is coming back to me now. Right here, on the island of our rededication. But it is not so much a conversation as it is a profound moment expressed through words of covenant, love, and vision for the years his mother and I will share in the future. Long before a crisis emerges, I need my son to know that, like my relationship with his mother, my relationship with him "is"—it is permanent. I need him to understand this: "Son, whatever the failure that may come, you are already forgiven. Son, I already see past your mistakes. And Son, no matter what happens on this earth with your imperfect father, there is an eternal father who loves you perfectly and will never forsake you. His love is perfect. His redemption of you is already complete. You are accepted by Him. You are loved perfectly and infinitely."

***

At the end of the trip, my firstborn told me that his favorite part of being on the island was seeing us rededicate ourselves to one another before God. I do not kid myself that a victory won today is a victory secured forever. My own journey has proven to me that hard-fought ground can be won, easily walked away from and lost, only to be recovered again. Victories must be won over and over again. The battle for our hearts and the hearts of our children is a fight for the eternally vigilant. The quest for an intentional family is a journey of ten thousand miles walked one step at a time. But the moments of victory are sweet and meant to be savored. In that moment, the words of my son became their own unique rock of remembrance in our family's legacy timeline.

I look at him now. There he is—my son, a man-in-the-making who through childlike simplicity has for this moment obtained the wisdom of a sage. Before me I experience a new twist on the visional ethic—I can imagine my boy radiating the glory of God as the man he will someday become . . .

***

Now he is a young man full of passion, learning, growing, discovering his own unique path. Now he is a man in his physical prime, in love with a woman with whom he will share his hopes and dreams. Now he is holding his own first-born son in his arms, lifting him up before God, and seeking blessings on that new life. Now he is at home opening the Word of God around the family table with his young children gathered around him. Now he is meeting the challenges of a life crisis, which he will conquer with the support of his family. Now his hair is graying, and he is having conversations similar to those we have shared, but with his own son who may someday pray over him, even as he has done for me. Now he is at rest, having completed a well-lived life, passing on an intentional legacy of culture, words, history, artifacts, and wealth to his own progeny . . .

***

Looking through the lens of a visional ethic, Mary-Catherine and I can see our best intentions and most hopeful dreams of a lasting multigenerational legacy personified in the life of this child—a man who carries a unique and powerful destiny. We want for each of our children not just to succeed, but to surpass their mother and me by going further and deeper, with greater beauty than we could imagine.

And I can see every bit of this as I look at the eight-year-old who is praying over us.

If he forgets everything else—I want him to know that there is a God who loves him perfectly and that he is never beyond hope and redemption.

I want him to know there is no chasm so deep that it could separate us from loving him. I want my son to run for his life from any vision of faith that is graceless. He must know that there is no sin, no disturbance that could break the bonds of sonship to his mother and father.

Someday my son may experience a life disturbance that threatens to shake him to the core. He may even disappoint his mother and father, as well as himself. Perhaps he will fall into a pit of despair or wrestle with a ferocious ethical crisis. Someday, he may forget the roots of his faith. But on this day—today—here at the end of the world on an island—through acts of testimony, confession, covenant, and prayer, we are accepting the forgiveness of Christ for that day in the future. We are declaring that our relationship "is." We affirm that the outcome is already settled in our mind—as nothing can separate us from the love of God, nothing will separate the love of this father for this son. If all else is forgotten, this much must be remembered: the love of God is greater than our shortcomings. The words of this boy echo in my ears: "Dad, we are McAlvanys, we don't give up."

"That is it, Son! We don't and we won't."

Some of us are thoughtful. Some of us are scrappy. All of us are fighters, but at the end of the day, we are sinful men and women. The victory will not be because of anything innately strong about our family, but because of Christ "who works in you, both to will and to work for his good pleasure," (Philippians 2:13). Christ in us, the hope of glory. My son was not alone. The prayer he offered was echoed by others. One of the most meaningful responses to the marriage rededication came from my brother, Scott, a man whose life has been about taking decisive action towards specific goals. Scott came to Mary-Catherine and me to give us a unique gift of legacy affirmation—the kind that one receives when another person not only understands the significance of words, but also interprets them in light of the very visional ethic advocated in this book.

Scott focused not just on the present reality, but also on how those words could mature and grow into something bigger than we might imagine: "Having this ceremony, bringing us all together here . . . the words, the vows . . . the careful thought you and Mary-Catherine put into this . . . the message you are sending, well, I believe God is going to use this. There will be ripple effects in each of our lives. None of us can be the same now. Our friends, our family . . . our children . . . our lives have changed because of this. It will affect our family for generations."

Scott saw the simple words of marriage rededication before God backed up by commitment and an integrity-aspiring vision for family legacy as having a multiplying effect. The heart of his message was this: something transformative has happened. A spiritual shift has taken place. There is a recalibration, which extends beyond David and Mary-Catherine and affects our entire tribe. God has done this, and today is a landmark to our legacy.

I needed to hear that. Those words are precious to me as is the recognition that I have a brother who intends to back me up by walking alongside me on a shared journey of intentionality. I think of the power of the words of a confession of faith or commitment and the profound statement made physically in baptism, which together, with word and deed, speak not only into our physical world as a testament, but also lay claim to a spiritual reality.

I am persuaded that one of the greatest acts of love an intentional family can perform is the daily ritual of speaking words of hope and affirmation into the lives of one another. It means looking your children in the eyes and affirming them as beings with souls of inestimable value and far-reaching potential. It means repeatable acts of meaningful recommitment to a non-contingent relationship based on a love that is selfless. It means appreciating other human beings not for what they can do for you, but for who they are and what they are meant to become before their God.

On an island at the end of the world, we gathered. We were surrounded by family: fathers, mothers, sisters, brothers, children, and friends, all who share in communion with Christ. Connected to the words spoken were the physical actions of the ceremony we experienced, speaking just as loudly to a claim being made: This shall flourish. This shall endure. This shall grow to something of beauty only the mind of God can conceive.

How can I explain it—the sublime influence on the soul and spirit of a broken family standing together with our closest family and friends, calling out as one to the Creator to bless a vision of marriage and family from one generation to the next? It was like being surrounded by an array of fearsome fighters. These are the people who pray for us. These are the people who fight for us. These are the people we walk with in life, as honestly as we can bear. This is the bulwark that would have to be torn down, to tear us down.

God help us. God protect us. We will be an intentional family.

Merciful father—Not unto us, O Lord, not unto us, But to thy name give the glory (Psalm 115:1). Amen.

NOTES

1. David Mitchell, *Cloud Atlas*, (New York: Random House, 2004).
2. C. S. Lewis, *The Weight of Glory*, (New York: Harper Collins, 2001, Originally published 1949).
3. Paul Vitz, T*rust: Faith of the Fatherless: The Psychology of Atheism*, (Dallas: Spence Pub. Co, 2000).
4. Omar Khayyam, *Rubaiyat of Omar Khayyam*, Translated by Edward Fitzgerald, (London and Glasgow: Collins' Clear Type Press, 1910).
5. Elizabeth Dodds, *Marriage to a Difficult Man: The Uncommon Union of Jonathan and Sarah Edwards*, (Philadelphia: The Westminster Press, 1971).
6. Alexander V.G. Allen, *Jonathan Edwards, The First Critical Biography*, (Boston: Houghton Mifflin 1889).
7. A. E. Winship, Jukes-Edwards, *A Study in Education and Heredity*, (Pennsylvania: R. L. Myers and Co., 1900).
8. *Ibid.*
9. James E. Hughes Jr., *Family Wealth: Keeping It in the Family*, (New York: Bloomberg Press, 2004).
10. William Strauss and Neil Howe, *The Fourth Turning*, (New York: Broadway Books, 1997).
11. Robert Penn Warren, *All The King's Men*, (New York: Harcourt, Brace, and Company, 1946).
12. Henry Pelling, *Winston Churchill*, (London: MacMillan Press, 1989).
13. Lori Grisham, "'I'm going to stay right here.' Lives Lost in Mount St. Helens eruption," *USA Today*, May 19, 2015.
14. Simon Winchester, *Krakatoa: The Day the World Exploded*, (London: Penguin, 2004).
15. Donald W. Olson, "When the Sky Ran Red: The Story behind The Scream," *Sky & Telescope Magazine*, February, 2004, p. 29.
16. "2004 Indian Ocean Earthquake," New World Encyclopedia, 20 June 2016, http://www.newworldencyclopedia.org/entry/2004_

Indian_Ocean_earthquake.

17. David Werner, Carol Thuman, and Jane Maxwell, *Where There is No Doctor: A Village Health Care Handbook*, (California: Hesperian Health Guides, 1992).

18. Robert Burns, "To a Mouse," *Poems, Chiefly in the Scottish Dialect*, (Kilmarnock edition, 1786).

19. Hugh Lofting, *The Voyages of Dr. Dolittle*, (New York: Frederick A. Stokes Company, 1922).

20. James Webb, *Born Fighting: How the Scots-Irish Shaped America*, (New York: Broadway Publishing Company, 2004).

21. Bernard Goldberg, *Bias*, (Washington, DC: Regnery Publishing, 2001).

22. Cecelia Ahern, *The Book of Tomorrow: A Novel*, (New York: Harper Collins, 2010).

23. Cassandra Clare, *Clockwork Prince*, (London: Walker Books, 2011).

24. Chris Hodges, *Fresh Air*, (Illinois: Tyndale, 2012).

25. Ralph Elison, *The Invisible Man*, (New York: Random House, 1952).

26. J. R. Miller, *The Family*, (San Antonio: The Vision Forum, 2009).

27. Mercola, Dr. Joseph, "When a Lile Poison is Good for You," August 30, 2008, http://www.mercola.com.

28. Francis Mallmann, *Seven Fires: Grilling the Argentine Way*, (Oklahoma: Artisan, 2009).

29. Andrew Julien, "Whatever Happened to Dinner?" *The Hartford Courant*, (December 18, 2002).

30. Roberto A. Ferdman, "The death of the American family dinner has been greatly exaggerated," Wonkblog, *The Washington Post*, 17 December 2014, https://www.washingtonpost.com/news/wonk.

31. Karen Page, and Andrew Dornenburg, *The Flavor Bible*, (Boston: Lile, Brown, 2008).

32. G.K. Chesterton, *Saint Thomas Aquinas*, (London: Hodder & Stoughton, 1933).

33. Umberto Eco, *Name of the Rose*, (New York: Harcourt, 1980).

34. Charles-Joseph Mathon de la Cour, *Testament de M. Fortuné Ricard* ("Last Will and Testament of Fortunate Richard"), (South Carolina: Nabu Press, 2013).

35. Angela Johnson, "76% of Americans are living paycheck to paycheck," CNNMoney, 24 June 2013, http://money.cnn.com/.

36. Chris Taylor, "70% of Rich Families Lose Their Wealth by the Second Generation," Money, 17 June, 2015, http://time.com/money.

37. "U.S. Trust Study of High Net Worth Investors Defines and Uncovers Planning Shortfalls in Reaching a 'Life Well-Lived,'" Bank of America Newsroom press release, May 28, 2015.

38. Chris Taylor, "70% of Families Lose Their Wealth by the Second Generation," *Money Magazine*, June 17, 2015.

39. Sun-tzu, *The Art of War*, (New York: Basic Books, 1994).

40. Bill Bonner and Will Bonner, *Family Fortunes: How to Build Family Wealth and Hold onto it for 100 Years*, (New Jersey: John Wiley & Sons, Inc., 2012).

41. Bill Federer, *America's God and Country: Encyclopedia of Quotations*, (Missouri: Amerisearch, Inc., 1994).

42. George Orwell, *Nineteen Eighty-Four*, (London: Secker & Warburg, 1949).

43. Marion F. Sturkey, *Warrior Culture of the U. S. Marines* (New York: Heritage Press, 2001).

44. Albert Grey, "The Common Denominator of Success," (Speech given at the National Association of Life Underwriters in 1940), *Laws of Leadership Series*, Volume IX, (Pennsylvania: Tremendous Life Books, 2008).

45. Carl Sandburg, *Remembrance Rock*. (New York: Harcourt, Brace and Company: 1948).

Bibliography
For Further Reading

- Allen, Alexander V. G. *Jonathan Edwards: The First Critical Biography*. Boston: Houghton Mifflin, 1889.
- Aristotle. *Nicomachean Ethics*. Translated by H. Rackham. Cambridge: Harvard University Press, 1926.
- Augustine. *Confessions*. Translated by Henry Chadwick. Oxford: Oxford World's Classics, 2009.
- Aquinas, Thomas. *The Summa Theologica of St. Thomas Aquinas*, 5 vols. Translated by the Fathers of the English Dominican Province. Ave Maria Press, 1981.
- Biggs, Barton. *Wealth, War and Wisdom*. Hoboken, New Jersey: John Wiley & Sons, Inc., 2008.
- Blue, Ron, with Jeremy White. *Splitting Heirs: Giving Your Money and Things to Your Children Without Ruining Their Lives*. Chicago: Northfield Publishing, 2004.
- Bernstein, Peter W., and Annalyn Swan, eds. *All the Money in the World: How the Forbes 400 Make—and Spend—Their Fortunes*. New York: Vintage Books, 2008.
- Birmingham, Stephan. *Our Crowd: The Great Jewish Families of New York*. London: Lowe and,Brydone, 1968.
- Bonhoeffer, Dietrich. *The Cost of Discipleship*. New York: Simon & Schuster, 1959.
- Buchanan, Mark. *Ubiquity: Why Catastrophes Happen*. New York: Three Rivers Press, 2001.
- Dodds, Elizabeth. *Marriage to a Difficult Man: The Uncommon Union of Jonathan and Sarah Edwards*. Philadelphia: The Westminster Press, 1971.
- Dornenburg, Karen, and Andrew Dornenburg. *The Flavor Bible*. Boston: Little, Brown and Company, 2008.
- Easterlin, Richard A. *Birth and Numbers: The Impact of Numbers on Personal Welfare*. Chicago: The University of Chicago Press, 1987.
- Eldred, Ken. *The Integrated Life: Experience the Powerful Advantage of Integrating You Faith and Work*. Colorado: Manna, 2007.

- Ferguson, Adam. *When Money Dies*. New York: Perseus Book Group, 2010.
- Fukuyama, Francis. *Trust: The Social Virtues and the Creation of Prosperity*. New York: The Free Press, 1995.
- Gersick, Kevin E., with Deanne Stone, Katherine Grady, Michele Desjardines, and Howard Muson. *Generations of Giving: Leadership and Continuity in Family Foundations*. Lanham, MD: Lexington Books, 2004.
- Gladwell, Malcolm. *Outliers: The Story of Success*. New York: Little, Brown and Company, 2008.
  ———. *The Tipping Point: How Little Things Can Make a Big Difference*. New York: Little, Brown and Company, 2008.
- Gonzales, Laurence. *Deep Survival*. New York: W.W. Norton and Company, 2004.
- Hayek, F. A. Profits, *Interest and Investment*. London: Routledge and Kegan Paul, 1939.
  ———. *The Road to Serfdom*. 2nd ed. London: Routledge and Kegan Paul, 1944.
- Hughes, James E., Jr. *Family Wealth: Keeping It in the Family*. New York: Bloomberg Press, 2004.
- Khayyam, Omar. *Rubaiyat of Omar Khayyam*. Translated by Edward FitzGerald. London and Glasgow: Collins' Clear-Type Press, 1910.
- Kubler-Ross, Elisabeth. *On Death and Dying*. New York: The Macmillan Company, 1969.
- Lewis, C. S. *The Weight of Glory*. New York: Harper Collins, 2001.
- Mahoney, Tom. *The Great Merchants*. New York: Harper and Row, 1966.
- Mallmann, Francis. *Seven Fires: Grilling the Argentine Way*. Oklahoma: Artisan, 2009.
- Maxwell, Jane. *Where There is No Doctor: A Village Health Care Notebook*. 1992.
- Maybury, Richard J. *Whatever Happened to Penny Candy? A Fast, Clear, and Fun Explanation of the Economics You Need For Success in Your Career, Business, and Investments*. Placerville, CA: Bluestocking Press, 2010.
- Miller, J. R. The Family. San Antonio: The Vision Forum, 2009.
- Mises, L. von, 1953, *The Theory of Money and Credit* (trans. H.E. Batson), J. Cape, London.

- Mises, L. 1977. *A Critique of Interventionism* (trans. H. F. Sennholz), Arlington House, NewRochelle, N.Y.
- Mises, L. 1996. *Human Action: A Treatise on Economics* (4th rev. edn), Fox and Wilkes, SanFrancisco.
- Pelling, Henry. *Winston Churchill.* London: MacMillan Press, 1989.
- Postman, Neil. *Amusing Ourselves to Death: Public Discourse in the Age of Show Business.* 20th anniversary ed. New York: Penguin Books, 2005.

  ———. *Technopoly: The Surrender of Culture to Technology.* New York: Vintage Books, 1993.
- Rickards, James. *The Death of Money.* New York: Portfolio Penguin, 2014.
- Robert, L. *Minding the Heart: The Way of Spiritual Formation,* Grand Rapids. MI: Kregel Publications. 2013. Print.
- Sandburg, Carl. *Remembrance Rock.* New York: Harcourt, Brace and Company, 1948.
- Saucy, Robert. *Minding the Heart: The Way of Spiritual Formation.* Grand Rapids, MI: Kregel Publications, 2013.
- Sowell, Thomas. *Intellectuals and Society.* New York: Basic Books, 2009.

  ———. *On Classical Economics.* New Haven, CT: Yale University Press, 2006.

  ———. *Wealth, Poverty and Politics: An International Perspective.* New York: Basic Books, 2015.
- Strauss, William, and Neil Howe. *The Fourth Turning: An American Prophecy.* New York: Broadway Books, 1997.
- Sturkey, Marion F. *Warrior Culture of the U. S. Marines.* New York: Heritage Press, 2001.
- Vitz, Paul. *Faith of the Fatherless: The Psychology of Atheism.* San Francisco: Ignatius, 2013.
- Von Mises, Ludwig. *A Critique of Interventionism.* Translated by Hans F. Sennholz. New York: Arlington House, 1977.

  ———. *Human Action: A Treatise on Economics.* 4th rev. ed. San Francisco: Fox and Wilkes,1996.

  ———. *The Theory of Money and Credit.* Translated by H. E. Batson. London: Jonathan Cape, London. 1953.
- Weaver, Henry Grady. *The Mainspring of Human Progress.* Atlanta:

Foundation for Economic Education, 1956.

- Weaver, Richard. *Ideas Have Consequences*. Chicago: University of Chicago Press, 1967.
- Warren, Robert Penn. *All The King's Men*. New York: Harcourt, Brace, and Company, 1946.
- Webb, James. *Born Fighting: How the Scots-Irish Shaped America*. New York: Broadway Publishing Company, 2004.
- Werner, David, Carol Thuman, and Jane Maxwell. *Where There Is No Doctor: A Village Health Care Handbook*. Berkeley, CA: Hesperian Foundation, 1992.
- Willard, Dallas. *Renovation of the Heart: Putting on the Character of Christ*. Colorado Springs, CO: Navpress, 2002.
- Winchester, Simon. *Krakatoa: The Day the World Exploded*. New York: Harper Perennial, 2005.
- Winship, A. E. Jukes-Edwards. *A Study in Education and Heredity*. Pennsylvania: R. L. Myers and Company, 1900.

ABOUT THE AUTHOR

For fifty years the McAlvany family has offered professional legacy and wealth management services to clients around the world. David McAlvany is the second generation CEO of McAlvany Financial Companies: International Collectors Associates, ICA Europe, and McAlvany Wealth Management. He has been featured as an economics commentator on CNBC, Fox News, Fox Business News, and Bloomberg; on national radio programs; and at financial seminars around the world, analyzing the impact of events and trends on the global economy. He can be heard weekly on his market commentary with world leaders, bankers, economists, and renowned investors at www.mcalvany.com.

David is also the creator and producer of *The Missing Chapter*, a distance learning-based video curriculum for students and families who want to grasp the basics of economics, wealth, and investment strategies. David has served as board member for private charitable organizations and is presently on the investment advisory board for the Ft. Lewis College Foundation. He is a graduate of Biola University and an associate member of Keble College, Oxford University, where he studied philosophy and political theory. David volunteered as an analyst in Chile with The Institute for Liberty and Development, dedicated to providing free market solutions throughout Latin America and the Third World. He also achieved honors as a top salesman with Southwestern Company and gained extensive business expertise with Morgan Stanley.

David is an avid reader, triathlete, and outdoorsman, with a keen passion for cycling and mountaineering. He spends his free time with his wife and their four children skiing, hiking, and enjoying the mountains of Colorado.

McALVANY COMPANIES

McAlvany Intelligence Advisor (MIA)
Don McAlvany's Monthly Newsletter
Website: mcalvanyintelligenceadvisor.com
Phone Number: 877-622-5826

McAlvany Weekly Commentary (MWC)
David McAlvany's Weekly Financial Podcast
Website: www.mcalvanyweeklycommentary.com

The Missing Chapter
Supplemental Financial Education Curriculum
developed for advanced students and high schoolers
Website: www.TheMissingChapter.net

The Intentional Legacy Resources
Blog, podcasts, and multi-copy discount ordering
Website: www.DavidMcAlvany.com

International Collectors Associates (ICA)
Precious Metals Brokerage
Retirement, private holdings, and foreign storage options
Website: www.mcalvanyica.com
Phone Number: 800-525-9556

McAlvany Wealth Management (MWM)
Alternative Asset Management
Conservative/Risk-Managed/Tactical Non-Correlated
Website: www.mwealthm.com
Phone Number: 866-211-8970